MOST
requested
RECIPES

167

Taste of Home®
RDA ENTHUSIAST BRANDS, LLC • MILWAUKEE, WI

SERVE UP THE VERY BEST DISHES

Your family deserves nothing but the most-loved, highest-rated recipes—and they're all right here inside *Taste of Home Most Requested Recipes*. With 368 irresistible dishes to choose from, you can create a menu for any occasion! Shared by home cooks just like you, these tasty favorites are ready to take center stage at your kitchen table.

With *Most Requested Recipes,* you can plan a stunning, simple meal in no time at all. Check out each chapter to discover appetizing snacks, sweet sips, sunny brunch offerings, comforting casseroles and main dishes, soothing soups and sandwiches, light salads, savory side dishes and dazzling desserts! And the bonus chapter of Seasonal Specialties provides a year's worth of ideas for holiday get-togethers.

Don't skip out on the helpful reviews and suggestions from *TasteofHome.com* throughout the book. Give them a read to find out why other family cooks loved these special recipes so much, then try them out for yourself!

To help you find dishes perfect for when you're in a pinch, look for two at-a-glance icons to get your meal on the table fast:

FAST FIX These recipes are ready in 30 minutes or less.

5 INGREDIENTS These recipes require no more than five items (not counting water, oil, salt, pepper and optional ingredients) to create a delicious dish.

Since every recipe inside has been tested and approved by the *Taste of Home* Test Kitchen and recommended by our readers, you can cook and bake your way through the book with confidence. With *Most Requested Recipes,* you've got 368 new ways to say "yum!"

MOST requested RECIPES

EDITORIAL

Editor-in-Chief	Catherine Cassidy
Vice President, Content Operations	Kerri Balliet
Creative Director	Howard Greenberg
Managing Editor, Print & Digital Books	Mark Hagen
Associate Creative Director	Edwin Robles Jr.
Editor	Hazel Wheaton
Associate Editors	Molly Jasinski, Julie Kuczynski
Art Director	Raeann Thompson
Graphic Designer	Courtney Lovetere
Editorial Services Manager	Dena Ahlers
Editorial Production Coordinator	Jill Banks
Copy Chief	Deb Warlaumont Mulvey
Copy Editors	Dulcie Shoener (senior), Ronald Kovach, Chris McLaughlin, Ellie Piper
Contributing Copy Editor	Michael Juley
Content Director	Julie Blume Benedict
Food Editors	Gina Nistico; James Schend; Peggy Woodward, RDN
Recipe Editors	Sue Ryon (lead), Irene Yeh
Editorial Services Administrator	Marie Brannon
Culinary Director	Sarah Thompson
Test Cooks	Nicholas Iverson (lead), Matthew Hass
Food Stylists	Kathryn Conrad (lead), Lauren Knoelke, Shannon Roum
Prep Cooks	Bethany Van Jacobson (lead), Melissa Hansen, Aria C. Thornton
Culinary Team Assistant	Maria Petrella
Photography Director	Stephanie Marchese
Photographers	Dan Roberts, Jim Wieland
Photographer/Set Stylist	Grace Natoli Sheldon
Set Stylists	Melissa Franco (lead), Stacey Genaw, Dee Dee Schaefer
Set Stylist Assistant	Stephanie Chojnacki
Business Architect, Publishing Technologies	Amanda Harmatys
Business Analyst, Publishing Technologies	Kate Unger
Junior Business Analyst, Publishing Technologies	Shannon Stroud
Editorial Business Manager	Kristy Martin
Rights & Permissions Associate	Samantha Lea Stoeger
Editorial Business Associate	Andrea Meiers
Editor, *Taste of Home*	Emily Betz Tyra
Art Director, *Taste of Home*	Kristin Bowker

BUSINESS

Vice President, Group Publisher	Kirsten Marchioli
Publisher, *Taste of Home*	Donna Lindskog
Business Development Director, Taste of Home Live	Laurel Osman
Strategic Partnerships Manager, Taste of Home Live	Jamie Piette Andrzejewski

TRUSTED MEDIA BRANDS, INC.

President & Chief Executive Officer	Bonnie Kintzer
Chief Financial Officer	Dean Durbin
Chief Marketing Officer	C. Alec Casey
Chief Revenue Officer	Richard Sutton
Chief Digital Officer	Vince Errico
Senior Vice President, Global HR & Communications	Phyllis E. Gebhardt, SPHR; SHRM-SCP
General Counsel	Mark Sirota
Vice President, Product Marketing	Brian Kennedy
Vice President, Operations	Michael Garzone
Vice President, Consumer Marketing Planning	Jim Woods
Vice President, Digital Product & Technology	Nick Contardo
Vice President, Financial Planning & Analysis	William Houston

COVER PHOTOGRAPHY

Photographer	Jim Wieland
Food Stylist	Shannon Roum
Set Stylist	Melissa Franco

© 2017 RDA Enthusiast Brands, LLC
1610 N. 2nd St., Suite 102, Milwaukee WI 53212-3906

International Standard Book Number: 978-1-61765-643-9
International Standard Serial Number: 2166-0522
Component Number: 119200022H

Pictured on the front cover: Cheesy Pizza Rolls (p. 5); Chocolate Chiffon Cake (p. 176); Apricot Lemonade Iced Tea (p. 14)
Pictured on the back cover: Refrigerator Jalapeno Dill Pickles (p. 79); Upside-Down Frito Pie (p. 127)
Pictured on title page: Simple Turtle Cheesecake (p. 167)

TABLE OF CONTENTS

82

117

224

APPETIZERS, SNACKS & BEVERAGES

It's time to get the party started! Mix and match to your heart's content with these tantalizingly tasty bites. Pick from cheesy dips, hot-from-the-oven sliders, fresh salsa and so much more! And don't forget about the beverages—there are both kid-approved and adult-only options inside.

CHEESY PIZZA ROLLS

The cast-iron skillet browns these rolls to perfection. My family can't get enough. Use whatever pizza toppings you like best.
—**DOROTHY SMITH** EL DORADO, AR

PREP: 15 MIN. • **BAKE:** 25 MIN.
MAKES: 8 APPETIZERS

- 1 loaf (1 pound) frozen pizza dough, thawed
- ½ cup pasta sauce
- 1 cup shredded part-skim mozzarella cheese, divided
- 1 cup coarsely chopped pepperoni (about 64 slices)
- ½ pound bulk Italian sausage, cooked and crumbled
- ¼ cup grated Parmesan cheese
  Minced fresh basil, optional
  Crushed red pepper flakes, optional

1. Preheat oven to 400°. On a lightly floured surface, roll the dough into a 16x10-in. rectangle. Brush with pasta sauce to within ½ in. of edges.

2. Sprinkle with ½ cup mozzarella cheese, pepperoni, sausage and Parmesan. Roll up jelly-roll style, starting with a long side; pinch seam to seal. Cut into eight slices. Place in a greased 9-in. cast-iron skillet or greased 9-in. round baking pan, cut side down.

3. Bake 20 minutes; sprinkle with remaining mozzarella cheese. Bake until golden brown, 5-10 minutes more. If desired, serve with minced fresh basil and red pepper flakes.

READER REVIEW

"Delicious and easy! My 2-year-old and 6-year-old gobbled them up! I served them with a Caesar salad for a wonderful, simple, family-pleasing meal."

ANNIEPANTS TASTEOFHOME.COM

SLOW COOKER SPINACH & ARTICHOKE DIP

With this creamy dip, my daughters will happily eat spinach and artichokes. We typically serve it with chips, toasted pita bread or fresh vegetables on the side.

—**JENNIFER STOWELL** MONTEZUMA, IA

PREP: 10 MIN. • **COOK:** 2 HOURS
MAKES: 32 SERVINGS (¼ CUP EACH)

- 2 cans (14 ounces each) water-packed artichoke hearts, drained and chopped
- 2 packages (10 ounces each) frozen chopped spinach, thawed and squeezed dry
- 1 jar (15 ounces) Alfredo sauce
- 1 package (8 ounces) cream cheese, cubed
- 2 cups shredded Italian cheese blend
- 1 cup shredded part-skim mozzarella cheese
- 1 cup shredded Parmesan cheese
- 1 cup 2% milk
- 2 garlic cloves, minced
  Assorted crackers and/or cucumber slices

In a greased 4-qt. slow cooker, combine first nine ingredients. Cook, covered, on low 2-3 hours or until heated through. Serve with crackers and/or cucumber slices.

⑤INGREDIENTS FAST FIX ▶
GARBANZO-STUFFED MINI PEPPERS

Mini peppers are so colorful and they're the perfect size for a two-bite appetizer. They have all the crunch of a pita chip without the extra calories.

—**CHRISTINE HANOVER** LEWISTON, CA

START TO FINISH: 20 MIN.
MAKES: 32 APPETIZERS

- 1 teaspoon cumin seeds
- 1 can (15 ounces) chickpeas, rinsed and drained
- ¼ cup fresh cilantro leaves
- 3 tablespoons water
- 3 tablespoons cider vinegar
- ¼ teaspoon salt
- 16 miniature sweet peppers, halved lengthwise
  Additional fresh cilantro leaves

1. In a dry small skillet, toast cumin seeds over medium heat 1-2 minutes or until aromatic, stirring frequently. Transfer to a food processor. Add the chickpeas, cilantro, water, vinegar and salt; pulse until blended.
2. Spoon into pepper halves. Top with the additional cilantro. Refrigerate until serving.

FAST FIX ▶
CREAMY LEMON MILK SHAKES

Several different recipes inspired the combination of ingredients I use in these shakes, and I'm glad they did! They're so refreshing.

—**CAROL GILLESPIE** CHAMBERSBURG, PA

START TO FINISH: 10 MIN.
MAKES: 4 SERVINGS

- 2 tablespoons crushed lemon drop candies
- 1 teaspoon sugar
- ½ small lemon, cut into six slices, divided
- ½ cup 2% milk
- 2 cups vanilla ice cream
- 2 cups lemon sorbet
- 3 ounces cream cheese, softened
- 2 teaspoons grated lemon peel
- ½ teaspoon vanilla extract

1. In a shallow dish, mix crushed lemon drops and sugar. Using 1 or 2 lemon slices, moisten the rims of four glasses; dip rims into candy mixture.
2. Place remaining ingredients (minus lemon slices) in a blender; cover and process until smooth. Pour into the prepared glasses; serve immediately with remaining lemon slices.

- 2 teaspoons butter
- 2 tablespoons chopped seeded jalapeno pepper
- 1 teaspoon minced fresh gingerroot
- ¾ cup orange marmalade
- 1 tablespoon lime juice
- 1 tablespoon thawed orange juice concentrate
- ¼ teaspoon salt

1. Preheat broiler. Pound chicken breasts with a meat mallet to ¼-in. thickness; cut lengthwise into 1-in.-wide strips. In a large resealable plastic bag, combine oil, soy sauce, garlic and pepper. Add the chicken; seal bag and turn to coat. Refrigerate 4 hours or overnight.

2. In a small saucepan, heat butter over medium-high heat. Add jalapeno; cook and stir until tender. Add ginger; cook 1 minute longer. Reduce heat; stir in marmalade, lime juice, orange juice concentrate and salt.

3. Drain the chicken, discarding the marinade. Thread chicken strips, weaving back and forth, onto eight metal or soaked wooden skewers. Place in a greased 15x10x1-in. baking pan. Broil 6 in. from heat 2-4 minutes on each side or until chicken is no longer pink. Serve with sauce.

NOTE *Wear disposable gloves when cutting hot peppers; the oils can burn skin. Avoid touching your face.*

SWISS MUSHROOM LOAF

I get lots of recipe requests when I serve this outstanding loaf stuffed with Swiss cheese and mushrooms. It's great as an appetizer or served with pasta.

—**HEIDI MELLON** WAUKESHA, WI

PREP: 15 MIN. • **BAKE:** 40 MIN.
MAKES: 10-12 SERVINGS

- 1 unsliced loaf (1 pound) Italian bread
- 1 block (8 ounces) Swiss cheese, cut into cubes
- 1 cup sliced fresh mushrooms
- ¼ cup butter, cubed
- 1 small onion, finely chopped
- 1½ teaspoons poppy seeds
- 2 garlic cloves, minced
- ½ teaspoon seasoned salt
- ½ teaspoon ground mustard
- ½ teaspoon lemon juice

1. Cut bread diagonally into 1-in. slices to within 1 in. of bottom. Repeat cuts in opposite direction. Place cheese cubes and mushrooms in each slit.

2. In a microwave-safe bowl, combine the remaining ingredients; cover and microwave on high for 30-60 seconds or until butter is melted; stir until blended. Spoon over bread.

3. Wrap the loaf in foil. Bake at 350° for 40 minutes or until the cheese is melted.

CHICKEN SKEWERS WITH MARMALADE

My father-in-law loved this chicken dish and said that it reminded him of growing up in southern California. What a great way to bring a dose of summer sunshine to cold winter days!

—**LAUREL DALZELL** MANTECA, CA

PREP: 25 MIN. + MARINATING • **BROIL:** 5 MIN.
MAKES: 8 SERVINGS (1 CUP SAUCE)

- 1 pound boneless skinless chicken breasts
- ¼ cup olive oil
- ¼ cup reduced-sodium soy sauce
- 2 garlic cloves, minced
- ⅛ teaspoon pepper

5 INGREDIENTS

CRANBERRY LIMEADE

When cranberry and lime juice get together, the result is thirst-quenching. Add ice and you've got a party in a glass.

—MICHAEL PASSOW POUGHKEEPSIE, NY

PREP: 15 MIN. + CHILLING
MAKES: 7 SERVINGS

- 2½ to 3½ cups water, divided
- 1¼ cups sugar
- 2 to 3 cups cranberry juice
- 1½ cups lime juice (10 to 12 medium limes)
- 1 tablespoon grated lime peel (2 medium limes)
  Ice cubes
  Lime slices, optional

Bring 1½ cups water and sugar to a boil. Remove from heat; stir in juices, lime peel and remaining water. Cover; refrigerate at least 1 hour. Serve over ice and, if desired, with lime slices.

FAST FIX

BLUEBERRY FRUIT DIP

After a long day at school, my kids like to snack on this fruit-filled dip.

—RENEE SEVIGNY WAYLAND, MI

START TO FINISH: 10 MIN.
MAKES: 1 CUP

- 4 ounces cream cheese, softened
- ½ cup confectioners' sugar
- ½ teaspoon ground cinnamon
- ½ teaspoon lemon juice
- ½ cup fresh blueberries
  Assorted fresh fruit, graham crackers and/or cookies

In a small bowl, beat the cream cheese, confectioners' sugar, cinnamon and lemon juice until smooth. Fold in blueberries. Serve with fruit, crackers and/or cookies.

GRILLED PINEAPPLE WITH LIME DIP

Serve this as an appetizer or dessert—the choice is yours! If you like, roll pineapple wedges in flaked coconut before throwing them on the grill.
—**TASTE OF HOME** TEST KITCHEN

PREP: 20 MIN. + MARINATING
GRILL: 10 MIN.
MAKES: 8 SERVINGS

- 1 fresh pineapple
- ¼ cup packed brown sugar
- 3 tablespoons honey
- 2 tablespoons lime juice

LIME DIP

- 3 ounces cream cheese, softened
- ¼ cup plain yogurt
- 2 tablespoons honey
- 1 tablespoon brown sugar
- 1 tablespoon lime juice
- 1 teaspoon grated lime peel

1. Peel and core the pineapple; cut into eight wedges. Cut each wedge into two spears. In a large resealable plastic bag, combine the brown sugar, honey and lime juice; add pineapple. Seal bag and turn to coat; refrigerate for 1 hour.
2. In a small bowl, beat cream cheese until smooth. Beat in yogurt, honey, brown sugar, lime juice and lime peel. Cover and refrigerate until serving.
3. Coat the grill rack with cooking spray before starting the grill. Drain and discard the marinade. Grill the pineapple, covered, over medium heat for 3-4 minutes on each side or until golden brown. Serve with lime dip.

BACON CHEESEBURGER SLIDER BAKE

 I created this dish to fill two pans because these sliders disappear in a flash. Just cut the recipe in half if you need only one pan's worth.
—**NICK IVERSON** MILWAUKEE, WI

PREP: 20 MIN. • **BAKE:** 25 MIN.
MAKES: 2 DOZEN

- 2 packages (18 ounces each) Hawaiian sweet rolls
- 4 cups shredded cheddar cheese, divided
- 2 pounds ground beef
- 1 cup chopped onion
- 1 can (14½ ounces) diced tomatoes with garlic and onion, drained
- 1 tablespoon Dijon mustard
- 1 tablespoon Worcestershire sauce
- ¾ teaspoon salt
- ¾ teaspoon pepper
- 24 bacon strips, cooked and crumbled

GLAZE

- 1 cup butter, cubed
- ¼ cup packed brown sugar
- 4 teaspoons Worcestershire sauce
- 2 tablespoons Dijon mustard
- 2 tablespoons sesame seeds

1. Preheat oven to 350°. Without separating rolls, cut each package of rolls horizontally in half; arrange bottom halves in two greased 13x9-in. baking pans. Sprinkle each pan of rolls with 1 cup cheese. Bake 3-5 minutes or until cheese is melted.
2. In a large skillet, cook beef and onion over medium heat 6-8 minutes or until meat is no longer pink and onion is tender, breaking up beef into crumbles; drain. Stir in the tomatoes, mustard, Worcestershire sauce, salt and pepper. Cook and stir 1-2 minutes or until combined.
3. Spoon beef mixture evenly over rolls; sprinkle with remaining cheese. Top with bacon. Replace tops. For the glaze, in a microwave-safe bowl, combine the butter, brown sugar, Worcestershire sauce and mustard. Microwave, covered, on high until butter is melted, stirring occasionally. Pour over rolls; sprinkle with sesame seeds. Bake, uncovered, 20-25 minutes or until sliders are golden brown and heated through.
FREEZE OPTION *Cover and freeze unbaked sandwiches; prepare and freeze glaze. To use, partially thaw in refrigerator overnight. Remove from refrigerator 30 minutes before baking. Preheat oven to 350°. Pour glaze over buns and sprinkle with sesame seeds. Bake as directed, increasing time by 10-15 minutes or until the cheese is melted and a thermometer inserted in the center reads 165°.*

MINIATURE SHEPHERD'S PIES

These mini pies are ideal for nibbling at holiday parties. If ground beef isn't your preference, change up the flavor with ground lamb and a teaspoon of dried rosemary instead.

—**SUZANNE BANFIELD** BASKING RIDGE, NJ

PREP: 40 MIN. • **BAKE:** 15 MIN.
MAKES: 4 DOZEN

- ½ **pound ground beef**
- ⅓ **cup finely chopped onion**
- ¼ **cup finely chopped celery**
- 3 **tablespoons finely chopped carrot**
- 1½ **teaspoons all-purpose flour**
- 1 **teaspoon dried thyme**
- ¼ **teaspoon salt**
- ⅛ **teaspoon ground nutmeg**
- ⅛ **teaspoon pepper**
- ⅔ **cup beef broth**
- ⅓ **cup frozen petite peas**
- 2 **packages (17.3 ounces each) frozen puff pastry, thawed**
- 3 **cups mashed potatoes**

1. Preheat oven to 400°. In a large skillet, cook beef, onion, celery and carrot over medium heat until beef is no longer pink; drain. Stir in flour, thyme, salt, nutmeg and pepper until blended; gradually add broth. Bring to a boil; cook and stir 2 minutes or until sauce is thickened. Stir in peas; heat through. Set aside.

2. Unfold puff pastry. Using a floured 2¼-in. round cutter, cut 12 circles from each sheet (save the scraps for another use). Press circles onto the bottoms and up the sides of ungreased miniature muffin cups.

3. Fill each with 1½ teaspoons beef mixture; top or pipe with 1 tablespoon mashed potatoes. Bake 13-16 minutes or until heated through and potatoes are lightly browned. Serve warm.

FAST FIX ▶

NUTTY STUFFED MUSHROOMS

Basil, Parmesan cheese and mushroom blend together well, while buttery pecans give these treats a surprising crunch. Our children, grandchildren and great-grandchildren always ask for them!

—**MILDRED ELDRED** UNION CITY, MI

START TO FINISH: 30 MIN.
MAKES: 18-20 SERVINGS

- 18 to 20 **large fresh mushrooms**
- 1 **small onion, chopped**
- 3 **tablespoons butter**
- ¼ **cup dry bread crumbs**
- ¼ **cup finely chopped pecans**
- 3 **tablespoons grated Parmesan cheese**
- ¼ **teaspoon salt**
- ¼ **teaspoon dried basil**
  Dash cayenne pepper

1. Remove stems from mushrooms; set caps aside. Finely chop the stems. In a large skillet, saute the chopped mushrooms and onion in butter for 5 minutes or until the liquid has evaporated. Remove from the heat; set aside.

2. In a bowl, combine bread crumbs, pecans, Parmesan cheese, salt, basil and cayenne; add mushroom mixture. Stuff firmly into mushroom caps.

3. Place in a greased 15x10x1-in. baking pan. Bake, uncovered, at 400° for 15-18 minutes or until tender. Serve mushrooms warm.

PEPPERONI STUFFED MUSHROOMS *Prepare mushroom caps as directed. Omit pecans, salt, basil and pepper. Add 1 minced garlic clove to the chopped mushrooms and onion when sauteing. Into mushroom mixture, stir bread crumbs, Parmesan, 3 ounces finely chopped pepperoni, 1 tablespoon minced parsley and ⅛ teaspoon pepper. Stuff into caps and bake at 375° for 15-20 minutes or until tender. Serve mushrooms warm.*

⑤INGREDIENTS **FAST FIX ▶**

SAUSAGE BISCUIT BITES

I sometimes bake these delightful little morsels the night before, refrigerate them, then put them in the slow cooker in the morning so my husband can share them with his co-workers. They're always gone in a hurry.

—AUDREY MARLER KOKOMO, IN

START TO FINISH: 30 MIN.
MAKES: 40 APPETIZERS

- 1 tube (7½ ounces) refrigerated buttermilk biscuits
- 1 tablespoon butter, melted
- 4½ teaspoons grated Parmesan cheese
- 1 teaspoon dried oregano
- 1 package (8 ounces) frozen fully cooked breakfast sausage links, thawed

1. On a lightly floured surface, roll each biscuit into a 4-in. circle; brush with butter. Combine the Parmesan cheese and oregano; sprinkle over biscuits. Place a sausage link in the center of each biscuit; roll up.

2. Cut each roll widthwise into four pieces; insert a toothpick into each. Place on an ungreased baking sheet. Bake at 375° for 8-10 minutes or until golden brown.

FAST FIX ▶
SALSA ROJA

With the help of my food processor, I can have fresh homemade salsa ready in 15 minutes. The lime juice works wonders bringing out all the flavors, and you can really taste the cilantro.

—AMBER MASSEY ARGYLE, TX

START TO FINISH: 15 MIN.
MAKES: 7 CUPS

- 1 can (28 ounces) whole tomatoes, drained
- 1 can (14½ ounces) diced tomatoes with garlic and onion, drained
- 1 can (14½ ounces) Mexican stewed tomatoes, drained
- 1 can (10 ounces) diced tomatoes and green chilies, drained
- 1 medium onion, quartered
- 2 banana peppers, seeded and coarsely chopped
- 2 jalapeno peppers, seeded and coarsely chopped
- 3 garlic cloves, minced
- 2 teaspoons salt
- ¼ teaspoon ground cumin
- ½ cup minced fresh cilantro
- ¼ cup lime juice
- 2 medium ripe avocados, peeled and cubed
  Tortilla chips

1. Place the first 10 ingredients in a food processor; cover and process until chopped. Add cilantro and lime juice; cover and pulse until combined.

2. Transfer to a bowl; stir in avocados. Serve with tortilla chips.

NOTE *Wear disposable gloves when cutting hot peppers; the oils can burn skin. Avoid touching your face.*

APPETIZER PIZZAS

To keep a summer kitchen cool, prepare pizzas on the grill. A variety of quick-prep ingredients allows you to create different flavor combinations—or let party guests build their own.

—*TASTE OF HOME* TEST KITCHEN

PREP: 30 MIN. • **GRILL:** 10 MIN.
MAKES: 9 APPETIZER PIZZAS

- 9   flour tortillas (6 inches)
- 3   tablespoons olive oil

TRADITIONAL PIZZAS
- ⅓   cup chopped pepperoni
- ¾   cup shredded Colby-Monterey Jack cheese
- 1   jar (14 ounces) pizza sauce

MEDITERRANEAN PIZZAS
- ½   cup chopped seeded tomato
- ⅓   cup sliced ripe olives
- ¾   cup crumbled feta cheese
- ¼   cup thinly sliced green onions
- 1   carton (7 ounces) hummus

MARGHERITA PIZZAS
- 9   thin slices tomato
- 1   package (8 ounces) small fresh mozzarella cheese balls, sliced
- 1   tablespoon minced fresh basil
- 1   cup prepared pesto

Brush one side of each tortilla with oil. Place oiled side down on grill rack. Grill, uncovered, over medium heat for 2-3 minutes or until puffed. Brush tortillas with oil; turn and top with pizza toppings.

FOR TRADITIONAL PIZZAS *Top three grilled tortillas with pepperoni and cheese. Cover and grill 2-3 minutes or until the cheese is melted. Cut into wedges; serve with pizza sauce.*

FOR MEDITERRANEAN PIZZAS *Top three grilled tortillas with tomato, olives, feta cheese and onions. Cover and grill 2-3 minutes or until cheese is heated through. Cut into wedges; serve with hummus.*

FOR MARGHERITA PIZZAS *Top three grilled tortillas with tomato slices, mozzarella cheese and basil. Cover and grill 2-3 minutes or until cheese is melted. Cut into wedges; serve with pesto.*

FAST FIX
LAYERED BLT DIP

When I throw a party for friends, I whip up this addictive three-cheese dip. It's always gone within the first 20 minutes.

—**JADE BENNETT** KINGWOOD, TX

START TO FINISH: 25 MIN.
MAKES: 20 SERVINGS (¼ CUP EACH)

- 1   package (8 ounces) cream cheese, softened
- ½   cup mayonnaise
- ¼   cup grated Parmesan cheese
- 1   cup finely chopped lettuce
- 8   bacon strips, cooked and crumbled
- 4   plum tomatoes, chopped
- 4   green onions, chopped
- 1½   cups shredded cheddar cheese
     Toasted French bread baguette slices

In a small bowl, beat cream cheese, mayonnaise and Parmesan cheese until blended; spread into a large shallow dish. Layer with lettuce, bacon, tomatoes, onions and cheddar cheese. Refrigerate until serving. Serve with bread slices.

FAST FIX
TOPSY-TURVY SANGRIA

I got this recipe from a friend a few years ago. It's perfect for relaxed get-togethers. It tastes best when you make it the night before and let the flavors steep. But be careful—it goes down easy!

—**TRACY FIELD** BREMERTON, WA

START TO FINISH: 10 MIN.
MAKES: 10 SERVINGS (¾ CUP EACH)

- 1   bottle (750 milliliters) merlot
- 1   cup sugar
- 1   cup orange liqueur
- ½   to 1 cup brandy
- 3   cups cold lemon-lime soda
- 1   cup sliced fresh strawberries
- 1   medium orange, sliced
- 1   medium lemon, sliced
- 1   medium peach, sliced
     Ice cubes

In a pitcher, stir first four ingredients until sugar is dissolved. Stir in soda and fruit. Serve over ice.

APPETIZERS, SNACKS & BEVERAGES

CUCUMBER FRUIT SALSA

We always have way more cucumbers and tomatoes from our garden than we can handle. This recipe is a delightful way to use them up. If making it ahead, stir in the banana and peach right before serving.

—ANNA DAVIS SPRINGFIELD, MO

PREP: 25 MIN. + CHILLING
MAKES: 24 SERVINGS (¼ CUP EACH)

- 1 **large cucumber, finely chopped**
- 2 **medium green peppers, finely chopped**
- 2 **medium tomatoes, finely chopped**
- 1 **small red onion, finely chopped**
- 1 **small navel orange, segmented and chopped**
- 2 **tablespoons lemon juice**
- 1 **tablespoon minced fresh cilantro**
- 1 **tablespoon minced fresh parsley**
- 1 **garlic clove, minced**
- ¼ **teaspoon salt**
- ¼ **teaspoon hot pepper sauce**
- ⅛ **teaspoon pepper**
- 1 **medium peach, peeled and finely chopped**
- 1 **small banana, finely chopped**

In a large bowl, combine the first 12 ingredients. Refrigerate at least 30 minutes to allow the flavors to blend. Just before serving, stir in peach and banana.

TOP TIP

Freeze Lemon Juice For Later

After juicing fresh lemons, I freeze some of the juice in ice cube trays. Then I simply defrost a few when I need lemon juice for a recipe.

—JUDY M. SOUTH BEND, IN

(5) INGREDIENTS

APRICOT LEMONADE ICED TEA

Every special occasion deserves a refreshing beverage. My tea has a tangy flavor from the lemonade, apricot nectar and mint.

—KAY CHON SHERWOOD, AR

PREP: 10 MIN. • **COOK:** 5 MIN. + COOLING
MAKES: 12 SERVINGS (¾ CUP EACH)

- 4 **cups water**
- 7 **individual tea bags**
- 1 **cup sugar**
- 1 **can (12 ounces) frozen lemonade concentrate, partially thawed**
- 1 **cup chilled apricot nectar**
- 4 **cups cold water**
   Ice cubes
   Mint sprigs

1. In a saucepan, bring 4 cups water to a boil; remove from heat. Add tea bags; steep, covered, 5 minutes.
2. Discard tea bags. Stir in sugar until dissolved; cool slightly. Transfer to a pitcher; cool completely.
3. Add lemonade concentrate and nectar to tea; stir in cold water. Serve over ice with mint.

GRILLED SHRIMP WITH SPICY-SWEET SAUCE

These finger-lickin' shrimp practically fly off the platter at my get-togethers. Play with the amount of Sriracha sauce to get the spice level just the way you like it.

—**SUSAN HARRISON** LAUREL, MD

START TO FINISH: 30 MIN.
MAKES: 15 SERVINGS (⅓ CUP SAUCE)

- 3 tablespoons reduced-fat mayonnaise
- 2 tablespoons sweet chili sauce
- 1 green onion, thinly sliced
- ¾ teaspoon Sriracha Asian hot chili sauce or ½ teaspoon hot pepper sauce
- 45 uncooked large shrimp (about 1½ pounds), peeled and deveined
- ¼ teaspoon salt
- ¼ teaspoon pepper

1. In a small bowl, mix mayonnaise, chili sauce, green onion and Sriracha. Sprinkle the shrimp with salt and pepper. Thread three shrimp onto each of 15 metal or soaked wooden skewers.
2. On a lightly greased grill rack, grill the shrimp, covered, over medium heat or broil 4 in. from heat 3-4 minutes on each side or until shrimp turn pink. Serve with sauce.

CHEESY MEATBALLS

Can meatballs be lucky? My guys think so, and they want them for game time. My beef, sausage and cheese recipe has a big fan following.

—**JILL HILL** DIXON, IL

PREP: 1 HOUR • **COOK:** 4 HOURS
MAKES: ABOUT 9 DOZEN

- 1 large egg
- ½ cup 2% milk
- 2 tablespoons dried minced onion
- 4 tablespoons chili powder, divided
- 1 teaspoon salt
- 1 teaspoon pepper
- 1½ cups crushed Ritz crackers (about 1 sleeve)
- 2 pounds ground beef
- 1 pound bulk pork sausage
- 2 cups shredded process cheese (Velveeta)
- 1 can (26 ounces) condensed tomato soup, undiluted
- 2½ cups water
- 1 cup packed brown sugar

1. Preheat oven to 400°. In a large bowl, whisk the egg, milk, minced onion, 2 tablespoons chili powder, salt and pepper; stir in crushed crackers. Add beef, sausage and cheese; mix lightly but thoroughly.
2. Shape mixture into 1-in. balls. Place meatballs on greased racks in 15x10x1-in. baking pans. Bake 15-18 minutes or until browned.
3. Meanwhile, in a 5- or 6-qt. slow cooker, combine soup, water, brown sugar and remaining chili powder. Gently stir in meatballs. Cook, covered, on low 4-5 hours or until meatballs are cooked through.

LOADED PULLED PORK CUPS

Potato nests are simple to make and surprisingly handy for pulled pork, cheese, sour cream and other toppings. Make, bake, then collect the compliments.

—MELISSA SPERKA GREENSBORO, NC

PREP: 40 MIN. • **BAKE:** 25 MIN.
MAKES: 1½ DOZEN

- 1 package (20 ounces) refrigerated shredded hash brown potatoes
- ¾ cup shredded Parmesan cheese
- 2 large egg whites, beaten
- 1 teaspoon garlic salt
- ½ teaspoon onion powder
- ¼ teaspoon pepper
- 1 carton (16 ounces) refrigerated fully cooked barbecued shredded pork
- 1 cup shredded Colby-Monterey Jack cheese
- ½ cup sour cream
- 5 bacon strips, cooked and crumbled Minced chives

1. Preheat oven to 450°. In a bowl, mix hash browns, Parmesan cheese, egg whites and seasonings until blended. Divide potatoes among 18 well-greased muffin cups; press onto bottoms and up sides to form cups.

2. Bake 22-25 minutes or until the edges are dark golden brown. Carefully run a knife around sides of each cup. Cool 5 minutes before removing from pans to a serving platter. Meanwhile, heat pulled pork according to package directions.

3. Sprinkle cheese into cups. Top with pork, sour cream and bacon; sprinkle with chives. Serve warm.

FAST FIX
GARLIC-CHEESE FLAT BREAD

As an appetizer or side, this cheesy flat bread will be devoured in less time than it takes to bake. And that's not long!

—SUZANNE ZICK MAIDEN, NC

START TO FINISH: 25 MIN.
MAKES: 12 SERVINGS

- 1 tube (11 ounces) refrigerated thin pizza crust
- 2 tablespoons butter, melted
- 1 tablespoon minced fresh basil
- 4 garlic cloves, minced
- ¾ cup shredded cheddar cheese
- ½ cup grated Romano cheese
- ¼ cup grated Parmesan cheese

1. Unroll dough into a greased 15x10x1-in. baking pan; flatten dough to 13x9-in. rectangle and build up edges slightly.

2. Drizzle with butter. Sprinkle with basil, garlic and cheeses.

3. Bake at 425° for 11-14 minutes or until bread is crisp. Cut into squares; serve warm.

CAPPUCCINO PUNCH

When I tried this punch at a friend's wedding shower, I had to have the recipe. Guests will eagerly gather around the punch bowl when you ladle out this frothy mocha ice cream drink.

—ROSE REICH NAMPA, ID

PREP: 10 MIN. + CHILLING
MAKES: ABOUT 1 GALLON

- ½ **cup sugar**
- ¼ **cup instant coffee granules**
- 1 **cup boiling water**
- 2 **quarts whole milk**
- 1 **quart vanilla ice cream, softened**
- 1 **quart chocolate ice cream, softened**
  Grated chocolate, optional

1. Combine sugar and coffee; stir in boiling water until dissolved. Cover and refrigerate until chilled.
2. Just before serving, pour coffee mixture into a 1-gal. punch bowl. Stir in milk. Add scoops of ice cream; stir until melted. If desired, sprinkle with grated chocolate.

WHITE CHOCOLATE BRIE CUPS

Try these unique little tarts as an appetizer before a special meal, or save them for a surprisingly different dinner finale. They're sweet, creamy and crunchy—and very addictive!

—ANGELA VITALE DELAWARE, OH

START TO FINISH: 25 MIN.
MAKES: 15 APPETIZERS

- 1 **package (1.9 ounces) frozen miniature phyllo tart shells**
- 1½ **ounces white baking chocolate, chopped**
- 2 **ounces Brie cheese, chopped**
- ⅓ **cup orange marmalade**
  Kumquat slices, optional

1. Preheat oven to 350°. Fill each tart shell with chocolate, then cheese. Place on an ungreased baking sheet. Top with marmalade.
2. Bake 6-8 minutes or until golden brown. Serve warm. If desired, top with kumquat.

APPETIZER BLUE CHEESE LOGS

Three kinds of cheese and a bit of curry powder make this cheese log a little more lively than most. Guests are sure to like the tasty surprise.

—ETHEL JOHNSON NORTH SAANICH, BC

PREP: 20 MIN. + CHILLING
MAKES: 2 CHEESE LOGS

- 1 package (8 ounces) cream cheese, softened
- 1 cup shredded sharp cheddar cheese
- ½ cup crumbled blue cheese
- 1½ teaspoons curry powder
- 1 tablespoon butter
- ½ cup finely chopped pecans
- 2 tablespoons minced fresh parsley
  Assorted crackers

1. In a bowl, beat the cream cheese. Fold in cheddar cheese and blue cheese. Cover and refrigerate for at least 2 hours.

2. In a small skillet, saute the curry powder in butter for 1-2 minutes. Stir in pecans; cook and stir for 1 minute. Stir in parsley. Cool slightly. Roll the cheese mixture into two logs, about 5 in. long. Roll logs in pecan mixture. Cover and refrigerate until serving. Serve with crackers.

FAST FIX ▶
GRILLED POTATO SKINS

The creamy topping on these potato skins is so delicious. These make an excellent summertime treat alongside your favorite grilled meat.

—STEPHANIE MOON BOISE, ID

START TO FINISH: 30 MIN.
MAKES: 4 SERVINGS

- 2 medium potatoes
- 1½ teaspoons butter, melted
- 2 tablespoons picante sauce
- ¼ cup shredded cheddar cheese
- 1 tablespoon real bacon bits
- ¼ cup chopped tomato
- 2 tablespoons chopped green onion

TOPPING

- 3 tablespoons mayonnaise
- 2 tablespoons sour cream
- 1 tablespoon prepared ranch salad dressing
- 1½ teaspoons real bacon bits
- ¼ teaspoon garlic powder

1. Cut each potato lengthwise into four wedges. Cut away white portion, leaving ¼ in. on the potato skins. Place skins on a microwave-safe plate.

2. Microwave, uncovered, on high for 8-10 minutes or until tender. Brush butter over shells; top with picante sauce, cheese and bacon bits.

3. Grill potatoes, skin side down, uncovered, over medium heat for 4-6 minutes or until lightly browned. Cover and grill 2-3 minutes longer or until cheese is melted. Sprinkle with tomato and onion. In a small bowl, combine topping ingredients. Serve with potato skins.

SWEET SRIRACHA WINGS

Serve my fiery hot wings whenever friends and family gather. If you don't like a ton of sweetness, add the honey slowly and taste as you go.
—**LOGAN HOLSER** CLARKSTON, MI

PREP: 20 MIN. + MARINATING
GRILL: 15 MIN.
MAKES: 1 DOZEN

- 12 chicken wings (about 3 pounds)
- 1 tablespoon canola oil
- 2 teaspoons ground coriander
- ½ teaspoon garlic salt
- ¼ teaspoon pepper

SAUCE
- ¼ cup butter, cubed
- ½ cup orange juice
- ⅓ cup Sriracha Asian hot chili sauce
- 3 tablespoons honey
- 2 tablespoons lime juice
- ¼ cup chopped fresh cilantro

1. Place chicken wings in a large bowl. Mix oil, coriander, garlic salt and pepper; add to wings and toss to coat. Refrigerate, covered, 2 hours or overnight.

2. For sauce, in a small saucepan, melt butter. Stir in orange juice, chili sauce, honey and lime juice until blended.

3. Grill wings, covered, over medium heat 15-18 minutes or until juices run clear, turning occasionally; brush with some of the sauce during last 5 minutes of grilling.

4. Transfer chicken to a large bowl; add remaining sauce and toss to coat. Sprinkle with cilantro.

SAVORY BLT CHEESECAKE

Served on lettuce, this savory cheesecake is great on its own, but it's also a tasty appetizer alongside crackers. It's a flexible recipe, so use another cheese in place of the Gruyere, or add olives, crab meat, cooked mushrooms—whatever strikes your fancy.
—**JONI HILTON** ROCKLIN, CA

PREP: 35 MIN. • **BAKE:** 45 MIN. + CHILLING
MAKES: 24 SERVINGS

- ¾ cup dry bread crumbs
- ½ cup grated Parmesan cheese
- 3 tablespoons butter, melted

FILLING
- 4 packages (8 ounces each) cream cheese, softened
- ½ cup heavy whipping cream
- 1½ cups crumbled cooked bacon
- 1 cup oil-packed sun-dried tomatoes, patted dry and chopped
- 1 cup shredded Gruyere or Swiss cheese
- 2 green onions, sliced
- 1 teaspoon freshly ground pepper
- 4 large eggs, lightly beaten
  Optional toppings: shredded iceberg lettuce, chopped cherry tomatoes and additional crumbled cooked bacon
  Assorted crackers, optional

1. Preheat oven to 325°. Place a greased 9-in. springform pan on a double thickness of heavy-duty foil (about 18 in. square). Securely wrap foil around pan.

2. In a small bowl, combine the bread crumbs, Parmesan cheese and butter. Press onto the bottom of prepared pan. Place the pan on a baking sheet. Bake 12 minutes. Cool on a wire rack.

3. In a large bowl, beat cream cheese and cream until smooth. Beat in bacon, tomatoes, Gruyere cheese, onions and pepper. Add eggs; beat on low speed just until combined. Pour over crust. Place springform pan in a large baking pan; add 1 in. of boiling water to the larger pan.

4. Bake 45-55 minutes or until center is just set and top appears dull. Remove the springform pan from water bath; remove foil. Cool cheesecake on a wire rack 10 minutes; loosen edges from the pan with a knife. Cool for 1 hour longer. Refrigerate overnight.

5. Remove rim from pan. Serve the cheesecake with toppings and crackers if desired.

ROASTED RED PEPPER TRIANGLES

Robust meats, cheeses and veggies fill a golden crust in this snack. I recommend using marinara sauce for dipping.
—AMY BELL ARLINGTON, TN

PREP: 35 MIN. • **BAKE:** 50 MIN.
MAKES: 2 DOZEN

- 2 tubes (8 ounces each) refrigerated crescent rolls
- 1½ cups finely diced fully cooked ham
- 1 cup shredded Swiss cheese
- 1 package (3 ounces) sliced pepperoni, chopped
- 8 slices provolone cheese
- 1 jar (12 ounces) roasted sweet red peppers, well drained and cut into strips
- 4 large eggs
- ¼ cup grated Parmesan cheese
- 3 teaspoons Italian salad dressing mix

1. Unroll one tube of crescent dough into a long rectangle; press onto the bottom and ¾ in. up the sides of a greased 13x9-in. baking dish. Seal seams and perforations. Top with half of the ham; layer with Swiss cheese, pepperoni, provolone cheese and remaining ham. Top with red peppers.
2. In a small bowl, whisk the eggs, Parmesan cheese and salad dressing mix; set aside ¼ cup. Pour remaining egg mixture over peppers.
3. On a lightly floured surface, roll out remaining crescent dough into a 13x9-in. rectangle; seal seams and perforations. Place over filling; pinch edges to seal.
4. Cover; bake at 350° for 30 minutes. Uncover; brush with the reserved egg mixture. Bake 20-25 minutes longer or until crust is golden brown. Cool on a wire rack for 5 minutes. Cut into triangles. Serve warm.

VIDALIA ONION SWISS DIP

I've got one of those sweet, creamy dips you can't resist. Bake it in the oven, or use the slow cooker to make it ooey-gooey marvelous.
—JUDY BATSON TAMPA, FL

PREP: 10 MIN. • **COOK:** 25 MIN.
MAKES: 20 SERVINGS (¼ CUP EACH)

- 3 cups chopped Vidalia or other sweet onion (about 1 large)
- 2 cups shredded Swiss cheese
- 2 cups mayonnaise
- ¼ cup prepared horseradish
- 1 teaspoon hot pepper sauce
  Fresh coarsely ground pepper, optional
  Assorted crackers or fresh vegetables

1. Preheat oven to 375°. In a large bowl, mix the first five ingredients. Transfer to a deep-dish pie plate.
2. Bake, uncovered, 25-30 minutes or until edges are golden brown and onion is tender. If desired, sprinkle with pepper. Serve warm with crackers.

⑤ INGREDIENTS   FAST FIX
CERVEZA MARGARITAS

One sip of this refreshing drink and you'll picture sand, sea and blue skies that stretch for miles. It's like a vacation in a glass, and you can mix it up in moments.
—CHRISTINA BREMSON PARKVILLE, MO

START TO FINISH: 10 MIN.
MAKES: 5 SERVINGS

- 1 can (12 ounces) lemon-lime soda, chilled
- 1 bottle (12 ounces) beer
- 1 can (12 ounces) frozen limeade concentrate, thawed
- ¾ cup tequila
  Lime slices and kosher salt, optional
  Crushed ice

In a pitcher, combine soda, beer, limeade concentrate and tequila. If desired, moisten the rims of five margarita or cocktail glasses with lime slices. Sprinkle salt on a plate; dip rims in salt. Serve over crushed ice with additional lime slices.

JALAPENO POPPER POCKET

For a fresh take on fried jalapeno poppers, we stuff chicken, cheeses and jalapenos into puff pastry and bake.

—**SALLY SIBTHORPE** SHELBY TOWNSHIP, MI

PREP: 15 MIN. • **BAKE:** 20 MIN. + STANDING
MAKES: 12 SERVINGS

- 2 **cups chopped rotisserie chicken (about 10 ounces)**
- 1 **carton (8 ounces) spreadable chive and onion cream cheese**
- 1 **cup shredded pepper jack or Monterey Jack cheese**
- 1 **can (4 ounces) diced jalapeno peppers**
- 1 **sheet frozen puff pastry, thawed**
- 1 **large egg, lightly beaten**

1. Preheat oven to 425°. In a bowl, mix chicken, cream cheese, pepper jack cheese and peppers.

2. On a lightly floured surface, unfold puff pastry; roll into a 13-in. square. Place on a parchment paper-lined baking sheet. Spread one half with chicken mixture to within ½ in. of edges. Fold remaining half over filling; press edges with a fork to seal.

3. Brush lightly with beaten egg. Cut slits in pastry. Bake 20-25 minutes or until pastry is golden brown. Let stand 10 minutes before cutting.

TOP TIP

Handle with Care

Puff pastry can be delicate, so try to handle it as little as possible to avoid stretching and tearing. As an additional help, be sure to thaw the pastry at room temperature for about 20 minutes before handling.

MARYLAND CORN POPS

Fresh-picked sweet corn is a big thing in Maryland. Here's my homespun version of Mexican street corn.

—**KRISTIE SCHLEY** SEVERNA PARK, MD

PREP: 25 MIN. • **GRILL:** 10 MIN.
MAKES: 2 DOZEN

- 8 **medium ears sweet corn, husks removed**
- 2 **tablespoons canola oil**
- 1½ **cups mayonnaise**
- 1½ **teaspoons garlic powder**
- ¼ **teaspoon freshly ground pepper**
- 24 **corncob holders**
- 2 **cups crumbled feta cheese**
- 2 **tablespoons seafood seasoning**
- ¼ **cup minced fresh cilantro**
  Lime wedges, optional

1. Brush all sides of the corn with oil. Grill corn, covered, over medium heat for 10-12 minutes or until tender and lightly browned, turning occasionally. Remove from grill; cool slightly.

2. Meanwhile, in a small bowl, mix mayonnaise, garlic powder and pepper. Cut each ear of corn into thirds. Insert one corncob holder into each piece. Spread the corn with the mayonnaise mixture; sprinkle with cheese, seafood seasoning and cilantro. If desired, serve with lime wedges.

SHRIMP CORN CAKES

- ½ cup chopped onion (about 1 small)
- 1 tablespoon oil plus additional oil for frying, divided
- 2 garlic cloves, minced
- ½ pound uncooked peeled and deveined shrimp, finely chopped
- ¾ cup all-purpose flour
- ¼ cup cornmeal
- 1 tablespoon cornstarch
- 1 teaspoon baking powder
- ¼ teaspoon salt
- ¼ teaspoon pepper
- 1 cup cream-style corn
- 1 cup whole kernel corn
- 1 large egg, lightly beaten

1. In a small bowl, combine the first seven ingredients. Cover and chill until serving.

2. In a large skillet, cook and stir the onion in 1 tablespoon oil over medium-high heat until tender. Add garlic; cook 1 minute longer. Add shrimp; cook and stir until shrimp turn pink. Remove from the heat.

3. In a large bowl, mix flour, cornmeal, cornstarch, baking powder, salt and pepper. In a small bowl, mix the corn, egg and shrimp mixture; stir into dry ingredients just until moistened.

4. In an electric skillet, heat ¼ in. of oil to 375°. In batches, drop corn mixture by rounded tablespoonfuls into oil; fry 1½ minutes on each side or until golden brown. Drain on paper towels. Serve with sauce.

DILLY VEGGIE PIZZA

Here's a fun way to use up leftover chopped veggies. It's a cinch to prepare and you can change the mixture to suit your kids' tastes. Always popular at special events, it tastes just as good the next day.

—**HEATHER AHRENS** COLUMBUS, OH

PREP: 20 MIN. • **BAKE:** 10 MIN. + COOLING
MAKES: 15 SERVINGS

- 1 tube (8 ounces) refrigerated crescent rolls
- 1½ cups vegetable dill dip
- 2 medium carrots, chopped
- 1 cup finely chopped fresh broccoli
- 1 cup chopped seeded tomatoes
- 4 green onions, sliced
- 1 can (2¼ ounces) sliced ripe olives, drained

1. Unroll crescent dough into one long rectangle. Press onto the bottom of a greased 13x9-in. baking pan; seal seams. Bake at 375° for 10-12 minutes or until golden brown. Cool completely on a wire rack.

2. Spread dip over crust; sprinkle with the carrots, broccoli, tomatoes, green onions and olives. Cut into squares. Refrigerate leftovers.

SHRIMP CORN CAKES WITH SOY MAYO

Feel free to add hot sauce to the dip that accompanies these savory corn cakes.

—**KATTY CHIONG** HOFFMAN ESTATES, IL

PREP: 30 MIN. • **COOK:** 5 MIN./BATCH
MAKES: 2 DOZEN (⅔ CUP SAUCE)

- ½ cup mayonnaise
- 1 tablespoon reduced-sodium soy sauce
- 1 tablespoon ketchup
- 2 teaspoons Dijon mustard
- ½ teaspoon garlic powder
- ½ teaspoon hot pepper sauce, optional
- ⅛ teaspoon pepper

BREAKFAST & BRUNCH

Whether you prefer sweet or savory with your morning cup of coffee, turn here to find just what you need to get going. It doesn't matter what side of the bed you woke up on—these delicious dishes will have you smiling and satisfied before you officially start the day!

PROSCIUTTO & CHEDDAR BREAKFAST BISCUITS

When family visits, I love to make my nephew happy by serving breakfast with pork and cheese. I created this as a twist on the traditional breakfast sandwich.
—KELLY BOE WHITELAND, IN

PREP: 30 MIN. • **BAKE:** 15 MIN.
MAKES: 6 SERVINGS

- 2⅓ cups biscuit/baking mix
- ½ cup 2% milk
- 3 tablespoons butter, melted
- 1 to 2 tablespoons minced fresh chives

EGGS

- 6 large eggs
- 2 tablespoons 2% milk
- ¼ teaspoon salt
- 2 ounces thinly sliced prosciutto or deli ham, cut into strips
- 2 green onions, chopped
- 1 tablespoon butter
- ½ cup shredded cheddar cheese

1. Preheat oven to 425°. In a large bowl, combine the biscuit mix, milk, melted butter and chives; mix just until moistened.

2. Turn dough onto a lightly floured surface; knead gently 8-10 times. Pat or roll dough to ¾-in. thickness; cut with a floured 2½-in. biscuit cutter. Place 2 in. apart on an ungreased baking sheet. Bake for 12-14 minutes or until golden brown.

3. Meanwhile, in a large bowl, whisk eggs, milk and salt. Place a large skillet over medium heat. Add prosciutto and green onions; cook until the prosciutto begins to brown, stirring occasionally. Stir in butter until melted. Add egg mixture; cook and stir until eggs are thickened and no liquid egg remains. Stir in cheese; remove from heat.

4. Split warm biscuits in half. Fill with egg mixture.

SPICY HASH BROWN WAFFLES WITH FRIED EGGS

Refrigerated hash brown potatoes help you make quick work of these waffles. Put out lots of toppings so everyone can customize his or her own.

—NANCY JUDD ALPINE, UT

START TO FINISH: 30 MIN.
MAKES: 4 SERVINGS

- 5 large eggs
- ½ teaspoon salt
- ½ teaspoon ground cumin
- ½ teaspoon pepper
- ¼ teaspoon chili powder
- 1¾ cups refrigerated shredded hash brown potatoes
- 1 small onion, finely chopped
- ¼ cup canned chopped green chilies
- 2 tablespoons salsa
- 2 tablespoons canola oil
- ½ cup shredded cheddar-Monterey Jack cheese
  Optional toppings: salsa, guacamole, sour cream and minced fresh cilantro

1. In a large bowl, whisk 1 egg, salt, cumin, pepper and chili powder. Stir in the potatoes, onion, green chilies and salsa. Bake in a preheated waffle iron coated with cooking spray until golden brown and potatoes are tender, 8-12 minutes.

2. In a large skillet, heat oil over medium-high heat. Break remaining eggs, one at a time, into pan. Reduce heat to low. Cook to desired doneness, turning after whites are set if desired. Remove from heat and sprinkle with cheese; cover and let stand 3 minutes or until cheese is melted.

3. Serve eggs with waffles and toppings of your choice.

ULTIMATE FRUITY GRANOLA

Honey, maple syrup and vanilla coat this wonderfully crunchy treat that's fantastic no matter how you serve it: on its own, with cold milk or in a yogurt parfait.

—SARAH VASQUES MILFORD, NH

PREP: 15 MIN. • **BAKE:** 20 MIN. + COOLING
MAKES: 9 CUPS

- 5 cups old-fashioned oats
- 1 cup sliced almonds
- ½ cup sunflower kernels
- ½ cup ground flaxseed
- ½ cup packed brown sugar
- ¼ cup maple syrup
- ¼ cup honey
- 2 tablespoons canola oil
- ½ teaspoon salt
- ½ teaspoon ground cinnamon
- 1 teaspoon vanilla extract
- ½ cup dried cranberries
- ½ cup dried banana chips
- ½ cup dried apricots, halved

1. In a large bowl, combine the oats, almonds, sunflower kernels and flax. In a small saucepan, combine brown sugar, maple syrup, honey, oil, salt and cinnamon. Cook and stir over medium heat for 2-3 minutes or until brown sugar is dissolved and the mixture is heated through. Remove from the heat; stir in vanilla. Pour over oat mixture and toss to coat.

2. Transfer to a 15x10x1-in. baking pan coated with cooking spray. Bake at 350° for 20-25 minutes or until golden brown, stirring every 8 minutes. Cool completely on a wire rack. Stir in dried fruits. Store in an airtight container.

APPLE-PEAR PUFF PANCAKE

Whenever I serve this fruity pancake, people think I worked on it for hours. They're surprised that such an attractive, scrumptious dish could be so easy.
—**CAROL WILLIAMS** ST. JOSEPH, MO

START TO FINISH: 30 MIN.
MAKES: 6 SERVINGS

- 3 **tablespoons butter**
- 4 **large eggs**
- 1 **cup 2% milk**
- 1 **cup all-purpose flour**
- 1 **tablespoon sugar**
- ⅛ **teaspoon ground nutmeg**

TOPPING
- 3 **tablespoons butter**
- 3 **medium apples, sliced**
- 3 **medium pears, sliced**
- 3 **tablespoons sugar**
  Maple syrup, optional

1. Preheat oven to 425°. Place the butter in a 10-in. ovenproof skillet; heat in the oven until butter is melted, 2-3 minutes. Tilt pan to coat evenly with butter.
2. Place eggs, milk, flour, sugar and nutmeg in a blender; cover and process until smooth. Pour batter into hot skillet. Bake 17-20 minutes or until puffed and browned.
3. Meanwhile, for the topping, heat butter in a large skillet over medium heat. Add the apples, pears and sugar; cook until the fruit is tender, stirring occasionally, 12-15 minutes.
4. Remove pancake from oven; fill with the fruit mixture and serve immediately. If desired, serve with maple syrup.

COFFEE-GLAZED DOUGHNUTS

The coffee-flavored glaze makes these tasty doughnuts a perfect way to start off the morning. They're also great for using up leftover potatoes.
—**PAT SIEBENALER** RANDOM LAKE, WI

PREP: 25 MIN. + RISING
COOK: 5 MIN./BATCH
MAKES: ABOUT 4 DOZEN

- 2 **packages (¼ ounce each) active dry yeast**
- ¼ **cup warm water (110° to 115°)**
- 2 **cups warm 2% milk (110° to 115°)**
- ½ **cup butter, softened**
- 1 **cup hot mashed potatoes (without added milk and butter)**
- 3 **large eggs**
- ½ **teaspoon lemon extract, optional**
- 1 **cup sugar**
- 1½ **teaspoons salt**
- ½ **teaspoon ground cinnamon**
- 9¼ to 9¾ **cups all-purpose flour**

COFFEE GLAZE
- 6 **to 8 tablespoons cold 2% milk**
- 1 **tablespoon instant coffee granules**
- 2 **teaspoons vanilla extract**
- ¾ **cup butter, softened**
- 6 **cups confectioners' sugar**
- ½ **teaspoon ground cinnamon**
  Dash salt
  Oil for deep-fat frying

1. In a large bowl, dissolve yeast in warm water. Add milk, butter, potatoes, eggs and, if desired, extract. Add sugar, salt, cinnamon and 3 cups flour. Beat until smooth. Stir in enough remaining flour to form a soft dough. Cover and let rise in a warm place until doubled, about 1 hour.
2. Stir down dough. On a well-floured surface, roll out to ½-in. thickness. Cut with a floured 2½-in. doughnut cutter. Place on greased baking sheets; cover and let rise for 45 minutes.
3. Meanwhile, for the glaze, combine 6 tablespoons milk, coffee and vanilla; stir to dissolve coffee. In a large bowl, beat butter, sugar, cinnamon and salt. Gradually add milk mixture; beat until smooth, adding milk to reach a good dipping consistency.
4. In an electric skillet or deep-fat fryer, heat oil to 375°. Fry doughnuts, a few at a time, about 1½ minutes per side or until golden. Drain on paper towels. Dip tops in glaze while warm.

CINNAMON-SUGAR DOUGHNUTS
Omit the glaze. Gently roll the warm doughnuts in a mixture of 2 cups sugar and 1 teaspoon ground cinnamon.

POPPY SEED DOUGHNUTS *Add ¼ cup poppy seeds to the dough along with the sugar. Substitute vanilla glaze for the coffee glaze. In a saucepan, bring ½ cup sugar, ¼ cup 2% milk and ¼ cup butter to a boil. Cook and stir for 1 minute. Remove from heat; let cool completely. Stir in ½ cup confectioners' sugar and ¼ teaspoon each salt and vanilla until smooth. Drizzle glaze over doughnuts.*

FAST FIX

PINEAPPLE OATMEAL

Oatmeal for breakfast is pretty standard, but I like to mix it up a bit. This version gets some natural sweetness from pineapple and pineapple juice. It is definitely worth the extra bit of effort!

—**MARIA REGAKIS** SAUGUS, MA

START TO FINISH: 15 MIN.
MAKES: 3 SERVINGS

- 1¼ cups water
- ½ cup unsweetened pineapple juice
- ¼ teaspoon salt
- 1 cup quick-cooking oats
- ¾ cup unsweetened pineapple tidbits
- ½ cup raisins
- 2 tablespoons brown sugar
- ¼ teaspoon ground cinnamon
- ¼ teaspoon vanilla extract
- ¼ cup chopped walnuts
  Fat-free milk, optional

1. In a large saucepan, bring water, pineapple juice and salt to a boil over medium heat. Stir in oats; cook and stir for 1-2 minutes or until thickened.
2. Remove from the heat. Stir in pineapple, raisins, brown sugar, cinnamon and vanilla. Cover and let stand for 2-3 minutes. Sprinkle with walnuts. Serve with milk if desired.

FAST FIX

ASPARAGUS CREAM CHEESE OMELET

When asparagus is in season, it makes an appearance in almost all of my meals. It tastes fantastic in this omelet, and it looks pretty, too.

—**JANE CAIN** JUNCTION CITY, OH

START TO FINISH: 20 MIN.
MAKES: 2 SERVINGS

- 4 fresh asparagus spears, trimmed and cut into 1-inch pieces
- 4 large eggs
- ¼ cup sour cream
- 2 teaspoons dried minced onion
- ¼ teaspoon salt
- ¼ teaspoon crushed red pepper flakes
- 2 teaspoons butter
- 2 ounces cream cheese, cubed and softened

1. Fill a small saucepan about three-fourths full with water; bring to a boil. Add the asparagus; cook, uncovered, for 2-4 minutes or until crisp-tender. Remove and immediately drop into ice water. Drain and pat dry.
2. In a small bowl, whisk eggs, sour cream, onion, salt and pepper flakes. In a large nonstick skillet, heat butter over medium-high heat. Pour in the egg mixture. The mixture should set immediately at edge. As eggs set, push cooked portions toward center, letting uncooked eggs flow underneath.
3. When eggs are thickened and no liquid egg remains, top one side with cream cheese and asparagus. Fold omelet in half. Reduce heat to low; let stand, covered, 1-2 minutes or until cream cheese is melted. Cut omelet in half before serving.

RAISIN BREAD & SAUSAGE MORNING CASSEROLE

When we used to have Sunday breakfasts with my grandparents, my mom often made this for Grandpa because he enjoyed it so much. Pork sausage and cinnamon bread go surprisingly well together.

—CAROLYN LEVAN DIXON, IL

PREP: 25 MIN. + CHILLING • **BAKE:** 35 MIN.
MAKES: 12 SERVINGS

- ½ **pound bulk pork sausage**
- 1 **loaf (1 pound) cinnamon-raisin bread, cubed**
- 6 **large eggs**
- 1½ **cups 2% milk**
- 1½ **cups half-and-half cream**
- 1 **teaspoon vanilla extract**
- ¼ **teaspoon ground cinnamon**
- ¼ **teaspoon ground nutmeg**

TOPPING
- 1 **cup chopped pecans**
- 1 **cup packed brown sugar**
- ½ **cup butter, softened**
- 2 **tablespoons maple syrup**

1. In a large skillet, cook sausage over medium heat 4-6 minutes or until no longer pink, breaking into crumbles; drain. In a greased 13x9-in. baking dish, combine bread and sausage.

2. In a large bowl, whisk eggs, milk, cream, vanilla, cinnamon and nutmeg until blended; pour over bread mixture. Refrigerate, covered, several hours or overnight.

3. Preheat oven to 350°. Remove casserole from refrigerator while oven heats. In a small bowl, beat topping ingredients until blended. Drop by tablespoonfuls over casserole.

4. Bake, uncovered, 35-45 minutes or until golden brown and a knife inserted in center comes out clean. Let stand 5-10 minutes before serving.

=== **READER REVIEW**

"Took this to a church brunch this morning— it was gone in no time. I upped the sausage to a full pound to make it meatier. Will make again."

LSHINPOCH TASTEOFHOME.COM

BACON ROLL-UPS

This family recipe dates back to the 1930s, when my grandmother started making these hearty breakfast rolls.

—JANET ABATE NORTH BRUNSWICK, NJ

PREP: 25 MIN. • **COOK:** 20 MIN.
MAKES: 10 ROLL-UPS

- ⅓ cup finely chopped onion
- 1 tablespoon butter
- 3 cups cubed day-old bread
- ¼ teaspoon celery salt
- ¼ teaspoon garlic powder
- ⅛ teaspoon salt
- ⅛ teaspoon pepper
- 1 large egg, lightly beaten
- 10 bacon strips

1. In a small skillet, saute onion in butter until tender. In a large bowl, combine the bread cubes, celery salt, garlic powder, salt, pepper and onion mixture; toss to mix evenly. Add the egg; toss to coat bread cubes. Roll into ten 1¼-in. balls. Wrap a bacon strip around each ball and secure with a toothpick. Repeat with remaining ingredients.

2. In a large skillet, cook bacon roll-ups on all sides over medium heat for 18 minutes or until bacon is crisp and a thermometer inserted into stuffing reads at least 160°. Drain on paper towels.

FAST FIX

FRESH STRAWBERRY BREAKFAST TACOS

When our son was growing up, this was one of his favorite breakfasts. I've used low-fat ingredients in the past with good results, too.

—JOAN HALLFORD NORTH RICHLAND HILLS, TX

START TO FINISH: 30 MIN.
MAKES: 6 SERVINGS

- 2 tablespoons butter, divided
- 6 flour tortillas (6 inches)
- ⅓ cup cream cheese, softened
- 1 tablespoon honey
- ½ teaspoon ground cinnamon
- ⅓ cup vanilla yogurt
- 1¾ cups quartered fresh strawberries

1. In a large skillet, heat 1 teaspoon butter over medium-low heat. Add one tortilla; cook each side until light golden, 1-2 minutes. Transfer to wire rack. Repeat with remaining butter and tortillas.

2. Beat together cream cheese, honey and cinnamon; slowly mix in yogurt until blended. Spread tortillas with cream cheese mixture; top with strawberries.

CHEESY POTATO EGG BAKE

I whip up this cozy egg bake with potato crowns for either breakfast or dinner.
—**AMY LENTS** GRAND FORKS, ND

PREP: 20 MIN. • **BAKE:** 45 MIN.
MAKES: 12 SERVINGS

- 1 **pound bulk lean turkey breakfast sausage**
- 1¾ **cups sliced baby portobello mushrooms, chopped**
- 4 **cups fresh spinach, coarsely chopped**
- 6 **large eggs**
- 1 **cup 2% milk**
  Dash seasoned salt
- 2 **cups shredded cheddar cheese**
- 6 **cups frozen potato crowns**

1. Preheat oven to 375°. In a large skillet, cook sausage over medium heat 5-7 minutes or until no longer pink, breaking into crumbles. Add the mushrooms and spinach and cook for 2-4 minutes more or until mushrooms are tender and spinach is wilted.
2. Spoon the sausage mixture into a greased 13x9-in. baking dish. In a large bowl, whisk eggs, milk and seasoned salt until blended; pour over sausage mixture. Layer with cheddar cheese and potato crowns.
3. Bake, uncovered, 45-50 minutes or until set and top is crisp.

MUSHROOM-GOUDA QUICHE

For a laid-back Sunday brunch, we make quiche using refrigerated pie pastry. Load it up with mushrooms, aromatic arugula and creamy Gouda.
—**THOMAS FAGLON** SOMERSET, NJ

PREP: 15 MIN. • **BAKE:** 30 MIN. + STANDING
MAKES: 6 SERVINGS

- 1 **sheet refrigerated pie pastry**
- 4 **large eggs**
- 1 **cup heavy whipping cream**
- ¼ **teaspoon salt**
- ¼ **teaspoon pepper**
- 2 **cups sliced fresh shiitake mushrooms (about 4 ounces)**
- 1 **cup shredded Gouda or Monterey Jack cheese**
- 1 **cup chopped arugula or fresh baby spinach**

1. Preheat oven to 350°. Unroll pastry sheet into a 9-in. pie plate; flute edge. Refrigerate while preparing filling.
2. In a large bowl, whisk eggs, cream, salt and pepper until blended. Stir in the remaining ingredients. Pour into pie shell.
3. Bake on a lower oven rack for 30-35 minutes or until crust is golden brown and a knife inserted in center comes out clean. Let stand 10 minutes before cutting.
FREEZE OPTION *Cover and freeze unbaked quiche. To use, remove from freezer 30 minutes before baking (do not thaw). Preheat oven to 350°. Place quiche on a baking sheet; cover edge loosely with foil. Bake as directed, increasing time as necessary for a knife inserted in center to come out clean.*

SAUSAGE & CRESCENT ROLL CASSEROLE

I made this tasty casserole for a baby shower. Preparing it ahead gave me more time to finish decorating for the party.
—**MELODY CRAFT** CONROE, TX

PREP: 15 MIN. • **BAKE:** 35 MIN.
MAKES: 12 SERVINGS

- 1 pound bulk pork sausage
- 1 tube (8 ounces) refrigerated crescent rolls
- 2 cups shredded part-skim mozzarella cheese
- 8 large eggs
- 2 cups 2% milk
- ½ teaspoon salt
- ¼ teaspoon pepper

1. Preheat oven to 375°. In a large skillet, cook sausage over medium heat 6-8 minutes or until no longer pink, breaking into crumbles; drain. Unroll the crescent roll dough into a greased 13x9-in. baking dish. Seal seams and perforations. Sprinkle with sausage and cheese.

2. In a large bowl, whisk eggs, milk, salt and pepper. Pour over sausage and cheese.

3. Bake, uncovered, 35-40 minutes or until a knife inserted in the center comes out clean. Let casserole stand 5-10 minutes before serving.

TO MAKE AHEAD *Refrigerate unbaked casserole, covered, several hours or overnight. To use, preheat oven to 375°. While the oven heats, remove the casserole from refrigerator. Bake as directed, increasing time as necessary until a knife inserted in the center comes out clean. Let stand 5-10 minutes before serving.*

━━━━ READER REVIEW

"I love this dish. I made it according to the recipe, except I added green peppers and onions. It was perfect."

KATHY TASTEOFHOME.COM

SOUTHERN BRUNCH PASTRY PUFF

My family just about jumps out of bed when the smell of eggs, sausage and this buttery pastry hits their noses. It's morning magic!
—**MISTY LEDDICK** CHESTER, SC

PREP: 30 MIN. • **BAKE:** 30 MIN. + STANDING
MAKES: 8 SERVINGS

- 2 cups plus 1 tablespoon water, divided
- ½ cup quick-cooking grits
- 1 cup shredded cheddar cheese
- ¼ cup butter, cubed
- 2 tablespoons prepared pesto
- ½ teaspoon salt, divided
- ¼ teaspoon coarsely ground pepper, divided
- ½ pound bulk pork sausage
- ¼ cup finely chopped sweet red pepper
- 7 large eggs, divided use
- 1 package (17.3 ounces) frozen puff pastry, thawed

1. Preheat oven to 375°. In a small saucepan, bring 2 cups water to a boil. Slowly stir in grits. Reduce heat to medium-low; cook, covered, about 5 minutes or until thickened, stirring occasionally. Remove from heat. Stir in cheese, butter, pesto, ¼ teaspoon salt and ⅛ teaspoon pepper until blended.

2. Meanwhile, in a large skillet, cook sausage and red pepper over medium heat 4-6 minutes or until the sausage is no longer pink and the red pepper is tender, breaking up sausage into crumbles; drain.

3. In a small bowl, whisk six eggs and the remaining salt and pepper until blended. Return sausage to skillet. Pour in egg mixture; cook and stir until the eggs are thickened and no liquid egg remains.

4. Unfold each puff pastry sheet onto a 12x10-in. sheet of parchment paper. Spread grits to within ½ in. of edges. Spoon sausage mixture over half of grits on each pastry. Fold pastries over sausage mixture to enclose; press the edges with a fork to seal. Transfer to a baking sheet.

5. In a small bowl, whisk remaining egg and water; brush over pastries. If desired, top with additional ground pepper. Bake 30-35 minutes or until golden brown. Let stand 10 minutes. Cut each pastry into four pieces.

RICOTTA-RAISIN COFFEE CAKE

Sharing this beautiful coffee cake with overnight guests is a joy. If you don't have cardamom or don't care for it, substitute nutmeg, cinnamon or allspice.

—CAROL GAUS ELK GROVE VILLAGE, IL

PREP: 15 MIN. + RISING
BAKE: 20 MIN. + COOLING
MAKES: 12 SERVINGS

- 1 loaf (1 pound) frozen bread dough, thawed
- 1 cup part-skim ricotta cheese
- ¼ cup honey
- ¼ teaspoon ground cardamom
- ¼ teaspoon almond extract
- 1 cup golden raisins
- ¼ cup confectioners' sugar
- 2 to 3 teaspoons fat-free milk

1. On a lightly floured surface, roll dough into a 15x9-in. rectangle. In a small bowl, combine cheese, honey, cardamom and almond extract. Spread the filling to within ½ in. of edges and sprinkle with raisins. Roll up jelly-roll style, starting with a long side; pinch seam to seal. Pinch ends together to form a ring.
2. Place ring seam side down in a parchment paper-lined 9-in. round baking pan. Cover and let rise until doubled, about 30 minutes.
3. Preheat oven to 350°. With a sharp knife, make 12 shallow slashes in top of coffee cake. Bake 20-25 minutes or until golden brown. Cool on a wire rack. In a small bowl, combine the confectioners' sugar and milk; drizzle over cake.

TOP TIP

Turn Coffee Cake Into Dessert

Have some leftover coffee cake? Transform it into a dessert! I serve extra slices of coffee cake with ice cream and a drizzle of caramel or hot fudge ice cream topping.
—CANDY G. TUCSON, AZ

---

5 INGREDIENTS | FAST FIX

PICANTE OMELET PIE

My daughter loves this egg bake. She visits for brunch every Sunday before church, so I serve it often.

—PHYLLIS CARLSON GARDNER, KS

START TO FINISH: 30 MIN.
MAKES: 6 SERVINGS

- ½ cup picante sauce
- 1 cup shredded Monterey Jack cheese
- 1 cup shredded cheddar cheese
- 6 large eggs
- 1 cup (8 ounces) sour cream
  Tomato slices and minced fresh cilantro, optional

1. Pour picante sauce into a lightly greased 9-in. pie plate. Sprinkle with the cheeses; set aside. In a blender, combine eggs and sour cream; cover and process until smooth. Pour over the cheese.
2. Bake at 375° for 20-25 minutes or until a knife inserted in the center comes out clean. Let stand 5 minutes before cutting. Garnish with tomato and cilantro if desired.

---

5 INGREDIENTS | FAST FIX

BRUNCH-STYLE PORTOBELLO MUSHROOMS

I've always loved portobellos for their stuffability. I combined my favorite ingredients for this rich dish that's ideal for breakfast, brunch or even dinner.

—SYLVIA WALDSMITH ROCKTON, IL

START TO FINISH: 30 MIN.
MAKES: 4 SERVINGS

- 4 large portobello mushrooms, stems removed
- 2 packages (10 ounces each) frozen creamed spinach, thawed
- 4 large eggs
- ¼ cup shredded Gouda cheese
- ½ cup crumbled cooked bacon
  Salt and pepper, optional

1. Place mushrooms, stem side up, in an ungreased 15x10x1-in. baking pan. Spoon spinach onto mushrooms, building up the sides. Carefully crack an egg into center of each mushroom; sprinkle with cheese and bacon.
2. Bake at 375° for 18-20 minutes or until eggs are set. Sprinkle with salt and pepper if desired.

FAVORITE LOADED BREAKFAST POTATOES

My four young children love to eat with their hands, and these potatoes make easy finger food. My kids like to call them "brunchskins."

—**MINDY CAMPBELL** RAPID CITY, MI

PREP: 45 MIN. • **BAKE:** 10 MIN.
MAKES: 6 SERVINGS

- 6 medium baking potatoes (about 3 pounds)
- 1 tablespoon butter
- 1 each small sweet red, orange and green pepper, finely chopped
- 1 cup finely chopped fresh mushrooms
- ¼ cup finely chopped red onion
- ½ teaspoon salt
- ¼ teaspoon pepper
- 6 large eggs, beaten
- 1¼ cups shredded cheddar cheese, divided
- ¼ cup plus 6 tablespoons sour cream, divided
- 6 bacon strips, cooked and crumbled or ⅓ cup bacon bits
- 3 green onions, chopped

1. Preheat oven to 375°. Scrub and pierce potatoes with a fork; place on a microwave-safe plate. Microwave, uncovered, on high 15-18 minutes or until tender, turning once.
2. When cool enough to handle, cut a thin slice off the top of each potato; discard slice. Scoop out pulp, leaving ¼-in.-thick shells. Set pulp aside.
3. In a skillet, heat butter over medium heat. Add peppers, mushrooms and red onion; cook and stir 4-6 minutes or until tender. Stir in salt, pepper and 1 cup pulp (save remaining pulp for another use). Add eggs; cook and stir until eggs are thickened and no liquid egg remains. Stir in ½ cup cheese and ¼ cup sour cream.
4. Spoon egg mixture into potato shells. Place on a 15x10x1-in. baking pan. Sprinkle with remaining ¾ cup cheese. Bake 10-12 minutes or until heated through and cheese is melted. Top with remaining sour cream; sprinkle with bacon and green onions.

GLAZED BACON

Brown sugar, mustard and wine help make bacon a little more special. It doesn't take too much effort to present bacon in a completely new way!

—**JUDITH DOBSON** BURLINGTON, WI

PREP: 10 MIN. • **BAKE:** 30 MIN.
MAKES: 8 SERVINGS

- 1 pound sliced bacon
- 1 cup packed brown sugar
- ¼ cup white wine or unsweetened apple juice
- 2 tablespoons Dijon mustard

1. Preheat oven to 350°. Place bacon on a rack in an ungreased 15x10x1-in. baking pan. Bake 10 minutes; drain.
2. Combine brown sugar, wine and mustard; drizzle half over bacon. Bake 10 minutes. Turn bacon and drizzle with remaining glaze. Bake 10 minutes or until golden brown. Place bacon on waxed paper until set. Serve warm.

ULTIMATE BACON-MAPLE FRENCH TOAST

A savory update to baked French toast, this is an easy make-ahead dish perfect for brunch and showers. The combination of maple syrup, bacon and nuts makes it impressive and satisfying.

—JOHN WHITEHEAD GREENVILLE, SC

PREP: 30 MIN. + CHILLING
BAKE: 40 MIN. + STANDING
MAKES: 10 SERVINGS

- 8 large eggs
- 2 cups half-and-half cream
- 1 cup 2% milk
- 1 tablespoon sugar
- 1 tablespoon brown sugar
- 1 teaspoon vanilla extract
- ½ teaspoon ground cinnamon
- ¼ teaspoon ground nutmeg
  Dash salt
  Dash cayenne pepper
- 1 loaf (1 pound) French bread, cut into 1-inch slices

TOPPING

- 6 thick-sliced bacon strips, cooked and crumbled
- 1 cup butter, melted
- 1 cup packed brown sugar
- ½ cup chopped pecans, toasted
- 2 tablespoons corn syrup
- 1 teaspoon ground cinnamon
- ½ teaspoon ground nutmeg
- ¼ teaspoon ground cloves
  Maple syrup

1. Grease a 13x9-in. baking dish; set dish aside.

2. In a large shallow bowl, whisk the first 10 ingredients. Dip each slice of bread into egg mixture. Arrange slices in prepared dish. Pour remaining egg mixture over top. Cover and refrigerate overnight.

3. Remove from the refrigerator 30 minutes before baking. Preheat oven to 350°. In a small bowl, combine the first eight topping ingredients. Spread over top.

4. Bake, uncovered, 40-45 minutes or until a knife inserted in the center comes out clean. Let stand 10 minutes before serving. Drizzle with syrup.

VERY VEGGIE FRITTATA

We enjoy this colorful frittata often. The wedges also make for a great meatless dinner. The sour cream gives the eggs a good boost.

—TERI CONDON BURLEY, ID

START TO FINISH: 25 MIN.
MAKES: 4 SERVINGS

- 5 **large eggs**
- ¼ **cup sour cream**
- ¼ **teaspoon salt**
- ⅛ **teaspoon pepper**
- 1 **cup shredded cheddar cheese, divided**
- 2 **green onions, chopped**
- 1 **cup chopped fresh mushrooms**
- ½ **cup each chopped sweet red, yellow and green pepper**
- ¼ **cup chopped onion**
- 1 **tablespoon butter**
  Hot pepper sauce, optional

1. In a large bowl, whisk the eggs, sour cream, salt and pepper. Stir in ¾ cup cheese and green onions; set aside. In a 9-in. ovenproof skillet, saute the mushrooms, sweet peppers and onion in butter until tender. Reduce heat; top with egg mixture. Cover and cook for 4-6 minutes or until nearly set.

2. Uncover skillet; sprinkle with remaining cheese. Broil 3-4 in. from the heat for 2-3 minutes or until the eggs are completely set. Let stand for 5 minutes. Cut into wedges. Serve with pepper sauce, if desired.

CHERRY CHEESE BLINTZES

You can serve these elegant blintzes as an attractive brunch entree or a fun dessert. The bright cherry sauce gives them a pop of freshness. I sometimes substitute other fruits, such as peaches, blueberries or raspberries.

—JESSICA VANTREASE ANDERSON, AK

PREP: 30 MIN. + CHILLING • **BAKE:** 10 MIN.
MAKES: 9 SERVINGS

- 1½ **cups 2% milk**
- 3 **large eggs**
- 2 **tablespoons butter, melted**
- ⅔ **cup all-purpose flour**
- ½ **teaspoon salt**

FILLING

- 1 **cup 4% cottage cheese**
- 3 **ounces cream cheese, softened**
- ¼ **cup sugar**
- ½ **teaspoon vanilla extract**

CHERRY SAUCE

- 1 **pound fresh or frozen pitted sweet cherries**
- ⅔ **cup plus 1 tablespoon water, divided**
- ¼ **cup sugar**
- 1 **tablespoon cornstarch**

1. In a small bowl, combine the milk, eggs and butter. Combine flour and salt; add to milk mixture and mix well. Cover and refrigerate for 2 hours.

2. Heat a lightly greased 8-in. nonstick skillet; pour 2 tablespoons batter into the center of skillet. Lift and tilt the pan to evenly coat the bottom. Cook until the top appears dry; turn and cook for 15-20 seconds longer. Remove to a wire rack. Repeat with remaining batter. When cool, stack crepes with waxed paper or paper towels in between. Wrap in foil; refrigerate.

3. In a blender, process cottage cheese until smooth. Transfer to a small bowl; add the cream cheese and beat until smooth. Beat in sugar and vanilla. Spread about 1 rounded tablespoonful onto each crepe. Fold opposite sides of the crepe over the filling, forming a little bundle.

4. Place blintzes seam side down in a greased 15x10x1-in. baking pan. Bake, uncovered, at 350° for 10 minutes or until heated through.

5. Meanwhile, in a large saucepan, bring cherries, ⅔ cup water and sugar to a boil over medium heat. Reduce heat; cover and simmer for 5 minutes or until heated through. Combine cornstarch and remaining water until smooth; stir into cherry mixture. Bring to a boil; cook and stir for 2 minutes or until thickened. Serve with crepes.

VEGGIE SAUSAGE STRATA

As a retired home economics teacher, I've made quite a few recipes through the years. This hearty casserole is a favorite in my family.

—**DOROTHY ERICKSON** BLUE EYE, MO

PREP: 15 MIN. + CHILLING
BAKE: 1 HOUR 20 MIN.
MAKES: 10-12 SERVINGS

- 2 pounds bulk Italian sausage
- 2 medium green peppers, coarsely chopped
- 1 medium onion, chopped
- 8 large eggs
- 2 cups whole milk
- 2 teaspoons salt
- 2 teaspoons white pepper
- 2 teaspoons ground mustard
- 12 slices bread, cut into ½-inch pieces
- 1 package (10 ounces) frozen chopped spinach, thawed and squeezed dry
- 2 cups shredded Swiss cheese
- 2 cups shredded cheddar cheese
- 1 medium zucchini, cut into ¼-inch slices

1. In a large skillet, cook the sausage, green peppers and onion over medium heat until meat is no longer pink; drain. Meanwhile, in a large bowl, whisk eggs, milk, salt, pepper and mustard. Stir in the sausage mixture, bread, spinach, cheeses and zucchini.

2. Transfer the mixture to a greased 13x9-in. baking dish. Cover dish and refrigerate overnight.

3. Remove from the refrigerator 30 minutes before baking. Cover and bake at 350° for 40 minutes. Uncover; bake 40-45 minutes longer or until a knife inserted in the center comes out clean.

---

(5) INGREDIENTS

GRANDMOTHER'S TOAD IN A HOLE

I cherish memories of my grandmother's Yorkshire pudding wrapped around sausages. My kids called this puffy dish "the boat."

—**SUSAN KIEBOAM** STREETSBORO, OH

PREP: 10 MIN. + STANDING • **BAKE:** 25 MIN.
MAKES: 6 SERVINGS

- 3 large eggs
- 1 cup 2% milk
- ½ teaspoon salt
- 1 cup all-purpose flour
- 1 package (12 ounces) uncooked maple breakfast sausage links
- 3 tablespoons olive oil
  Butter and maple syrup, optional

1. Preheat oven to 400°. In a small bowl, whisk the eggs, milk and salt. Whisk flour into the egg mixture until blended. Let stand 30 minutes. Meanwhile, cook sausage according to package directions; cut each sausage into three pieces.

2. Place oil in a 12-in. nonstick ovenproof skillet. Place in the oven 3-4 minutes or until hot. Stir batter and pour into prepared skillet; top with sausage. Bake 20-25 minutes or until golden brown and puffed. Remove from skillet; cut into wedges. If desired, serve with butter and syrup.

HAM 'N' EGG CASSEROLE

I turn to this bake when I have leftover ham and day-old bread on hand. I love that it's prepared the night before, because it allows me to focus on making other dishes for the meal.

—**ELIZABETH HESSE** SPRINGVILLE, NY

PREP: 15 MIN. + CHILLING • **BAKE:** 45 MIN.
MAKES: 10-12 SERVINGS

- ½ cup chopped green pepper
- ½ cup butter, cubed
- 10 slices white bread, cubed
- 2 cups cubed fully cooked ham
- ½ pound process American cheese, cubed
- 6 large eggs
- 2 cups whole milk
- 1 teaspoon ground mustard

1. In a large skillet, saute green pepper in butter until tender. Remove green pepper, reserving drippings. Combine the green pepper, bread and ham; place in an ungreased 13x9-in. baking dish.
2. Add cheese to drippings; cook and stir over low heat until cheese melts. Pour over bread mixture. Whisk eggs, milk and mustard; pour over cheese. Cover and refrigerate overnight.
3. Remove the baking dish from the refrigerator 30 minutes before baking. Bake, uncovered, at 350° for 45-55 minutes or until a knife inserted in the center comes out clean. Let stand for 5 minutes before serving.

CHORIZO & EGG BREAKFAST RING

Friends flip for this loaded crescent ring when I bring it to brunch. It's the result of my love for Mexican food and quick-fix recipes.

—**FRANCES BLACKWELDER**
GRAND JUNCTION, CO

PREP: 25 MIN. • **BAKE:** 15 MIN.
MAKES: 8 SERVINGS

- 2 tubes (8 ounces each) refrigerated crescent rolls
- ½ pound uncooked chorizo, casings removed, or bulk spicy pork sausage
- 8 large eggs
- ¼ teaspoon salt
- ¼ teaspoon pepper
- 1 tablespoon butter
- 1 cup shredded pepper Jack cheese
- 1 cup salsa

1. Preheat oven to 375°. Unroll crescent dough and separate into triangles. On an ungreased 12-in. pizza pan, arrange triangles in a ring with points toward the outside and wide ends overlapping. Press overlapping dough to seal.
2. In a large skillet, cook chorizo over medium heat 6-8 minutes or until cooked through, breaking meat into crumbles. Remove with a slotted spoon; drain on paper towels. Discard drippings, wiping skillet clean.
3. In a small bowl, whisk eggs, salt and pepper until blended. In same skillet, heat butter over medium heat. Pour in egg mixture; cook and stir until eggs are thickened and no liquid egg remains.
4. Spoon egg mixture, chorizo and cheese across wide end of triangles. Fold pointed end of triangles over filling, tucking points under to form a ring (filling will be visible).
5. Bake 15-20 minutes or until golden brown. Serve with salsa.

SMOKED GOUDA & SWISS CHARD STRATA

I shared this impressive strata with friends at their new home. You can always change up the veggies and cheese—I've used tomatoes, spinach and cheddar.

—KIM FORNI LACONIA, NH

PREP: 30 MIN. + CHILLING • **BAKE:** 1 HOUR
MAKES: 10 SERVINGS

- 10 bacon strips, chopped
- 1 pound Swiss chard, leaves chopped and stems julienned
- 1 large sweet onion, thinly sliced
- ½ cup chopped roasted sweet red peppers
- 12 slices white bread, toasted and cubed
- 2 cups smoked Gouda or smoked Gruyere cheese, shredded
- 2 cups Swiss cheese, shredded
- 10 large eggs
- 3½ cups 2% milk
- 2 teaspoons prepared mustard
- 1 teaspoon salt
- ½ teaspoon coarsely ground pepper
- ½ teaspoon cayenne pepper

1. In a large skillet, cook bacon over medium heat until crisp; drain on paper towels, reserving 1 tablespoon drippings. Cook chard stems and onion in reserved drippings over medium heat until tender, about 4 minutes. Add the chard leaves and red pepper; cook 2 minutes. Drain.

2. Lightly grease a 13x9-in. baking dish. Layer with half of the bread cubes, half of the vegetable mixture and half of the cheeses. Repeat layers.

3. Mix remaining ingredients until well blended. Pour over layers; press down slightly. Sprinkle bacon over top. Cover and refrigerate several hours or overnight.

4. Preheat oven to 325°. Bake until strata is puffy, lightly browned and set, about 1 hour.

HOMEMADE BISCUITS & MAPLE SAUSAGE GRAVY

I remember digging into flaky, gravy-smothered biscuits on Christmas morning and other special occasions when I was a child. What a satisfying, lovely way to start the day!

—JENN TIDWELL FAIR OAKS, CA

PREP: 30 MIN. • **BAKE:** 15 MIN.
MAKES: 8 SERVINGS

- 2 cups all-purpose flour
- 3 teaspoons baking powder
- 1 tablespoon sugar
- 1 teaspoon salt
- ¼ teaspoon pepper, optional
- 3 tablespoons cold butter, cubed
- 1 tablespoon shortening
- ¾ cup 2% milk

SAUSAGE GRAVY
- 1 pound bulk maple pork sausage
- ¼ cup all-purpose flour
- 3 cups 2% milk
- 2 tablespoons maple syrup
- ½ teaspoon salt
- ¼ teaspoon ground sage
- ¼ teaspoon coarsely ground pepper

1. Preheat oven to 400°. In a large bowl, whisk flour, baking powder, sugar, salt and, if desired, pepper. Cut in butter and shortening until mixture resembles coarse crumbs. Add milk; stir just until moistened. Turn onto a lightly floured surface; knead gently 8-10 times.

2. Pat or roll dough to 1-in. thickness; cut with a floured 2-in. biscuit cutter. Place 1 in. apart on an ungreased baking sheet. Bake 15-17 minutes or until golden brown.

3. Meanwhile, in a large skillet, cook sausage over medium heat 6-8 minutes or until no longer pink, breaking into crumbles. Stir in flour until blended; gradually stir in the milk. Bring to a boil, stirring constantly; cook and stir 4-6 minutes or until sauce is thickened. Stir in remaining ingredients. Serve with warm biscuits.

PEAR-STUFFED FRENCH VANILLA TOAST

My handyman, who is originally from Nicaragua, shared this classic breakfast dish his mother use to prepare. He says he makes it frequently for his children and they clean their plates.

—GAIL BORCZYK BOCA RATON, FL

PREP: 20 MIN. + CHILLING • **BAKE:** 40 MIN.
MAKES: 6 SERVINGS

- 1 cup packed brown sugar
- ½ cup butter, melted
- 1 large pear, peeled and sliced (about 1½ cups)
- ¾ cup raisins
- 4 cups cubed day-old French bread (1½-inch pieces)
- ¾ cup finely chopped pecans
- 4 large eggs
- 2 cups French vanilla ice cream, melted
- 2 teaspoons ground cinnamon
- 2 teaspoons vanilla extract

1. In a small bowl, mix the brown sugar and butter. Spread onto bottom of a greased 8-in. square baking dish. Layer with pear, raisins, bread cubes and pecans.

2. In a large bowl, whisk eggs, ice cream, cinnamon and vanilla until blended; pour over top. Refrigerate, covered, several hours or overnight.

3. Preheat oven to 350°. Remove casserole from refrigerator while oven heats. Bake, uncovered, 40-45 minutes or until golden brown and a knife inserted in center comes out clean. Let stand 5-10 minutes before serving.

FAST FIX

SAUSAGE BREAKFAST BURRITOS

Here's a totally new way to serve scrambled eggs. The zippy flavor will awaken your taste buds.

—BRENDA SPANN GRANGER, IN

START TO FINISH: 20 MIN.
MAKES: 8 SERVINGS

- 1 pound bulk pork sausage
- 1 small onion, chopped
- ½ green pepper, chopped
- 1 can (4 ounces) mushroom stems and pieces, drained
- 1 tablespoon butter
- 6 large eggs, beaten
- 8 flour tortillas (8 inches), warmed
- 1 cup shredded cheddar cheese
  Salsa, optional

1. In a large skillet, brown sausage. Drain, reserving 2 tablespoons of the drippings. Saute the onion, green pepper and mushrooms in drippings until tender.

2. In another skillet, melt butter over medium-high heat. Add eggs; cook and stir until set.

3. Divide sausage mixture among tortillas; top with eggs and cheese. Fold bottom of tortilla over filling and roll up. Serve with salsa if desired.

ZUCCHINI EGG SKILLET

My neighbor shared more zucchini from his garden than I knew what to do with. He loved this recipe—it's great for brunch or a special breakfast.

—DARCY KENNEDY HENDERSONVLLE, NC

START TO FINISH: 30 MIN.
MAKES: 4 SERVINGS

- 2 tablespoons olive oil
- 2 medium red potatoes (about ½ lb.), cut into ¼-inch cubes
- 1 medium onion, chopped
- 2 small zucchini, shredded (about 3 cups)
- 4 frozen fully cooked breakfast sausage links, thawed and cut into ½-inch slices
- ½ cup chopped roasted sweet red peppers
- 6 cherry tomatoes, quartered
- ¼ teaspoon salt
- ⅛ teaspoon pepper
- ½ cup shredded cheddar cheese
- 4 large eggs

1. In a large skillet, heat oil over medium-high heat. Add the potatoes and onion; cook and stir 4-6 minutes or until the potatoes are crisp-tender. Stir in zucchini and sausage; cook for 4-6 minutes longer or until vegetables are tender.

2. Gently stir in red peppers, tomatoes, salt and pepper; sprinkle with cheese. With back of spoon, make four wells in potato mixture; break an egg into each well. Reduce heat to medium. Cook, covered, 4-6 minutes or until egg whites are completely set and yolks begin to thicken but are not hard.

MINI HAM & CHEESE QUICHES

We bake mini quiches with ham and cheddar in muffin pans. Salad croutons replace the need for a crust.

—LOIS ENGER COLORADO SPRINGS, CO

START TO FINISH: 30 MIN.
MAKES: 1 DOZEN

- 1 cup salad croutons
- 1 cup shredded cheddar cheese
- 1 cup chopped fully cooked ham
- 4 large eggs
- 1½ cups 2% milk

- 1½ teaspoons dried parsley flakes
- ½ teaspoon Dijon mustard
- ¼ teaspoon salt
- ⅛ teaspoon onion powder
  Dash pepper

1. Preheat oven to 325°. Divide croutons, cheese and ham among 12 greased muffin cups. In a large bowl, whisk remaining ingredients until blended. Divide egg mixture among prepared muffin cups.

2. Bake 15-20 minutes or until a knife inserted in the center comes out clean. Let stand 5 minutes before removing from pan. Serve warm.

CORNMEAL-WHEAT HOTCAKES

Drizzled with a touch of honey butter, these tasty hotcakes will brighten the day for everyone at the breakfast table. We sometimes add fruit on the side.

—ELISABETH LARSEN PLEASANT GROVE, UT

PREP: 15 MIN. • **COOK:** 5 MIN./BATCH
MAKES: 12 PANCAKES (½ CUP HONEY BUTTER)

- ¾ cup all-purpose flour
- ½ cup whole wheat flour
- ¼ cup cornmeal
- 2 teaspoons sugar
- 1 teaspoon salt
- 1 teaspoon baking powder
- ¾ teaspoon baking soda
- 2 large eggs
- 1½ cups buttermilk
- ¼ cup canola oil

HONEY BUTTER

- ¼ cup butter, softened
- ¼ cup honey
- 1 teaspoon ground cinnamon

1. In a large bowl, combine the first seven ingredients. Combine eggs, buttermilk and oil; add to the dry ingredients just until moistened.

2. Pour batter by ¼ cupfuls onto a greased hot griddle; turn when bubbles form on top. Cook until the second side is golden brown.

3. In a small bowl, combine butter, honey and cinnamon. Serve with pancakes.

SOUPS & SANDWICHES

Cozy up with terrifically scrumptious soups and sandwiches. Many of these recipes are fast fixes for when you're in a pinch and still want a flavorful meal, and some you can make ahead and freeze to enjoy whenever you'd like. If you're looking for a fresh way to make a hearty meal, this is where it's at. Enjoy!

CHEESY BROCCOLI SOUP IN A BREAD BOWL

Try this creamy, rich, cheesy broccoli soup that tastes just like it's from a restaurant! My family requests it all the time. Make homemade bread bowls if you so desire.
—RACHEL PREUS MARSHALL, MI

PREP: 5 MIN. • **COOK:** 30 MIN.
MAKES: 6 SERVINGS

- ¼ cup butter, cubed
- ½ cup chopped onion
- 2 garlic cloves, minced
- 4 cups fresh broccoli florets (about 8 ounces)
- 1 large carrot, finely chopped
- 3 cups chicken stock
- 2 cups half-and-half cream
- 2 bay leaves
- ½ teaspoon salt
- ¼ teaspoon ground nutmeg
- ¼ teaspoon pepper
- ¼ cup cornstarch
- ¼ cup water or additional chicken stock
- 2½ cups shredded cheddar cheese
- 6 small round bread loaves (about 8 ounces each)

1. In a 6-qt. stockpot, heat butter over medium heat; saute onion and garlic until tender, 6-8 minutes. Stir in broccoli, carrot, stock, cream and seasonings; bring to a boil. Simmer, uncovered, until vegetables are tender, 10-12 minutes.

2. Mix cornstarch and water until smooth; stir into soup. Bring to a boil, stirring occasionally; cook and stir until thickened, 1-2 minutes. Remove bay leaves. Stir in cheese until melted.

3. Cut a slice off the top of each bread loaf; hollow out the bottoms, leaving ¼-in.-thick shells (save removed bread for another use). Fill with soup just before serving.

READER REVIEW

"A hearty soup to make for lunch at the cabin. I topped it with crumbled bacon. Will definitely make again!"

KARENKEEFE TASTEOFHOME.COM

QUICK PEPPERONI CALZONES

These toasty pockets come together in no time. Take them to the next level by sprinkling herbs and Parmesan on top.

—SHANNON ROUM MILWAUKEE, WI

START TO FINISH: 30 MIN.
MAKES: 4 SERVINGS

- 1 **cup chopped pepperoni**
- ½ **cup pasta sauce with meat**
- ¼ **cup shredded part-skim mozzarella cheese**
- 1 **loaf (1 pound) frozen bread dough, thawed**
- 1 **to 2 tablespoons 2% milk**
- 1 **tablespoon grated Parmesan cheese**
- ½ **teaspoon Italian seasoning, optional**

1. Preheat oven to 350°. In a small bowl, mix pepperoni, pasta sauce and mozzarella cheese.

2. On a lightly floured surface, divide dough into four portions. Roll each into a 6-in. circle; top each with a scant ⅓ cup pepperoni mixture. Fold dough over filling; pinch edges to seal. Place on a greased baking sheet.

3. Brush milk over tops; sprinkle with Parmesan cheese and, if desired, Italian seasoning. Bake 20-25 minutes or until golden brown.

TOP TIP

Make Your Own Seasoning

If you don't have Italian seasoning, you can mix up your own with equal amounts of basil, thyme, rosemary and oregano. You can also add parsley flakes, marjoram, sage, savory or garlic powder.

TURKEY CHILI WITH PASTA

Some may call it witches' stew, but we think this hearty chili is the ultimate comfort food. It's a perfect warmer on chilly autumn nights.

—PAT SCHMELING GERMANTOWN, WI

PREP: 10 MIN. • **COOK:** 30 MIN.
MAKES: 10 SERVINGS (4 QUARTS)

- 1 package (20 ounces) lean ground turkey
- 3 celery ribs with leaves, chopped
- 1 large green pepper, chopped
- 1 large onion, chopped
- 2 garlic cloves, minced
- 1 can (46 ounces) tomato juice
- 1 can (11½ ounces) V8 juice
- 2 cans (8 ounces each) tomato sauce
- 2 tablespoons brown sugar
- 2 tablespoons chili powder
- ½ teaspoon salt
- ½ teaspoon ground cumin
- ¼ teaspoon pepper
- 1 bay leaf
- 1 cup uncooked elbow macaroni
- 2 cans (16 ounces each) kidney beans, rinsed and drained
  Optional toppings: sour cream, shredded cheddar cheese, thinly sliced green onions and ripe olives

1. In a Dutch oven, cook the turkey, celery, green pepper, onion and garlic over medium heat until meat is no longer pink. Add the juices, tomato sauce, brown sugar, seasonings and bay leaf. Bring to a boil. Reduce heat; simmer, uncovered, for 20 minutes.
2. Meanwhile, cook the macaroni according to package directions; drain. Add beans and macaroni to turkey mixture; heat through. Discard bay leaf before serving. Garnish with toppings of your choice.

NEBRASKA'S STUFFED BEEF SANDWICHES

When I moved to Nebraska, a friend introduced me to this German-Russian beef sandwich, and now my family requests it often.

—DOLLY CROGHAN MEAD, NE

PREP: 35 MIN. + RISING • **BAKE:** 20 MIN.
MAKES: 12 SERVINGS

- 4½ cups all-purpose flour, divided
- ¼ cup sugar
- 2 packages (¼ ounce each) active dry yeast
- 1 teaspoon salt
- ¾ cup whole milk
- ½ cup water
- ½ cup shortening
- 2 large eggs

FILLING

- 2 pounds lean ground beef (90% lean)
- 2 medium onions, chopped
- 4 cups chopped cabbage
- 2 teaspoons seasoned salt
- 1 teaspoon garlic powder
- 1 teaspoon pepper

1. Place 1¾ cups flour, sugar, yeast and salt in a large bowl. Heat milk, water and shortening to 120°-130°. Pour over flour mixture; add the eggs. Beat with an electric mixer on low speed until blended. Beat 3 additional minutes on high. Stir in the remaining flour; knead until smooth and elastic, 6-8 minutes.
2. Place dough in a greased bowl; cover and let rise in a warm place until doubled, about 1 hour.
3. Meanwhile, in a large skillet, cook beef and onions over medium heat until the meat is no longer pink; drain. Add cabbage, seasoned salt, garlic powder and pepper; cook until cabbage is wilted.
4. Punch the dough down; divide into 12 portions and cover with plastic wrap. Working with one piece at a time, roll into a 6-in. square. Place ¾ cup meat mixture in the center of each square. Fold dough over filling, forming a rectangle. Pinch edges tightly to seal and place on greased baking sheets.
5. Bake at 350° for 18-20 minutes or until golden brown. Serve hot.

SPICY BARLEY & LENTIL SOUP

My family has been making lentil soup every New Year's since I was little. We have tweaked it over time, and all of our family and friends love it.

—KRISTEN HEIGL STATEN ISLAND, NY

PREP: 15 MIN. • **COOK:** 55 MIN.
MAKES: 12 SERVINGS (4½ QUARTS)

- 1 tablespoon olive oil
- 1 package (14 ounces) smoked kielbasa or Polish sausage, halved lengthwise and sliced
- 4 medium carrots, chopped
- 1 medium onion, chopped
- 2 garlic cloves, minced
- ¾ teaspoon ground cumin
- 1 can (28 ounces) crushed tomatoes
- 1 package (16 ounces) dried lentils, rinsed
- 1 can (15 ounces) black beans, rinsed and drained
- ¾ cup medium pearl barley
- ½ cup frozen corn
- 10 cups reduced-sodium chicken broth

1. In a 6-qt. stockpot, heat oil over medium heat. Add kielbasa; cook and stir for 6-8 minutes or until browned. Remove from pan with a slotted spoon.
2. Add carrots and onion to same pot; cook and stir for 6-8 minutes or until tender. Add the garlic and cumin; cook 1 minute longer. Stir in kielbasa and remaining ingredients; bring to a boil. Reduce heat; simmer, covered, for 35-45 minutes or until the lentils and barley are tender, stirring occasionally.

FAST FIX ▶
CHICKEN SALAD CROISSANT SANDWICHES

Parmesan cheese and dill make this the most incredible chicken salad I've ever tasted. For the no-cook version, use canned chicken. These sandwiches are a simple entree to serve at parties, showers or picnics.

—JACLYN BELL LOGAN, UT

START TO FINISH: 25 MIN.
MAKES: 4 SERVINGS

- 2 cups shredded cooked chicken breast
- 1 cup seedless red grapes, halved
- ½ cup chopped cashews
- 1 celery rib, chopped
- ⅓ cup grated Parmesan cheese
- 1 green onion, chopped
- ½ cup mayonnaise
- ⅓ cup buttermilk
- 2 teaspoons lemon juice
- 1 teaspoon dill weed
- 1 teaspoon dried parsley flakes
- ¼ teaspoon salt
- ¼ teaspoon garlic powder
- ¼ teaspoon pepper
- 4 croissants, split

In a small bowl, combine the first six ingredients. In another bowl, whisk mayonnaise, buttermilk, lemon juice and seasonings. Pour over chicken mixture; mix well. Spoon chicken salad onto croissant bottoms. Replace tops.

FAST FIX ▶

MUSHROOM TORTELLINI SOUP

This nutritious veggie soup is a meal in itself thanks to cheese tortellini. It's a real comfort on a cold or rainy day.

—**JEN LUCAS** BALDWINVILLE, MA

START TO FINISH: 25 MIN.
MAKES: 6 SERVINGS

- 2 **tablespoons olive oil**
- ½ **pound sliced fresh mushrooms**
- 2 **garlic cloves, minced**
- 4 **cups vegetable broth**
- 1 **can (14½ ounces) diced tomatoes with basil, oregano and garlic, undrained**
- 1 **package (19 ounces) frozen cheese tortellini**
- 2 **cups fresh baby spinach, coarsely chopped**
- ⅛ **teaspoon pepper**
  Shredded Parmesan cheese, optional

1. In a Dutch oven, heat the oil over medium-high heat. Add mushrooms; cook and stir for 6-8 minutes or until tender. Add minced garlic; cook for 1 minute longer.

2. Add broth and tomatoes; bring to a boil. Add tortellini; cook, uncovered, 3-4 minutes or just until tortellini float (do not boil). Stir in baby spinach and pepper; cook just until spinach is wilted. If desired, serve with cheese.

FAST FIX ▶

ASIAN TURKEY BURGER WITH APPLE SLAW

I wanted to make turkey burgers a lot more fun. On a whim, I added hoisin sauce, gingerroot and garlic. Now we eat them about once a week.

—**ASHLEY GAYLE** ELLICOTT CITY, MD

START TO FINISH: 30 MIN.
MAKES: 4 SERVINGS

- 3 **green onions, finely chopped**
- 2 **tablespoons hoisin sauce**
- 1 **tablespoon minced fresh gingerroot**
- 2 **garlic cloves, minced**
- ½ **teaspoon salt**
- ¼ **teaspoon pepper**
- 1¼ **pounds ground turkey**
- 1 **tablespoon olive oil**

SLAW
- 3 **tablespoons olive oil**
- 1 **tablespoon cider vinegar**
- 1 **teaspoon Dijon mustard**
- ¼ **teaspoon salt**
- ⅛ **teaspoon pepper**
- 2 **medium apples, julienned**
- 2 **green onions, finely chopped**

ASSEMBLY
- 4 **hamburger buns, split and toasted**
- 2 **tablespoons hoisin sauce**

1. In a large bowl, mix green onions, hoisin sauce, ginger, garlic, salt and pepper. Add the turkey; mix lightly but thoroughly. Shape into four ¾-in.-thick patties.

2. In a large nonstick skillet, heat oil over medium heat. Cook burgers 7-9 minutes on each side or until a thermometer reads 165°.

3. Meanwhile, for slaw, in a large bowl, whisk oil, vinegar, mustard, salt and pepper. Add apples and green onions; toss to coat.

4. To assemble, spread bun bottoms with hoisin sauce. Top with burgers; replace tops. Serve with apple slaw.

FREEZE OPTION *Place patties on a plastic wrap-lined baking sheet; wrap and freeze until firm. Remove from pan and transfer to a resealable plastic freezer bag; return to freezer. To use, cook frozen patties as directed, increasing time as necessary for a thermometer to read 165°.*

MUSHROOM & ONION GRILLED CHEESE SANDWICHES

We took grilled cheese up a notch with baby portobello mushrooms, bacon and cheddar. For weeknight comfort food, it's good to the very last crumb.

—**BLAIR LONERGAN** ROCHELLE, VA

START TO FINISH: 25 MIN.
MAKES: 4 SERVINGS

- 3 **tablespoons butter, softened, divided**
- 8 **ounces sliced baby portobello mushrooms**
- 1 **small onion, halved and thinly sliced**
- 8 **thin slices cheddar cheese (about 3 ounces)**
- 8 **slices Texas toast**
- 4 **bacon strips, cooked and crumbled**

1. In a large nonstick skillet coated with cooking spray, heat 1 tablespoon butter over medium-high heat. Add mushrooms and onion; cook and stir 4-5 minutes or until tender. Remove from pan. Wipe skillet clean.

2. Place one slice cheese on each of four bread slices. Top with mushroom mixture, bacon and remaining cheese and bread. Lightly spread outsides of sandwiches with the remaining butter.

3. In the same skillet, toast the sandwiches in batches over medium heat for 45-60 seconds on each side or until golden brown and cheese is melted.

CHEDDAR POTATO CHOWDER

I would only make this soup occasionally because the original recipe was quite high in fat. I doctored it up a bit, using healthier ingredients, and now my family eats this rich, flavorful chowder much more often.

—**ELLIE RAUSCH** GOODSOIL, SK

PREP: 20 MIN. • **COOK:** 20 MIN.
MAKES: 7 SERVINGS

- 2 **cups water**
- 2 **cups diced unpeeled red potatoes**
- 1 **cup diced carrot**
- ½ **cup diced celery**
- ¼ **cup chopped onion**
- 1 **teaspoon salt**
- ¼ **teaspoon pepper**
- ¼ **cup all-purpose flour**
- 2 **cups 2% milk**
- 2 **cups shredded reduced-fat cheddar cheese**
- 1 **cup cubed fully cooked lean ham**

1. In a Dutch oven, combine the first seven ingredients. Bring to a boil. Reduce heat; cover and simmer for 10-12 minutes or until tender.

2. Meanwhile, place flour in a large saucepan; gradually whisk in milk. Bring to a boil over medium heat; cook and stir for 2 minutes or until thickened. Remove from heat. Add cheese; stir until melted. Add the ham and the cheese sauce to the undrained vegetables; stir until combined.

━━━━━━━ READER REVIEW

"I used evaporated milk because we were low on 2% at the time. Still turned out great."

DILIGENTFROG TASTEOFHOME.COM

SPICE IT UP SOUP

Turkey Italian sausage and jalapeno peppers add kick to this chunky soup. The original recipe called for a lot of butter and required the use of three cooking pots. I eliminated the butter and tossed the ingredients together in just one pot. My husband really enjoys this meaty soup, so I make plenty and freeze what's left over in individual servings for his lunches.

—**GUYLA COOPER** ENVILLE, TN

PREP: 10 MIN. • **COOK:** 40 MIN.
MAKES: 8 SERVINGS (2½ QUARTS)

- 1 **pound uncooked hot turkey Italian sausage links, sliced**
- ½ **pound lean ground beef (90% lean)**
- 1 **large onion, chopped**
- 1 **medium green pepper, chopped**
- 3 **garlic cloves, minced**
- 2 **cans (14½ ounces each) beef broth**
- 2 **cups water**
- 2 **cups fresh or frozen corn**
- 1 **can (14½ ounces) diced tomatoes with green chilies, undrained**
- 1 **cup diced carrots**
- ⅓ **cup minced fresh cilantro**
- 2 **jalapeno peppers, seeded and chopped**
- ½ **teaspoon salt**
- ½ **teaspoon ground cumin**

1. In a Dutch oven, cook the sausage, beef, onion and green pepper over medium heat until the meat is no longer pink. Add garlic; cook for 1 minute longer. Drain.

2. Stir in the remaining ingredients. Bring to a boil. Reduce heat; cover and simmer for 30-40 minutes to allow flavors to blend.

NOTE *Wear disposable gloves when cutting hot peppers; the oils can burn skin. Avoid touching your face.*

TURKEY & SWISS BISCUIT SLIDERS

I love to come up with new recipe ideas; I'm always experimenting. One of my favorite things to make is buttermilk biscuits. I created this sandwich combo to perfectly complement the homemade biscuits.

—**CINDY ESPOSITO** BLOOMFIELD, NJ

PREP: 35 MIN. + RISING • **BAKE:** 10 MIN.
MAKES: 16 SERVINGS

- 1 **package (¼ ounce) active dry yeast**
- ⅔ **cup warm buttermilk (110° to 115°)**
- 2 **tablespoons warm water (110° to 115°)**
- 2 **cups bread flour**
- 3 **tablespoons sugar**
- 1½ **teaspoons baking powder**
- ½ **teaspoon salt**
- ½ **cup shortening**
- ¾ **pound thinly sliced deli smoked turkey**
- ½ **pound sliced Swiss cheese Dijon mustard, optional**

1. In a small bowl, dissolve yeast in warm buttermilk and water. Place flour, sugar, baking powder and salt in a food processor; pulse until blended. Add shortening; pulse until shortening is the size of peas. While processing, gradually add yeast mixture and process just until dough forms a ball.

2. Turn dough onto a lightly floured surface; knead 8-10 times. Pat or roll to ½-in. thickness; cut with a floured 2-in. biscuit cutter. Place 2 in. apart on greased baking sheets. Let rise until almost doubled, about 30 minutes.

3. Preheat oven to 425°. Bake biscuits for 7-9 minutes or until golden brown. Remove to wire racks to cool slightly. Preheat broiler.

4. Split biscuits in half; place bottoms on greased baking sheets. Layer with turkey and cheese. Broil 3-4 in. from heat for 2-3 minutes or until cheese is melted. Replace tops. If desired, serve with mustard.

CHUNKY TACO SOUP

I get a happy response at church suppers and potlucks whenever I bring this easy-to-fix soup featuring a Southwestern zip. The flavor seems to improve in leftovers—if there are any!
—EVELYN BUFORD BELTON, MO

PREP: 20 MIN. • **COOK:** 20 MIN.
MAKES: 12 SERVINGS (ABOUT 3 QUARTS)

- 1½ **pounds beef top sirloin or round steak, cut into ¾-inch cubes**
- 1 **medium onion, chopped**
- 1 **tablespoon olive oil**
- 2 **cans (15 ounces each) pinto beans, rinsed and drained**
- 2 **cans (14½ ounces each) diced tomatoes and green chilies, undrained**
- 2 **cups water**
- 1 **can (15 ounces) black beans, rinsed and drained**
- 1 **can (14¾ ounces) cream-style corn**
- 1 **envelope ranch salad dressing mix**
- 1 **envelope taco seasoning**
- ¼ **cup minced fresh cilantro**

In a large stockpot or Dutch oven, brown beef and onion in oil. Add pinto beans, tomatoes, water, black beans, corn, salad dressing mix and taco seasoning. Bring to a boil. Reduce heat; cover and simmer for 20-30 minutes or until the meat is tender. Sprinkle with cilantro.

SAUSAGE BREAD SANDWICHES

I make these sandwiches in my spare time and freeze them so they're ready when needed. We use them for tailgating when we attend Kansas State games.
—DONNA ROBERTS MANHATTAN, KS

PREP: 30 MIN. • **BAKE:** 20 MIN.
MAKES: 4 SANDWICH LOAVES (3 PIECES EACH)

- 1 **package (16 ounces) hot roll mix**
- 2 **pounds reduced-fat bulk pork sausage**
- 2 **tablespoons dried parsley flakes**
- 2 **teaspoons garlic powder**
- 1 **teaspoon onion powder**
- ½ **teaspoon dried oregano**
- 2 **cups shredded part-skim mozzarella cheese**

- ½ **cup grated Parmesan cheese**
- 1 **large egg**
- 1 **tablespoon water**

1. Preheat oven to 350°. Prepare the roll mix dough according to package directions.

2. Meanwhile, in a large skillet, cook the sausage over medium heat for 8-10 minutes or until no longer pink, breaking into crumbles; drain. Stir in seasonings.

3. Divide dough into four portions. On a lightly floured surface, roll each into a 14x8-in. rectangle. Top each with 1¼ cups sausage mixture to within 1 inch of edges; sprinkle each with ½ cup mozzarella cheese and

2 tablespoons Parmesan cheese. Roll up jelly-roll style, starting with a long side; pinch seams and ends to seal.

4. Transfer to greased baking sheets, seam side down. In a small bowl, whisk egg with water; brush over loaves. Bake 20-25 minutes or until golden brown and heated through. Cool for 5 minutes before slicing.

FREEZE OPTION *Cool cooked sandwiches 1 hour on wire racks. Cut each sandwich into thirds; wrap each securely in foil. Freeze until serving. To reheat sandwiches in the oven, place wrapped frozen sandwiches on a baking sheet. Heat in a preheated 375° oven for 20-25 minutes or until heated through.*

TURKEY GYROS

Greek seasoning, cucumber sauce and feta cheese give my lightened-up gyros an authentic taste. I sometimes use cheddar or Monterey Jack instead of feta cheese.

—DONNA GARVIN GLENS FALLS, NY

START TO FINISH: 25 MIN.
MAKES: 4 SERVINGS

- 1 medium cucumber, peeled
- ⅔ cup reduced-fat sour cream
- ¼ cup finely chopped onion
- 2 teaspoons dill weed
- 2 teaspoons lemon juice
- 1 teaspoon olive oil
- ½ pound turkey breast tenderloin, cut into ¼-inch slices
- 1½ teaspoons salt-free Greek seasoning
- 8 thin tomato slices
- 4 pita breads (6 inches), warmed
- 1½ cups shredded lettuce
- 2 tablespoons crumbled feta cheese

1. Finely chop one-third of the cucumber; place in a small bowl. Toss with sour cream, onion, dill and lemon juice. Thinly slice the remaining cucumber.
2. In a nonstick skillet, heat oil over medium-high heat. Add turkey; cook and stir 5-7 minutes or until no longer pink. Sprinkle with Greek seasoning.
3. Serve turkey, tomato and sliced cucumber on pita breads. Top with lettuce, cheese and sauce.

TO MAKE YOUR OWN SALT-FREE GREEK SEASONING *In a small bowl, combine 1½ teaspoons dried oregano, 1 teaspoon each dried mint and dried thyme and ½ teaspoon each dried basil, dried marjoram and dried minced onion and ¼ teaspoon dried minced garlic. Keep airtight in a cool dry place for up to 6 months. Makes 2 tablespoons.*

QUICK & EASY TURKEY SLOPPY JOES

When I was first married, I found this simple recipe and adjusted it to taste. The fresh bell pepper and red onion give it a wonderful flavor.

—KALLEE TWINER MARYVILLE, TN

START TO FINISH: 30 MIN.
MAKES: 8 SERVINGS

- 1 pound lean ground turkey
- 1 large red onion, chopped
- 1 large green pepper, chopped
- 1 can (8 ounces) tomato sauce
- ½ cup barbecue sauce
- 1 teaspoon dried oregano
- 1 teaspoon ground cumin
- 1 teaspoon chili powder
- ¼ teaspoon salt
- 8 hamburger buns, split

1. In a large skillet, cook the turkey, onion and pepper over medium heat for 6-8 minutes or until turkey is no longer pink and vegetables are tender, breaking up turkey into crumbles.
2. Stir in tomato sauce, barbecue sauce and seasonings. Bring to a boil. Reduce heat; simmer, uncovered, 10 minutes to allow flavors to blend, stirring occasionally. Serve on buns.

EASY MINESTRONE

This recipe is special because it's one of the few dinners my entire family loves. And I can feel good about serving it because it's nutritious and low in fat.

—LAUREN BRENNAN HOOD RIVER, OR

PREP: 25 MIN. • **COOK:** 40 MIN.
MAKES: 11 SERVINGS (2¾ QUARTS)

- 2 **large carrots, diced**
- 2 **celery ribs, chopped**
- 1 **medium onion, chopped**
- 1 **tablespoon olive oil**
- 1 **tablespoon butter**
- 2 **garlic cloves, minced**
- 2 **cans (14½ ounces each) reduced-sodium chicken broth**
- 2 **cans (8 ounces each) no-salt-added tomato sauce**
- 1 **can (16 ounces) kidney beans, rinsed and drained**
- 1 **can (15 ounces) chickpeas, rinsed and drained**
- 1 **can (14½ ounces) diced tomatoes, undrained**
- 1½ **cups shredded cabbage**
- 1 **tablespoon dried basil**
- 1½ **teaspoons dried parsley flakes**
- 1 **teaspoon dried oregano**
- ½ **teaspoon pepper**
- 1 **cup uncooked whole wheat elbow macaroni**
- 11 **teaspoons grated Parmesan cheese**

1. In a large saucepan, saute the carrots, celery and onion in oil and butter until tender. Add garlic; cook 1 minute longer.

2. Stir in the broth, tomato sauce, kidney beans, chickpeas, tomatoes, cabbage, basil, parsley, oregano and pepper. Bring to a boil. Reduce heat; cover and simmer for 15 minutes. Add macaroni; cook, uncovered, 6-8 minutes or until macaroni and vegetables are tender.

3. Ladle soup into bowls. Sprinkle with cheese.

FREEZE OPTION *Before adding cheese, freeze cooled soup in freezer containers. To use, partially thaw in refrigerator overnight. Heat through in a saucepan, stirring occasionally and adding a little broth or water if necessary.*

ITALIAN SAUSAGE & ZUCCHINI SOUP

Everyone in my family likes this soup. Sometimes I use mini farfalle in this soup because my grandchildren say it looks like tiny butterflies. The recipe also works in a slow cooker.

—NANCY MURPHY ONEONTA, NY

START TO FINISH: 30 MIN.
MAKES: 6 SERVINGS

- ½ pound bulk Italian sausage
- 1 medium onion, chopped
- 1 medium green pepper, chopped
- 3 cups beef broth
- 1 can (14½ ounces) diced tomatoes, undrained
- 1 tablespoon minced fresh basil or 1 teaspoon dried basil
- 1 tablespoon minced fresh parsley or 1 teaspoon dried parsley flakes
- 1 medium zucchini, cut into ½-inch pieces
- ½ cup uncooked orzo pasta

1. In a large saucepan, cook sausage, onion and pepper over medium heat for 4-6 minutes or until sausage is no longer pink and vegetables are tender, breaking up sausage into crumbles; drain.

2. Add broth, tomatoes, basil and parsley; bring to a boil. Stir in the zucchini and orzo; return to a boil. Cook, covered, 10-12 minutes or until zucchini and orzo are tender.

=== READER REVIEW

"Very simple, and using garden-fresh veggies and herbs makes this soup burst with flavor!"

REDHEN1970 TASTEOFHOME.COM

FAST FIX

CILANTRO-AVOCADO TUNA SALAD SANDWICHES

Lime juice and cilantro in tuna salad— who knew? This recipe came to me as a way to have a protein-packed meal with lots of pizzazz.

—HEATHER WALDORF BLACK MOUNTAIN, NC

START TO FINISH: 15 MIN.
MAKES: 4 SERVINGS

- 2 pouches (5 ounces each) albacore white tuna in water
- ⅓ cup mayonnaise
- 3 tablespoons minced fresh cilantro
- 2 tablespoons lime juice
- 2 garlic cloves, minced
- ¼ teaspoon salt
- ⅛ teaspoon pepper
- 8 slices whole wheat bread, toasted if desired
- 4 slices Muenster or provolone cheese
- 1 medium ripe avocado, peeled and sliced

In a small bowl, mix the first seven ingredients. Spread tuna mixture over four slices of bread; top with cheese, avocado and remaining bread. Serve immediately.

MIXED VEGGIE TUNA SALAD SANDWICHES *Mix tuna and mayonnaise with ½ cup frozen mixed vegetables, thawed and chopped; 2 tablespoons chopped onion and 1 tablespoon ranch salad dressing mix. Serve on buns.*

GRANDMA'S SEAFOOD CHOWDER

My grandmother makes this recipe every year for Christmas morning—the only time I've ever had it. Why wait when you can enjoy this satisfying chowder anytime?

—MELISSA OBERNESSER UTICA, NY

PREP: 15 MIN. • **COOK:** 25 MIN.
MAKES: 10 SERVINGS (3¼ QUARTS)

- 3 tablespoons plus ¼ cup butter, divided
- 1 pound sliced fresh mushrooms
- ⅓ cup all-purpose flour
- 1 teaspoon salt
- ⅛ teaspoon pepper
- 4 cups half-and-half cream
- 1½ cups 2% milk
- 1 pound haddock fillets, skin removed, cut into 1-inch pieces
- 1 pound uncooked medium shrimp, peeled and deveined
- 2 cups frozen peas (about 10 ounces)
- ¾ cup shredded cheddar cheese
- 1 cup lump crabmeat (about 5 ounces), drained
- 1 jar (4 ounces) diced pimientos, drained
- 1 teaspoon paprika

1. In a 6-qt. stockpot, heat 3 tablespoons butter over medium-high heat. Add mushrooms; cook and stir for 8-10 minutes or until tender. Remove from pot.
2. In the same pot, heat remaining butter over medium heat. Stir in flour, salt and pepper until smooth; gradually whisk in cream and milk. Bring to a boil, stirring constantly; cook and stir for 2-3 minutes or until thickened.
3. Stir in the haddock, shrimp, peas and sauteed mushrooms; cook for 5-7 minutes or until fish just begins to flake easily with a fork and shrimp turn pink. Add cheese, crab and pimientos; stir gently until cheese is melted. Sprinkle servings with paprika.

ROOT BEER PULLED PORK SANDWICHES

My husband is a huge fan of pulled pork sandwiches, so my sister shared this easy recipe with me. At potlucks and family dinners, nobody can get enough of this root beer-braised version.

—CAROLYN PALM WALTON, NY

PREP: 20 MIN. • **COOK:** 8½ HOURS
MAKES: 12 SERVINGS

- 1 boneless pork shoulder butt roast (3 to 4 pounds)
- 1 can (12 ounces) root beer or cola
- 1 bottle (18 ounces) barbecue sauce
- 12 kaiser rolls, split

1. Place roast in a 4- or 5-qt. slow cooker. Add root beer; cook, covered, on low for 8-10 hours or until meat is tender.
2. Remove roast; cool slightly. Discard cooking juices. Shred pork with two forks; return to slow cooker. Stir in barbecue sauce. Cook, covered, until heated through, about 30 minutes. Serve on rolls.
FREEZE OPTION *Freeze cooled meat mixture in freezer containers. To use, partially thaw in the refrigerator overnight. Heat through in a saucepan, stirring occasionally and adding a little water if necessary.*

CRISPY BUFFALO CHICKEN WRAPS

I'm big on wraps, even when I go out to eat. As a busy stay-at-home mom, I flip to this family favorite a lot. It's so good with chips and salsa on the side.

—CHRISTINA ADDISON BLANCHESTER, OH

START TO FINISH: 30 MIN.
MAKES: 4 SERVINGS

- 1 package (12 ounces) frozen popcorn chicken
- 1 package (8 ounces) shredded lettuce
- 2 medium tomatoes, finely chopped
- 1 cup shredded cheddar cheese
- ⅓ cup Buffalo wing sauce
- 4 flour tortillas (10 inches), warmed
   Ranch or chipotle ranch salad dressing, optional

1. Cook chicken according to package directions; coarsely chop chicken. In a large bowl, mix the chicken, lettuce, tomatoes and cheese. Drizzle with wing sauce; toss to coat.
2. Spoon 1½ cups chicken mixture in the center of each tortilla. Fold bottom of tortilla over filling; fold both sides to close. Serve immediately with salad dressing if desired.

CUBAN-STYLE PORK SANDWICHES

Loaded with tangy flavor, this is a lighter version of a favorite restaurant-style sandwich. If you don't have a panini maker, tuck the sandwiches under the broiler until the bread is browned and the cheese melted.

—**ROBIN HAAS** CRANSTON, RI

PREP: 20 MIN. • **COOK:** 6 HOURS + STANDING
MAKES: 10 SERVINGS

- 1 large onion, cut into wedges
- ¾ cup reduced-sodium chicken broth
- 1 cup minced fresh parsley
- 7 garlic cloves, minced and divided
- 2 tablespoons cider vinegar
- 1 tablespoon plus 1½ teaspoons lemon juice, divided
- 2 teaspoons ground cumin
- 1 teaspoon ground mustard
- 1 teaspoon dried oregano
- ½ teaspoon salt
- ½ teaspoon pepper
- 1 boneless pork shoulder butt roast (3 to 4 pounds)
- 1¼ cups fat-free mayonnaise
- 2 tablespoons Dijon mustard
- 10 whole wheat hamburger buns, split
- 1¼ cups shredded reduced-fat Swiss cheese
- 1 medium onion, thinly sliced and separated into rings
- 2 whole dill pickles, sliced

1. Place onion wedges and broth in a 5-qt. slow cooker. In a small bowl, combine the parsley, 5 garlic cloves, vinegar, 1 tablespoon lemon juice, cumin, mustard, oregano, salt and pepper; rub over pork. Add to slow cooker. Cover and cook on low for 6-8 hours or until meat is tender.

2. Remove the meat; let stand for 10 minutes before slicing. In another small bowl, combine the mayonnaise, mustard and remaining garlic and lemon juice; spread over buns. Layer bun bottoms with pork, cheese, sliced onion and pickles; replace tops.

3. Cook on a panini maker or indoor grill for 2-3 minutes or until buns are browned and cheese is melted.

FAST FIX ▶

SOUTHWEST MEATBALL SOUP

I turned leftover hamburgers into meatballs and dreamed up this cozy Southwestern soup. Now my Italian family favors it over traditional wedding soup.

—**TEENA PETRUS** JOHNSTOWN, PA

START TO FINISH: 30 MIN.
MAKES: 6 SERVINGS

- 1 tablespoon canola oil
- 2 medium carrots, chopped
- 2 medium celery ribs, chopped
- ½ cup frozen corn, thawed
- 2 quarts chicken stock
- 1 cup soft bread crumbs
- 1 envelope reduced-sodium taco seasoning
- 1 large egg
- 1 pound ground chicken
- 1½ cups acini di pepe pasta
- 2 tablespoons minced fresh cilantro
- ¼ teaspoon salt
    Cubed avocado and sour cream

1. In a Dutch oven, heat the oil over medium heat. Add carrots, celery and corn; cook until tender. Stir in stock. Increase heat to high; bring to a boil.

2. Meanwhile, combine bread crumbs, taco seasoning, egg and chicken; mix lightly. With wet hands, shape into 1½-in. balls. Reduce heat to simmer; gently drop meatballs into stock. Cook, covered, until meatballs are no longer pink, 8-10 minutes. Stir in pasta. Simmer, covered, until pasta is tender, 6-8 minutes. Sprinkle with cilantro and salt.

3. Serve with avocado and sour cream.
NOTE *To make soft bread crumbs, tear bread into pieces and place in a food processor or blender. Cover and pulse until crumbs form. One slice of bread yields ½ to ¾ cup crumbs.*

BEEF STROGANOFF SANDWICHES

For an American take on classic Russian comfort food, I turn beef Stroganoff into a sandwich. It comes together fast, and my family devours it.

—ALISON GARCIA BEATRICE, NE

START TO FINISH: 25 MIN.
MAKES: 6 SERVINGS

- 1 **pound ground beef**
- 1 **cup sliced fresh mushrooms**
- 1 **small green pepper, finely chopped**
- 1 **small onion, finely chopped**
- 1 **envelope ranch dip mix**
- ¾ **cup sour cream**
- 1 **loaf (about 8 ounces) French bread**
- 2 **cups shredded part-skim mozzarella cheese**

1. Preheat broiler. In a large skillet, cook beef, mushrooms, pepper and onion over medium-high heat for 8-10 minutes or until beef is no longer pink, breaking up beef into crumbles; drain. Stir in dip mix and sour cream.

2. Cut French bread horizontally in half; place halves on a baking sheet, cut side up. Broil 3-4 in. from heat for 1-2 minutes or until lightly toasted. Remove from broiler.

3. Spoon the beef mixture over bread. Sprinkle with cheese. Broil 1-2 minutes longer or until the cheese is lightly browned. To serve, cut each bread half into three pieces.

CRISPY PITA BLT'S

Pack this sandwich full of fresh produce from your garden or a local farmers market. You'll wow lunch guests with just-picked flavor.

—MARY MILLER POPLARVILLE, MS

PREP: 35 MIN. • **BAKE:** 15 MIN.
MAKES: 4 SERVINGS

- ⅓ **cup mayonnaise**
- 1 **garlic clove, minced**
- ¼ **teaspoon grated lemon peel**
- ¼ **cup all-purpose flour**
- ¾ **cup fat-free milk**
- 1 **cup panko (Japanese) bread crumbs**
- 2 **medium yellow summer squash, cut into ¼-inch slices**
- 2 **jalapeno peppers, seeds removed and cut into ¼-inch slices Cooking spray**
- 8 **pita pocket halves**
- 8 **romaine leaves**
- 8 **slices tomato**
- 16 **cooked bacon strips, halved**

1. In a small bowl, mix mayonnaise, garlic and lemon peel. Cover and chill until serving.

2. Place flour, milk and bread crumbs in three separate shallow bowls. Coat squash and jalapeno slices with flour, then dip in milk and coat with bread crumbs. Place on baking sheets coated with cooking spray. Spritz vegetables with additional cooking spray.

3. Bake at 475° for 12-14 minutes or until golden brown, turning once.

4. Spread mayonnaise mixture inside pita halves; fill with lettuce, tomatoes, bacon and breaded vegetables. Serve immediately.

AVOCADO QUESADILLAS

Avocado slices give these quesadillas a nutritional boost and, fortunately, my son likes them, too. Add chicken or beef for extra protein.

—**DEBBIE LIMAS** NORTH ANDOVER, MA

START TO FINISH: 20 MIN.
MAKES: 4 SERVINGS (2 QUESADILLAS EACH)

  1 **tablespoon canola oil**
16 **corn tortillas (6 inches)**
  2 **cups shredded Mexican cheese blend**
  1 **cup pico de gallo**
  1 **large ripe avocado, peeled and thinly sliced**
  3 **tablespoons minced fresh cilantro**
     Additional pico de gallo

1. Grease a griddle with oil; heat over medium heat. Lightly sprinkle tortillas with water to moisten.
2. Place eight tortillas on griddle; sprinkle with cheese. After cheese has melted slightly, top with 1 cup pico de gallo, avocado and cilantro. Top with remaining tortillas.
3. Cook for 3-4 minutes on each side or until lightly browned and cheese is melted. Serve with additional pico de gallo.

ORANGE TURKEY CROISSANTS

Here's an easy, amazing sandwich that feels special. Sweet and tangy orange and crunchy pecans make it truly delicious. And only five ingredients!

—**JENNIFER MOORE** CENTERVILLE, IA

START TO FINISH: 10 MIN.
MAKES: 6 SERVINGS

  6 **tablespoons spreadable cream cheese**
  6 **tablespoons orange marmalade**
  6 **croissants, split**
  ½ **cup chopped pecans**
  1 **pound thinly sliced deli turkey**

Spread the cream cheese and marmalade onto the bottom half of croissants. Sprinkle with chopped pecans. Top with turkey; replace tops of croissants.

ROASTED TOMATO AND PEPPER SOUP

You'll want to capture everything the roasted tomatoes, pepper, onion and garlic have to offer in this colorful soup. Add cubed bread pieces to soak up some of the soup.

—**DEBBY HARDEN** LANSING, MI

PREP: 45 MIN. • **COOK:** 45 MIN.
MAKES: 4 SERVINGS

- 2 **pounds plum tomatoes, halved lengthwise**
- 2 **medium sweet red peppers, quartered and seeded**
- 2 **medium onions, finely chopped**
- 2 **tablespoons olive oil**
- 3 **garlic cloves, minced**
- 2 **teaspoons ground cumin**
- 1 **teaspoon ground coriander**
- 1 **carton (32 ounces) reduced-sodium chicken broth**
- 3 **slices day-old French bread (1 inch thick), crusts removed and cubed**
- 1 **tablespoon balsamic vinegar**
- ¼ **teaspoon salt**
- ¼ **teaspoon pepper**
  Shaved Parmesan cheese

1. Place the tomatoes and peppers, cut side down, in a 15x10x1-in. baking pan. Bake at 425° for 20 minutes. Turn tomatoes and peppers; bake 10-15 minutes longer or until skins are blistered and blackened.

2. Immediately place peppers and tomatoes in a large bowl; cover and let stand for 10 minutes. Peel off and discard skins; coarsely chop tomatoes and peppers.

3. In a large saucepan, saute onions in oil until tender. Add garlic, cumin and coriander; saute 1 minute longer. Add the broth, tomatoes and peppers. Bring to a boil. Reduce heat; simmer, uncovered, for 30 minutes.

4. Stir in the bread, vinegar, salt and pepper; heat through. Sprinkle servings with cheese.

BBQ BACON BURGER

Every family has a burger of choice, and this is ours. It's stacked tall with bacon and crunchy onion rings.

—**PAULA HOMER** NAMPA, ID

START TO FINISH: 30 MIN.
MAKES: 6 SERVINGS

- 12 **frozen onion rings**
- 2 **pounds ground beef**
- ¼ **teaspoon garlic salt**
- ¼ **teaspoon pepper**
- 6 **slices pepper jack cheese**
- 6 **hamburger buns, split and toasted**
- 1 **cup barbecue sauce**
- 6 **cooked bacon strips**
  Optional toppings: lettuce leaves, sliced tomato and dill pickles

1. Bake the onion rings according to package directions. Meanwhile, in a large bowl, combine beef, garlic salt and pepper; mix lightly but thoroughly. Shape into six ¾-in.-thick patties.

2. In a large nonstick skillet, cook burgers over medium heat 5-7 minutes on each side or until a thermometer reads 160°, adding cheese during the last minute of cooking. Serve on buns with barbecue sauce, bacon, onion rings and toppings as desired.

HEARTY CHICKEN & WILD RICE SOUP

Garlic and herb cream cheese adds subtle notes of flavor to this creamy, hearty soup. On a chilly day, it's like having a bowlful of comfort.

—**SHELISA TERRY** HENDERSON, NV

START TO FINISH: 25 MIN.
MAKES: 6 SERVINGS (2¼ QUARTS)

- 1 **package (6.2 ounces) fast-cooking long grain and wild rice mix**
- 2 **cans (10¾ ounces each) condensed cream of chicken and mushroom soup, undiluted**
- 3 **cups 2% milk**
- 2 **packages (6 ounces each) ready-to-use grilled chicken breast strips**
- 2 **cups frozen California-blend vegetables, thawed and coarsely chopped**
- ¾ **cup spreadable garlic and herb cream cheese**

Prepare the rice mix according to package directions using a Dutch oven. Stir in remaining ingredients; heat through.

GRANDMA'S PEA SOUP

Mondays were wash days at our house when I was a child, and because they were busy days, we ate soup on Mondays. My grandma's pea soup was a family favorite. What makes it different from other pea soups I have tried is the addition of whole peas, spaetzle-like dumplings and sausage.
—**CAROLE TALCOTT** DAHINDA, IL

PREP: 15 MIN. + SOAKING • **COOK:** 2¾ HOURS
MAKES: 4 QUARTS

- ½ **pound dried whole peas**
- ½ **pound dried green split peas**
- 1 **meaty ham bone**
- 3 **quarts water**
- 1 **large onion, chopped**
- 1 **medium carrot, chopped**
- 2 **celery ribs, chopped**
- ½ **cup chopped celery leaves**
- 1 **teaspoon bouquet garni (mixed herbs)**
- 1 **tablespoon minced fresh parsley**
- 1 **bay leaf**
- 1 **teaspoon salt**
- ¼ **teaspoon pepper**
- ½ **pound smoked sausage, chopped, optional**

SPAETZLE DUMPLINGS
- 1 **cup all-purpose flour**
- 1 **large egg, beaten**
- ⅓ **cup water**

1. Cover peas with water and soak overnight. Drain, rinse and place in a Dutch oven.
2. Add the ham bone, water and remaining soup ingredients except sausage and dumplings. Bring to a boil. Reduce heat; cover and simmer for 2 to 2½ hours.
3. Remove ham bone and skim fat. Remove meat from bone; dice. Add ham and sausage if desired to pan.
4. For dumplings, place flour in a small bowl; make a depression in the center of the flour; add egg and water and stir until smooth.
5. Place a colander with 3/16-in.- diameter holes over simmering soup; transfer the dough to the colander and press through with a wooden spoon. Cook, uncovered, for 10-15 minutes. Discard bay leaf.
FREEZE OPTION *Prepare soup without dumplings and freeze in serving-size portions to enjoy for months to come.*

MOM'S ITALIAN BEEF SANDWICHES

My mom made the best Italian beef. I've added to it over the years, but it's still her recipe. She made this for family reunions, and there were never leftovers.
—**MARY MCVEY** COLFAX, NC

PREP: 20 MIN. • **COOK:** 8 HOURS
MAKES: 16 SERVINGS

- 1 **boneless beef rump roast or bottom round roast (2 pounds), halved**
- 1 **boneless beef chuck roast (2 pounds), halved**
- 1 **beef sirloin tip roast (1 pound)**
- 2 **tablespoons canola oil**
- 2 **cups water**
- 1 **medium onion, chopped**
- 4 **garlic cloves, minced**
- 2 **envelopes Italian salad dressing mix**
- 1 **envelope zesty Italian salad dressing mix**
- 1 **envelope (0.87 ounce) brown gravy mix**
- 1 **to 2 tablespoons crushed red pepper flakes**
- 1 **tablespoon Italian seasoning**
- 2 **teaspoons Worcestershire sauce**
- 16 **hoagie buns, split**
  Sliced provolone cheese, optional
  Giardiniera, optional

1. In a large skillet, brown each roast in oil on all sides. Drain. Transfer the meat to a 7-qt. slow cooker. Combine the water, onion, garlic, salad dressing and gravy mixes, pepper flakes, Italian seasoning and Worcestershire sauce; pour over beef. Cover and cook on low for 8-10 hours or until meat is tender.
2. Remove beef; cool slightly. Skim fat from cooking juices. Pour juices into a large bowl. Shred beef with two forks; add to bowl. Using a slotted spoon, place ½ cup on each bun. Top with cheese and giardiniera if desired.
FREEZE OPTION *Cool meat and juices; transfer to freezer containers. Freeze for up to 3 months. To use, thaw in the refrigerator overnight. Place in a Dutch oven; heat through. Using a slotted spoon, place ½ cup on each bun. Top with cheese and giardiniera if desired.*

SIDE DISHES, SALADS & MORE

It's time to meet your new best selections for picnics, parties and so much more. Turn the pages to discover creamy coleslaws, garden fresh salads, flame-kissed veggies and homemade jam, pickles and dressings. Simple yet satisfying, any of these recipes will make you the talk of the potluck.

THREE BEAN SALAD

Fresh herbs and cayenne pepper provide the fantastic flavor in this marinated salad featuring fresh veggies and canned beans.

—**CAROL TUCKER** WOOSTER, OH

PREP: 20 MIN. + CHILLING
MAKES: 8 SERVINGS

- 1 can (15½ ounces) great northern beans, rinsed and drained
- 1 can (15 ounces) chickpeas, rinsed and drained
- 1 can (15 ounces) black beans, rinsed and drained
- 1 medium tomato, chopped
- 1 medium onion, chopped
- 1 celery rib, chopped
- ⅓ cup each chopped green, sweet red and yellow pepper
- ½ cup water
- 3 tablespoons minced fresh basil or 1 tablespoon dried basil
- 2 tablespoons minced fresh parsley
- 2 tablespoons lemon juice
- 2 tablespoons olive oil
- 1½ teaspoons minced fresh oregano or ½ teaspoon dried oregano
- ½ teaspoon salt
- ½ teaspoon pepper
- ¼ teaspoon cayenne pepper

In a large bowl, combine beans, tomato, onion, celery and peppers. In a small bowl, whisk the remaining ingredients; gently stir into the bean mixture. Cover and refrigerate for 4 hours, stirring the salad occasionally.

=== **READER REVIEW**

"This is a great summer dish to bring to potluck dinners. It's refreshing, light and full of color. My family loves it and always asks for more."

NANCYMAY70 TASTEOFHOME.COM

FAST FIX

LIME AND SESAME GRILLED EGGPLANT

When I lived in Greece, I fell in love with eggplant. My recipe's seasonings have an Asian theme, but the dish still makes me think Greek.

—**ALLYSON MEYLER** GREENSBORO, NC

START TO FINISH: 20 MIN.
MAKES: 6 SERVINGS

- 3 tablespoons lime juice
- 1 tablespoon sesame oil
- 1½ teaspoons reduced-sodium soy sauce
- 1 garlic clove, minced
- ½ teaspoon grated fresh gingerroot or ¼ teaspoon ground ginger
- ½ teaspoon salt
- ⅛ teaspoon pepper
- 1 medium eggplant (1¼ pounds), cut lengthwise into ½-inch slices
- 2 teaspoons honey
- ⅛ teaspoon crushed red pepper flakes
  Thinly sliced green onion and sesame seeds

1. In a small bowl, whisk first seven ingredients until blended; brush 2 tablespoons juice mixture over both sides of eggplant slices. Grill, covered, over medium heat 4-6 minutes on each side or until tender.

2. Transfer eggplant to a serving plate. Stir honey and pepper flakes into the remaining juice mixture; drizzle over eggplant. Sprinkle with green onion and sesame seeds.

⑤ INGREDIENTS FAST FIX

BACON-TOMATO SALAD

We love this wonderful salad that tastes like a piled-high BLT. It doesn't take much effort, and you can make it hours ahead and keep it in the fridge until mealtime.

—**DENISE THURMAN** COLUMBIA, MO

START TO FINISH: 15 MIN.
MAKES: 6 SERVINGS

- 1 package (12 ounces) iceberg lettuce blend
- 2 cups grape tomatoes, halved
- ¾ cup coleslaw salad dressing
- ¾ cup shredded cheddar cheese
- 12 bacon strips, cooked and crumbled

In a large bowl, combine lettuce blend and tomatoes. Drizzle with dressing; sprinkle with cheese and bacon.

BAKED PARMESAN BREADED SQUASH

Yellow summer squash crisps beautifully when baked. You don't have to turn the pieces, but do keep an eye on them.
—**DEBI MITCHELL** FLOWER MOUND, TX

PREP: 20 MIN. • **BAKE:** 20 MIN.
MAKES: 6 SERVINGS

- 4 **cups thinly sliced yellow summer squash (3 medium)**
- 3 **tablespoons olive oil**
- ½ **teaspoon salt**
- ½ **teaspoon pepper**
- ⅛ **teaspoon cayenne pepper**
- ¾ **cup panko (Japanese) bread crumbs**
- ¾ **cup grated Parmesan cheese**

1. Preheat oven to 450°. Place squash in a large bowl. Add oil and seasonings; toss to coat.
2. In a shallow bowl, mix the bread crumbs and cheese. Dip the squash in the crumb mixture to coat both sides, patting to help coating adhere. Place on parchment paper-lined baking sheets. Bake 20-25 minutes or until golden brown, rotating the pans halfway through baking.

PATIO PINTOS

Whenever Mom had everyone over for dinner, she made these pinto beans. Once, she made a batch for my cousin's birthday, and he ate the entire thing himself!
—**JOAN HALLFORD** NORTH RICHLAND HILLS, TX

PREP: 25 MIN. • **BAKE:** 1 HOUR
MAKES: 10 SERVINGS

- ½ **pound bacon strips, chopped**
- 1 **large onion, chopped**
- 2 **garlic cloves, minced**
- 6 **cans (15 ounces each) pinto beans, rinsed and drained**
- 4 **cans (8 ounces each) tomato sauce**
- 2 **cans (4 ounces each) chopped green chilies**
- ⅓ **cup packed brown sugar**
- 1 **teaspoon chili powder**
- ¾ **teaspoon salt**
- ½ **teaspoon dried oregano**
- ¼ **teaspoon pepper**

1. Preheat oven to 350°. In a Dutch oven, cook the bacon over medium heat until crisp, stirring occasionally. Remove with a slotted spoon; drain on paper towels. Discard the drippings, reserving 2 tablespoons in pan.
2. Add onion to drippings; cook and stir over medium heat 6-8 minutes or until tender. Add garlic; cook 1 minute longer. Stir in beans, tomato sauce, chilies, brown sugar and seasonings. Sprinkle top with bacon. Bake, covered, 60-70 minutes or until heated through.
FREEZE OPTION *Freeze the cooled bean mixture in freezer containers. To use, partially thaw in the refrigerator overnight. Heat through in a saucepan, stirring occasionally and adding a little water if necessary.*

FAST FIX ▶

BRUSSELS SPROUTS & KALE SAUTE

This colorful side dish is filled with healthy greens. The crispy salami, my kid's favorite ingredient, makes it over-the-top delicious.

—JENNIFER MCNABB BRENTWOOD, TN

START TO FINISH: 30 MIN.
MAKES: 12 SERVINGS (½ CUP EACH)

- ¼ pound thinly sliced hard salami, cut into ¼-inch strips
- 1½ teaspoons olive oil
- 2 tablespoons butter
- 2 pounds fresh Brussels sprouts, thinly sliced
- 2 cups shredded fresh kale
- 1 large onion, finely chopped
- ½ teaspoon kosher salt
- ⅛ teaspoon cayenne pepper
- ¼ teaspoon coarsely ground pepper
- 1 garlic clove, minced
- ½ cup chicken broth
- ½ cup chopped walnuts
- 1 tablespoon balsamic vinegar

1. In a Dutch oven, cook and stir salami in oil over medium-high heat for 3-5 minutes or until crisp. Remove to paper towels with a slotted spoon; reserve drippings in pan.

2. Add butter to drippings; heat over medium-high heat. Add the Brussels sprouts, kale, onion, salt, cayenne and black pepper; cook and stir until the vegetables are crisp-tender. Add garlic; cook 1 minute longer.

3. Stir in broth; bring to a boil. Reduce heat; cover and cook for 4-5 minutes or until Brussels sprouts are tender. Stir in walnuts and vinegar. Serve with salami strips.

HOW-TO

Quick Garlic Swap

In a pinch? You can use ½ teaspoon minced garlic from a jar to replace 1 fresh garlic clove, minced.

EDDIE'S FAVORITE FIESTA CORN

When fresh sweet corn is available, I love making this splurge of a side dish. Frozen corn works in a pinch, just be sure to taste as you go and add sugar if needed.

—ANTHONY BOLTON BELLEVUE, NE

PREP: 15 MIN. • **COOK:** 25 MIN.
MAKES: 8 SERVINGS

- ½ pound bacon strips, chopped
- 5 cups fresh or frozen super sweet corn
- 1 medium sweet red pepper, finely chopped
- 1 medium sweet yellow pepper, finely chopped
- 1 package (8 ounces) reduced-fat cream cheese
- ½ cup half-and-half cream
- 1 can (4 ounces) chopped green chilies, optional
- 2 teaspoons sugar
- 1 teaspoon pepper
- ¼ teaspoon salt

1. In a 6-qt. stockpot, cook the bacon over medium heat until crisp, stirring occasionally. Remove with a slotted spoon; drain on paper towels. Discard the drippings, reserving 1 tablespoon in the pan.

2. Add corn, red pepper and yellow pepper to drippings; cook and stir over medium-high heat 5-6 minutes or until tender. Stir in remaining ingredients until blended; bring to a boil. Reduce heat; simmer, covered, 8-10 minutes or until thickened.

FAST FIX ▶

FRESH HEIRLOOM TOMATO SALAD

Consider this tomato salad a summertime must. The standout dressing takes these tasty ingredients to a brand-new level.
—*TASTE OF HOME* TEST KITCHEN

START TO FINISH: 20 MIN.
MAKES: 12 SERVINGS

- 1 package (5 ounces) spring mix salad greens
- 3 tablespoons olive oil
- 2 tablespoons balsamic vinegar
- 1 teaspoon Dijon mustard
- 1 garlic clove, minced
- ½ teaspoon sugar
- ¼ teaspoon dried oregano
- 3 large heirloom tomatoes, sliced
- ½ cup fresh basil leaves
- ⅓ cup pine nuts, toasted
- 3 tablespoons chopped red onion
- 2 ounces fresh goat cheese, crumbled

Place salad greens in a large bowl. In a small bowl, whisk oil, vinegar, mustard, garlic, sugar and oregano until blended. Pour over salad greens; toss to coat.

Transfer to a large platter. Arrange tomato slices over greens. Top with basil, pine nuts, onion and cheese. Serve immediately.
NOTE *To toast nuts, bake in a shallow pan in a 350° oven for 5-10 minutes or cook in a skillet over low heat until lightly browned, stirring occasionally.*

SAUSAGE & CORN BREAD DRESSING

At our house, we add sausage and a little steak sauce to our corn bread dressing. It warms us up on even the coldest days.
—**MANDY NALL** MONTGOMERY, AL

PREP: 30 MIN. • **BAKE:** 40 MIN.
MAKES: 12 SERVINGS

- 1 package (19½ ounces) Italian turkey sausage links, casings removed
- 4 medium onions, chopped (about 3 cups)
- ½ cup chopped celery
- 6 cups cubed day-old white or French bread
- 6 cups coarsely crumbled corn bread
- 2 large eggs
- 2 tablespoons steak sauce
- 2 teaspoons onion salt
- 2 teaspoons poultry seasoning
- 2 teaspoons dried parsley flakes
- 1 teaspoon garlic powder
- 1 teaspoon baking powder
- 2½ to 3 cups reduced-sodium chicken broth

1. Preheat oven to 350°. In a 6-qt. stockpot, cook sausage over medium heat 6-8 minutes or until no longer pink, breaking into crumbles. Remove with a slotted spoon, reserving the drippings in the pot.
2. Add onions and celery to drippings; cook and stir for 6-8 minutes or until tender. Remove from heat; stir in sausage. Add cubed bread and corn bread; toss to combine.
3. In a small bowl, whisk eggs, steak sauce, seasonings and baking powder until blended; stir into bread mixture. Stir in enough broth to reach desired moistness.
4. Transfer to a greased 13x9-in. or 3-qt. baking dish. Bake 40-50 minutes or until lightly browned.

LIME-HONEY FRUIT SALAD

Nothing is more refreshing to me than a seasonal fruit salad enhanced with this simple honey lime dressing.

—VICTORIA SHEVLIN CAPE CORAL, FL

PREP: 20 MIN. + CHILLING
MAKES: 12 SERVINGS (¾ CUP EACH)

- 1 teaspoon cornstarch
- ¼ cup lime juice
- ¼ cup honey
- ½ teaspoon poppy seeds
- 3 medium Gala or Red Delicious apples, cubed
- 2 medium pears, cubed
- 2 cups seedless red grapes
- 2 cups green grapes

1. In a small microwave-safe bowl, combine cornstarch and lime juice until smooth. Microwave, uncovered, on high for 20 seconds; stir. Cook for 15 seconds longer; stir. Stir in honey and poppy seeds.

2. In a large bowl, combine apples, pears and grapes. Pour dressing over fruit; toss to coat. Cover and refrigerate overnight.

NOTE *This recipe was tested in an 1,100-watt microwave.*

READER REVIEW

"I halved the salad for just the two of us by using one apple, one pear and one clump of grapes. I also cut the dressing in half, and it was perfect."

MARINEMOM_TEXAS TASTEOFHOME.COM

ZESTY GARLIC GREEN BEANS

If you've got side-dish duty, change up the usual green bean casserole. These beans travel well, too.

—CHRISTINE BERGMAN SUWANEE, GA

START TO FINISH: 25 MIN.
MAKES: 10 SERVINGS

- 2 tablespoons oil from oil-packed sun-dried tomatoes
- 1 cup sliced sweet onion
- ½ cup oil-packed sun-dried tomatoes, chopped
- 3 garlic cloves, minced
- 1½ teaspoons lemon-pepper seasoning
- 2 packages (16 ounces each) frozen french-style green beans

1. In a Dutch oven, heat the oil over medium heat. Add onion; cook and stir 3-4 minutes or until tender. Add tomatoes, garlic and lemon pepper; cook and stir 2 minutes longer.
2. Stir in frozen green beans; cook, covered, 7-9 minutes or until beans are heated through, stirring occasionally. Uncover; cook 2-3 minutes longer or until liquid is almost evaporated.

ROASTED CABBAGE & ONIONS

I roast veggies to bring out their sweetness, and it works wonders with onions and cabbage. The puckery vinegar-mustard sauce makes this dish similar to a slaw.

—ANN SHEEHY LAWRENCE, MA

PREP: 10 MIN. • **COOK:** 30 MIN. + STANDING
MAKES: 6 SERVINGS

- 1 medium head cabbage (about 2 pounds), coarsely chopped
- 2 large onions, chopped
- ¼ cup olive oil
- ¾ teaspoon salt
- ¾ teaspoon pepper
- 3 tablespoons minced fresh chives
- 3 tablespoons minced fresh tarragon

DRESSING
- 2 tablespoons white balsamic vinegar or white wine vinegar
- 2 tablespoons olive oil
- 2 tablespoons Dijon mustard
- 1 tablespoon lemon juice
- ½ teaspoon salt
- ½ teaspoon pepper

1. Preheat oven to 450°. Place cabbage and onions in a large bowl. Drizzle with oil; sprinkle with salt and pepper and toss to coat. Transfer to a shallow roasting pan, spreading evenly. Roast 30-35 minutes or until vegetables are tender and lightly browned, stirring halfway through cook time.
2. Transfer cabbage mixture to a large bowl. Add chives and tarragon; toss to combine. In a small bowl, whisk the dressing ingredients until blended. Drizzle over cabbage mixture; toss to coat. Let stand for 10 minutes to allow the flavors to blend. Serve warm or at room temperature.

WATERMELON & SPINACH SALAD

Now's the perfect time to toss this melon salad together. Quite unexpectedly, the spinach is awesome in this recipe. You'll eat it and feel cool on even the hottest days.

—MARJORIE AU HONOLULU, HI

START TO FINISH: 30 MIN.
MAKES: 8 SERVINGS

- ¼ cup rice vinegar or white wine vinegar
- 1 tablespoon grated lime peel
- 2 tablespoons lime juice
- 2 tablespoons canola oil
- 4 teaspoons minced fresh gingerroot
- 2 garlic cloves, minced
- ½ teaspoon salt
- ¼ teaspoon sugar
- ¼ teaspoon pepper

SALAD

- 4 cups fresh baby spinach or arugula
- 3 cups cubed seedless watermelon
- 2 cups cubed cantaloupe
- 2 cups cubed English cucumber
- ½ cup chopped fresh cilantro
- 2 green onions, chopped

In a small bowl, whisk the first nine ingredients. In a large bowl, combine salad ingredients. Drizzle with dressing and toss to coat; serve immediately.

PESTO BUTTERMILK DRESSING

A good homemade dressing is hard to beat. We love this tangy blend of buttermilk and Greek yogurt.

—LIZ BELLVILLE HAVELOCK, NC

PREP: 10 MIN. + CHILLING
MAKES: 1¾ CUPS

- ⅔ cup buttermilk
- ½ cup fat-free plain Greek yogurt
- ½ cup prepared pesto
- ¼ cup shredded Parmesan cheese
- 1 tablespoon white wine vinegar
- 1 tablespoon grated lemon peel
- 1 garlic clove, minced
- ½ teaspoon coarsely ground pepper
- ⅛ teaspoon salt

Place all ingredients in a jar with a tight-fitting lid; shake well. Refrigerate 1 hour. Just before serving, shake the dressing again.

BUTTERY HORSERADISH CORN ON THE COB

For a July Fourth barbecue, I whipped up a butter and horseradish topping to spice up grilled corn. People actually formed a line to get seconds.

—TRISH LOEWEN BAKERSFIELD, CA

START TO FINISH: 30 MIN.
MAKES: 12 SERVINGS

- ¾ cup butter, softened
- ¼ cup shredded pepper jack cheese
- ¼ cup prepared horseradish
- 1 tablespoon dried parsley flakes
- 3 teaspoons salt
- 2 teaspoons balsamic vinegar
- ½ teaspoon pepper
- ¼ teaspoon dried thyme
- 12 medium ears sweet corn, husks removed

1. In a small bowl, mix the first eight ingredients until blended; spread over corn. Wrap each corncob with a piece of heavy-duty foil (about 14 in. square), sealing tightly.
2. Grill corn, covered, over medium heat 15-20 minutes or until tender, turning occasionally. Open the foil carefully to allow steam to escape.

GREAT GRAIN SALAD

I can't think of a better dish to round out a meal. This grain salad features all my favorite nuts, seeds and fruits. Try adding grilled chicken to make it a meal on its own.

—**RACHEL DUEKER** GERVAIS, OR

PREP: 15 MIN. • **COOK:** 1 HOUR + CHILLING
MAKES: 12 SERVINGS (¾ CUP EACH)

- 3 **cups water**
- ½ **cup medium pearl barley**
- ½ **cup uncooked wild rice**
- ⅔ **cup uncooked basmati rice**
- ½ **cup slivered almonds**
- ½ **cup sunflower kernels**
- ½ **cup salted pumpkin seeds or pepitas**
- ½ **cup each golden raisins, chopped dried apricots and dried cranberries**
- ⅓ **cup minced fresh parsley**
- 4 **teaspoons grated orange peel**

VINAIGRETTE

- ⅔ **cup walnut oil**
- ⅔ **cup raspberry vinegar**
- 2 **teaspoons orange juice**
- 2 **teaspoons pepper**
- 1 **teaspoon salt**

1. In a large saucepan, bring water to a boil. Add barley and wild rice. Reduce heat; cover and simmer 55-65 minutes or until tender. Meanwhile, cook the basmati rice according to the package directions. Cool pearl barley and rices to room temperature.

2. In a large bowl, combine almonds, sunflower kernels, pumpkin seeds, dried fruit, parsley and orange peel; add barley and rices.

3. In a small bowl, whisk vinaigrette ingredients. Pour over the salad and toss to coat. Cover and refrigerate for at least 2 hours.

ZESTY COLESLAW

This easy slaw tastes best after it's been refrigerated for at least one hour. The mixture seems to get creamier as it sits.

—**MICHELLE GAUER** SPICER, MN

PREP: 15 MIN. + CHILLING
MAKES: 12 SERVINGS (⅔ CUP EACH)

- 1 **cup mayonnaise**
- ⅓ **cup sugar**
- 3 **tablespoons cider vinegar**
- 1 **teaspoon seasoned salt**
- ¾ **teaspoon pepper**
- ½ **teaspoon celery seed**
- 2 **packages (14 ounces each) coleslaw mix**
- 1 **small sweet red pepper, chopped**
- ½ **cup thinly sliced sweet onion**

In a large bowl, mix the first six ingredients. Add the coleslaw mix, red pepper and onion; toss to coat. Refrigerate slaw for at least 1 hour before serving.

DILL SMASHED POTATOES *Boil, flatten and season the potatoes, adding ¼ teaspoon garlic powder. Butter, season and roast. Sprinkle potatoes with 2-3 teaspoons snipped fresh dill instead of the chives and parsley.*

ARTICHOKE SMASHED POTATOES *Boil, flatten and season the potatoes, adding ¾ teaspoon dried thyme. Butter, season and roast, adding a drained 7½-ounce jar of marinated quartered artichoke hearts during last 5 minutes. Omit herbs.*

⑤INGREDIENTS **FAST FIX**

HERBED BUTTERNUT SQUASH

Here's one of many ways we prepare butternut squash—it's a staple in our household.
—**JENN TIDWELL** FAIR OAKS, CA

START TO FINISH: 25 MIN.
MAKES: 6 SERVINGS

- 1 medium butternut squash (about 3 pounds)
- 1 tablespoon olive oil
- 1½ teaspoons dried oregano
- 1 teaspoon dried thyme
- ½ teaspoon salt
- ¼ teaspoon pepper

Peel and cut squash crosswise into ½-in.-thick slices; remove and discard seeds. In a large bowl, toss squash with remaining ingredients. Grill, covered, over medium heat or broil 4 in. from heat 6-8 minutes on each side or until squash is tender.

⑤INGREDIENTS

CRISPY SMASHED HERBED POTATOES

Golden brown and buttery, these spuds live up to their tantalizing name. A sprinkle of fresh herbs when they're hot out of the oven maximizes the flavor...and the pretty.
—**ALTHEA DYE** HOWARD, OH

PREP: 25 MIN. • **BAKE:** 20 MIN.
MAKES: 4 SERVINGS

- 12 small red potatoes (about 1½ pounds)
- 3 tablespoons olive oil
- ¼ cup butter, melted
- ¾ teaspoon salt
- ¼ teaspoon pepper
- 3 tablespoons minced fresh chives
- 1 tablespoon minced fresh parsley

1. Preheat oven to 450°. Place the potatoes in a large saucepan; add water to cover. Bring to a boil. Reduce heat; cook, uncovered, 15-20 minutes or until tender. Drain.

2. Drizzle the olive oil over the bottom of a 15x10x1-in. baking pan; arrange potatoes over the oil. Using a potato masher, flatten the potatoes to ½-in. thickness. Brush potatoes with butter; sprinkle with salt and pepper.

3. Roast potatoes 20-25 minutes or until golden brown. Sprinkle with chives and parsley.

LEMON-ROSEMARY SMASHED POTATOES *Boil and flatten potatoes; add 1 small halved and sliced lemon and 1½ teaspoons minced fresh rosemary. Butter, season and roast. Omit herbs.*

WARM SQUASH & QUINOA SALAD

Butternut squash is amazing when tossed with earthy quinoa, Italian spices and crunchy pine nuts. And don't get me started on the browned butter! Yum.

—**CARLY TAYLOR** LIBERTYVILLE, IL

START TO FINISH: 30 MIN.
MAKES: 6 SERVINGS

- 2 **cups quinoa, rinsed**
- 3 **teaspoons ground cumin**
- 3 **cups water**
- 2 **tablespoons butter**
- 3½ **cups cubed peeled butternut squash (about ½ medium)**
- 1 **teaspoon sea salt**
- ¾ **teaspoon Italian seasoning**
- ¼ **teaspoon coarsely ground pepper**
- ½ **cup crumbled feta cheese**
  Toasted pine nuts, optional

1. In a large saucepan, combine quinoa, cumin and water; bring to a boil. Reduce heat; simmer, covered, until liquid is absorbed, 10-13 minutes. Remove from heat; keep warm.

2. Meanwhile, in a large skillet, heat butter over medium-low heat until golden brown, 3-5 minutes, stirring constantly. Immediately stir in the squash and seasonings; cook, covered, until tender, 10-12 minutes, stirring occasionally. Stir into quinoa. Sprinkle with cheese and, if desired, pine nuts.

GRANDMA'S CRANBERRY STUFF

My grandmother's classic recipe makes the best cranberry dish to share with your loved ones during the holidays.

—**CATHERINE CASSIDY** MILWAUKEE, WI

START TO FINISH: 10 MIN.
MAKES: 3 CUPS

- 1 **medium navel orange**
- 1 **package (12 ounces) fresh or frozen cranberries, thawed**
- 1 **cup sugar**
- 1 **cup chopped walnuts, toasted**

Cut unpeeled orange into wedges, removing any seeds, and place in a food processor. Add cranberries and sugar; pulse until chopped. Add walnuts; pulse just until combined.

NOTE *To toast nuts, bake in a shallow pan in a 350° oven for 5-10 minutes or cook in a skillet over low heat until lightly browned, stirring occasionally.*

TOP TIP

Cranberry Facts

Want to use fresh cranberries when you make Grandma's Cranberry Stuff? They're in season from early fall through December, so stock up while you can. Fresh, unwashed cranberries can be refrigerated for about 1 month.

VEGGIE CHOPPED SALAD

My husband's aunt gave me this recipe in 1987, and it's been a staple at our house ever since. I like to prepare it a day ahead, because some time in the fridge makes it even better. Be sure to save yourself some leftovers, too.

—**MADELINE ETZKORN** BURIEN, WA

START TO FINISH: 25 MIN.
MAKES: 12 SERVINGS (¾ CUP EACH)

- 3 cups finely chopped fresh broccoli
- 3 cups finely chopped cauliflower
- 3 cups finely chopped celery
- 2 cups frozen peas (about 8 ounces), thawed
- 6 bacon strips, cooked and crumbled
- 1⅓ cups mayonnaise
- ¼ cup sugar
- 2 tablespoons grated Parmesan cheese
- 1 tablespoon cider vinegar
- ¼ teaspoon salt
- ¾ cup salted peanuts

In a large bowl, combine the first five ingredients. In a small bowl, mix mayonnaise, sugar, cheese, vinegar and salt until blended. Add to salad and toss to coat. Just before serving, stir in peanuts. Refrigerate leftovers.

SPRING GREEN RISOTTO

I came up with this risotto when I needed something cheerful and satisfying. It would be fantastic with asparagus, zucchini or summer squash, but use whatever veggies are in season.

—**DEANNA MCDONALD** GRAND RAPIDS, MI

PREP: 15 MIN. • **COOK:** 30 MIN.
MAKES: 8 SERVINGS

- 1 carton (32 ounces) vegetable stock
- 1 to 1½ cups water
- 1 tablespoon olive oil
- 2 cups sliced fresh mushrooms
- 1 medium onion, chopped
- 1½ cups uncooked arborio rice
- 2 garlic cloves, minced
- ½ cup white wine or additional vegetable stock
- 1 teaspoon dried thyme
- 3 cups fresh baby spinach
- 1 cup frozen peas
- 3 tablespoons grated Parmesan cheese
- 1 tablespoon red wine vinegar
- ½ teaspoon salt
- ¼ teaspoon pepper

1. In a large saucepan, bring stock and water to a simmer; keep hot. In a Dutch oven, heat oil over medium-high heat. Add the mushrooms and onion; cook and stir 5-7 minutes or until tender. Add the rice and garlic; cook and stir 1-2 minutes or until rice is coated.
2. Stir in wine and thyme. Reduce heat to maintain a simmer; cook and stir until wine is absorbed. Add hot stock mixture, ½ cup at a time, cooking and stirring after each addition until stock has been absorbed; continue until the rice is tender but firm to the bite and the mixture is creamy. Stir in the remaining ingredients; heat through. Serve immediately.

BLUE CHEESE & GRAPE COLESLAW

Dishes like coleslaw beg for a fresh approach. I update mine with almonds, grapes, blue cheese and bacon for a grand bowl of color and crunch.

—**JEANNINE BUNGE** HARTLEY, IA

PREP: 10 MIN. + CHILLING
MAKES: 8 SERVINGS

- 1 package (14 ounces) coleslaw mix
- ¾ cup sliced almonds, toasted
- ¾ cup quartered green grapes
- ¾ cup quartered seedless red grapes
- ½ cup crumbled blue cheese
- 3 bacon strips, cooked and crumbled
- ¼ teaspoon pepper
- ¾ cup coleslaw salad dressing

Combine the first seven ingredients. Pour dressing over salad; toss to coat. Refrigerate 1 hour.

NOTE *To toast nuts, bake in a shallow pan in a 350° oven for 5-10 minutes or cook in a skillet over low heat until lightly browned, stirring occasionally.*

MICHIGAN CHERRY SALAD

This recipe reminds me of what I love about my home state: apple picking with my children, buying greens at the farmers market and tasting cherries on vacations.

—**JENNIFER GILBERT** BRIGHTON, MI

START TO FINISH: 15 MIN.
MAKES: 8 SERVINGS

- 7 ounces fresh baby spinach (about 9 cups)
- 3 ounces spring mix salad greens (about 5 cups)
- 1 large apple, chopped
- ½ cup coarsely chopped pecans, toasted
- ½ cup dried cherries
- ¼ cup crumbled Gorgonzola cheese

DRESSING

- ¼ cup fresh raspberries
- ¼ cup red wine vinegar
- 3 tablespoons cider vinegar
- 3 tablespoons cherry preserves
- 1 tablespoon sugar
- 2 tablespoons olive oil

1. In a large bowl, combine the first six ingredients.

2. Place the raspberries, vinegars, preserves and sugar in a blender. While processing, gradually add oil in a steady stream. Drizzle over salad; toss to coat.

NOTE *To toast nuts, bake in a shallow pan in a 350° oven for 5-10 minutes or cook in a skillet over low heat until lightly browned, stirring occasionally.*

REFRIGERATOR JALAPENO DILL PICKLES

I'm passionate about making pickles; my husband is passionate about eating them. He's too impatient to let them cure on the shelf, so I found this quick recipe to make him happy. Add hotter peppers if you like the heat.

—**ANNIE JENSEN** ROSEAU, MN

PREP: 20 MIN. + CHILLING
MAKES: ABOUT 4 DOZEN PICKLE SPEARS

- 3 **pounds pickling cucumbers (about 12)**
- 1 **small onion, halved and sliced**
- ¼ **cup snipped fresh dill**
- 1 **to 2 jalapeno peppers, sliced**
- 3 **garlic cloves, minced**
- 2½ **cups water**
- 2½ **cups cider vinegar**
- ⅓ **cup canning salt**
- ⅓ **cup sugar**

1. Cut each cucumber lengthwise into four spears. In a very large bowl, combine cucumber spears, onion, dill, sliced jalapenos and garlic. In a large saucepan, combine water, vinegar, salt and sugar. Bring to a boil; cook and stir just until salt and sugar are dissolved. Pour over cucumber mixture; cool.

2. Cover tightly and refrigerate for at least 24 hours. Store in the refrigerator for up to 2 months.

NOTE *Wear disposable gloves when cutting hot peppers; the oils can burn skin. Avoid touching your face.*

=== READER REVIEW

"These were great! My whole family (and friends and neighbors) loved them, and they were so simple to make!"

CNERAK99 TASTEOFHOME.COM

DAD'S GREEK SALAD

The heart of a Greek salad is the olives, feta, cucumbers and tomatoes. Dress it with olive oil and vinegar, then add more olives and cheese.

—ARGE SALVATORI WALDWICK, NJ

START TO FINISH: 20 MIN.
MAKES: 8 SERVINGS

- 4 **large tomatoes, seeded and coarsely chopped**
- 2½ **cups (about 6) thinly sliced English cucumbers**
- 1 **small red onion, halved and thinly sliced**
- ¼ **cup olive oil**
- 3 **tablespoons red wine vinegar**
- ¼ **teaspoon salt**
- ⅛ **teaspoon pepper**
- ¼ **teaspoon dried oregano, optional**
- ¾ **cup pitted Greek olives**
- ¾ **cup crumbled feta cheese**

Place the tomatoes, cucumbers and onion in a large bowl. In a small bowl, whisk the oil, vinegar, salt and pepper and, if desired, oregano until blended. Drizzle over salad; toss to coat. Top with olives and cheese.

LOADED SMASHED POTATOES

If mashed potatoes are a must at your family gatherings, then why not go all out with the works? I love garlic, onions and bacon—this dish has all three!

—KATHY HARDING RICHMOND, MO

PREP: 40 MIN. • **BAKE:** 10 MIN.
MAKES: 15 SERVINGS

- 2 **whole garlic bulbs**
- 1 **tablespoon canola oil**
- 8 **bacon strips**
- 3 **green onions, chopped**
- 4 **pounds small red potatoes**
- 1 **container (16 ounces) sour cream**
- 1½ **cups shredded cheddar cheese, divided**
- ⅓ **cup butter, softened**
- ¼ **cup 2% milk**
- ½ **teaspoon salt**
- ¼ **teaspoon pepper**
  Minced chives, optional

1. Remove papery outer skin from garlic (do not peel or separate cloves). Cut tops off garlic bulbs. Brush with oil. Wrap each bulb in heavy-duty foil.

2. Bake at 425° for 30-35 minutes or until softened. Cool for 10 minutes.

3. Meanwhile, in a large skillet, cook the bacon over medium heat until crisp. Remove to paper towels; drain, reserving 2 tablespoons drippings. In the same skillet, cook the onions in reserved drippings for 2 minutes or until tender; set aside. Crumble bacon.

4. Place potatoes in a large saucepan and cover with water. Bring to a boil.

Reduce the heat; cover and cook for 10-15 minutes or until tender. Drain and transfer to a large bowl.

5. Mash potatoes. Squeeze softened garlic over top. Stir in bacon, onions with drippings, sour cream, 1 cup of cheese, butter, milk, salt and pepper; combine. Spoon mixture into a greased 13x9-in. baking dish; top with the remaining cheese.

6. Bake, uncovered, at 350° for 10-15 minutes or until the cheese is melted. Garnish with chives if desired.

⑤ INGREDIENTS

LUSCIOUS BLUEBERRY JAM

Enjoy this perfectly spreadable jam that boasts a beautiful dark color with a sweetly seasonal flavor.

—**KAREN HAEN** STURGEON BAY, WI

PREP: 20 MIN. • **COOK:** 20 MIN. + STANDING
MAKES: 8 CUPS

- 8 cups fresh blueberries
- 2 tablespoons lemon juice
- 1 package (1¾ ounces) powdered fruit pectin
- 7 cups sugar

1. Mash blueberries; transfer to a Dutch oven. Add lemon juice; stir in pectin. Bring to a full rolling boil over high heat, stirring constantly.
2. Stir in the sugar; return to a full rolling boil. Boil for 1 minute, stirring constantly. Remove from the heat; skim off foam. Ladle jam into jars or freezer containers and cool to room temperature, about 1 hour.
3. Cover and let stand overnight or until set, but not longer than 24 hours. Refrigerate for up to 3 weeks or freeze for up to 12 months.

MOM'S SUPER STUPENDOUS POTATO SALAD

In college, my best friend and I debated whose mom made the best potato salad. Turns out they were almost identical! Even though I've since tweaked our recipe, it still takes me home again.

—**ELLIE MARTIN CLIFFE** MILWAUKEE, WI

PREP: 20 MIN. • **COOK:** 15 MIN. + CHILLING
MAKES: 12 SERVINGS

- 1 garlic clove, peeled
- 3 pounds small red potatoes, quartered
- 2 tablespoons cider vinegar, divided
- 1½ teaspoons salt, divided
- 6 hard-cooked large eggs, divided
- 1 cup mayonnaise
- ½ cup sour cream
- 1 tablespoon Dijon mustard
- ½ teaspoon paprika
- ¼ teaspoon pepper
- 1 medium sweet onion, finely chopped
- 2 celery ribs, finely chopped
- 2 tablespoons minced fresh parsley

1. Skewer garlic with a toothpick (to make it easy to find after cooking). Place the potatoes, 1 tablespoon vinegar, 1 teaspoon salt and skewered garlic in a Dutch oven; add water to cover. Bring to a boil. Reduce heat; simmer until tender, 10-12 minutes. Drain potatoes, reserving garlic; remove skewer and crush garlic.
2. Meanwhile, chop five eggs. Whisk together mayonnaise, sour cream, mustard, paprika, pepper, garlic and the remaining vinegar and salt. Stir in potatoes, chopped eggs, onion and celery. Refrigerate for 4 hours or until salad is cold.
3. Just before serving, slice remaining egg. Top salad with egg slices; sprinkle with minced parsley and, if desired, additional paprika.

BLT TWICE-BAKED POTATOES

Two favorites— BLTs and twice-baked potatoes—come together in this hearty dish. I like to serve them with grilled steaks or barbecued chicken.

—MARY SHENK DEKALB, IL

PREP: 25 MIN. • **BAKE:** 15 MIN.
MAKES: 8 SERVINGS

- 4 medium potatoes (about 8 ounces each)
- ½ cup mayonnaise
- 1 cup shredded cheddar cheese
- 8 bacon strips, cooked and crumbled
- ⅓ cup oil-packed sun-dried tomatoes, patted dry and chopped
- 1 green onion, thinly sliced
- ½ teaspoon salt
- ¼ teaspoon pepper
- 1 cup shredded lettuce

1. Preheat oven to 400°. Scrub the potatoes; pierce several times with a fork. Place on a microwave-safe plate. Microwave potatoes, uncovered, on high 12-15 minutes or until tender, turning once.

2. When cool enough to handle, cut each potato lengthwise in half. Scoop out pulp, leaving ¼-in.-thick shells. In a small bowl, mash pulp with the mayonnaise, adding cheese, bacon, tomatoes, green onion, salt and pepper.

3. Spoon mixture into the potato shells. Place on a baking sheet. Bake 12-15 minutes or until heated through. Sprinkle with lettuce.

ITALIAN SALAD WITH LEMON VINAIGRETTE

For an Italian twist on salad, I mix greens with red onion, mushrooms, pepperoncini, olives and lemon juice. Add tomatoes and carrots if you like.

—DEBORAH LOOP CLINTON TOWNSHIP, MI

START TO FINISH: 20 MIN.
MAKES: 8 SERVINGS (½ CUP VINAIGRETTE)

- 1 package (5 ounces) spring mix salad greens
- 1 small red onion, thinly sliced
- 1 cup sliced fresh mushrooms
- 1 cup assorted olives, pitted and coarsely chopped
- 8 pepperoncini
  Optional toppings: chopped tomatoes, shredded carrots and grated Parmesan cheese

VINAIGRETTE

- ⅓ cup extra virgin olive oil
- 3 tablespoons lemon juice
- 1 teaspoon Italian seasoning
- ¼ teaspoon salt
- ¼ teaspoon pepper

1. In a large bowl, combine the first five ingredients; toss lightly. If desired, add toppings.

2. In a small bowl, whisk vinaigrette ingredients until blended. Serve with the salad.

SWEET ONION & RED BELL PEPPER TOPPING

When Vidalia onions hit the spring market, this is one of the first recipes I make. I use it on hot dogs, bruschetta, cream cheese and crackers.

—PAT HOCKETT OCALA, FL

PREP: 20 MIN. • **COOK:** 4 HOURS
MAKES: 4 CUPS

- 4 large sweet onions, thinly sliced (about 8 cups)
- 4 large sweet red peppers, thinly sliced (about 6 cups)
- ½ cup cider vinegar
- ¼ cup packed brown sugar
- 2 tablespoons canola oil
- 2 tablespoons honey
- 2 teaspoons celery seed
- ¾ teaspoon crushed red pepper flakes
- ½ teaspoon salt

In a 5- or 6-qt. slow cooker, combine all ingredients. Cook, covered, on low 4-5 hours or until the vegetables are tender. Serve with a slotted spoon.

HEARTY MAIN DISHES

Think back to some of the best meals you remember having—there's probably a main dish or two that comes to mind immediately! It's time for a creation of your own to take center stage at your next special meal, and these recipes are all ready for their moment in the spotlight.

FIESTA BEEF & CHEESE SKILLET COBBLER

I tweaked my beefy skillet cobbler until it achieved the wow factor. Top it off with lettuce, avocado, cherry tomatoes and a dollop of sour cream if you'd like.

—**GLORIA BRADLEY** NAPERVILLE, IL

PREP: 40 MIN. • **BAKE:** 15 MIN. + STANDING
MAKES: 8 SERVINGS

- 1 **pound ground beef**
- 1 **can (15 ounces) black beans, rinsed and drained**
- 1 **can (14½ ounces) diced tomatoes with mild green chilies**
- 1 **can (10 ounces) enchilada sauce**
- 1 **teaspoon ground cumin**
- 4 **tablespoons chopped fresh cilantro or parsley, divided**
- 1½ **cups biscuit/baking mix**
- 1½ **cups shredded Colby-Monterey Jack cheese, divided**
- 4 **bacon strips, cooked and crumbled**
- ⅔ **cup 2% milk**
- 1 **large egg, lightly beaten**
  Sour cream, optional

1. Preheat oven to 400°. In a 10-in. ovenproof skillet, cook beef over medium heat 5-7 minutes or until no longer pink, breaking into crumbles; drain. Stir in the beans, tomatoes, enchilada sauce and cumin; bring to a boil. Reduce heat; simmer, uncovered, 20 minutes to allow the flavors to blend, stirring occasionally. Stir in 2 tablespoons cilantro.

2. In a bowl, combine the baking mix, ½ cup cheese, bacon and remaining cilantro. Add milk and beaten egg; stir just until a soft dough is formed. Spoon over beef mixture.

3. Bake, uncovered, 13-15 minutes or until golden brown. Sprinkle with remaining cheese; bake 2-3 minutes longer or until cheese is melted. Let stand 10 minutes before serving. If desired, serve with sour cream.

==== READER REVIEW

"Big hit with all the family! Thank you for the great meal!"

SARAHJO83 TASTEOFHOME.COM

MY BEST-EVER JAMBALAYA

I tried to mimic jambalaya from my favorite restaurant, and it turned out so well that my daughter and husband now prefer my recipe. They won't order the jambalaya when we go out to eat!

—ALEXIS VAN VULPEN ST. ALBERT, AB

PREP: 20 MIN. • **COOK:** 40 MIN.
MAKES: 10 SERVINGS

- 2 tablespoons canola oil
- ½ pound fully cooked Spanish chorizo links, sliced
- 2 cups cubed fully cooked ham
- ¾ pound boneless skinless chicken breasts, cubed
- 1 can (28 ounces) diced tomatoes, undrained
- 3 cups chicken broth
- 2 large green peppers, chopped
- 1 large onion, chopped
- 1 tablespoon Cajun seasoning
- 2 teaspoons hot pepper sauce
- 3 cups instant brown rice
- ½ pound uncooked medium shrimp, peeled and deveined

1. In a Dutch oven, heat oil over medium-high heat. Add chorizo and ham; cook and stir for 3-4 minutes or until browned.

2. Add chicken to the pan; cook 5-7 minutes or until no longer pink. Stir in tomatoes, broth, peppers, onion, Cajun seasoning and pepper sauce. Bring to a boil. Reduce heat; simmer, uncovered, 8-10 minutes or until peppers are crisp-tender.

3. Return to a boil; stir in rice and shrimp. Reduce heat; simmer, covered, 7-9 minutes or until shrimp turn pink. Remove from heat; let stand, covered, 5 minutes or until rice is tender.

FAST FIX ▶

SLOPPY JOE BISCUIT CUPS

I'm a busy teacher and mom, so weekday meals with shortcuts like this are definitely a huge help to me. I always have to share the recipe when I take these to school.

—JULIE AHERN WAUKEGAN, IL

START TO FINISH: 30 MIN.
MAKES: 5 SERVINGS

- 1 pound lean ground beef (90% lean)
- ¼ cup each finely chopped celery, onion and green pepper
- ½ cup barbecue sauce
- 1 tube (12 ounces) refrigerated flaky biscuits (10 count)
- ½ cup shredded cheddar cheese

1. Heat oven to 400°. In a large skillet, cook beef and vegetables over medium heat 5-7 minutes or until beef is no longer pink, breaking up beef into crumbles; drain. Stir in barbecue sauce; bring to a boil. Reduce heat; simmer, uncovered, 2 minutes, stirring the mixture occasionally.

2. Separate dough into 10 biscuits; flatten to 5-in. circles. Press onto bottom and up sides of greased muffin cups. Fill with beef mixture.

3. Bake 9-11 minutes or until biscuits are golden brown. Sprinkle with cheese; bake 1-2 minutes longer or until cheese is melted.

ULTIMATE GRILLED PORK CHOPS

A little brining and a special dry rub go a long way to making the perfect pork chop. Once you've mastered the techniques, you'll be using them all summer long.

—**MATTHEW HASS** FRANKLIN, WI

PREP: 20 MIN. + BRINING • **GRILL:** 10 MIN.
MAKES: 4 SERVINGS

- ¼ **cup kosher salt**
- ¼ **cup sugar**
- 2 **cups water**
- 2 **cups ice water**
- 4 **bone-in pork center-cut rib chops (1 inch thick and 8 ounces each)**
- 2 **tablespoons canola oil**

BASIC RUB
- 3 **tablespoons paprika**
- 1 **teaspoon each garlic powder, onion powder, ground cumin and ground mustard**
- 1 **teaspoon coarsely ground pepper**
- ½ **teaspoon ground chipotle pepper**

1. In a large saucepan, combine salt, sugar and 2 cups water; cook and stir over medium heat until salt and sugar are dissolved. Remove from the heat. Add 2 cups ice water to cool brine to room temperature.

2. Place the pork chops in a large resealable plastic bag; add cooled brine. Seal bag, pressing out as much air as possible; turn to coat the chops. Place in a 13x9-in. baking dish. Refrigerate 8-12 hours.

3. Remove the chops from brine; rinse and pat dry. Discard brine. Brush both sides of the chops with oil. In a small bowl, mix rub ingredients; rub over the pork chops. Let stand at room temperature 30 minutes. Grill the chops on an oiled rack, covered, over medium heat 4-6 minutes on each side or until a thermometer reads 145°. Let stand 5 minutes before serving.

FOR SMOKY PORK RUB *Prepare rub as directed, using smoked paprika in place of regular paprika.*

FOR SPICY PORK RUB *Add ½ teaspoon cayenne pepper to rub mixture.*

FOR SWEET PORK RUB *Add 3 tablespoons brown sugar to rub mixture.*

FAST FIX ▶

EASY MEATBALL STROGANOFF

This recipe has fed not only my own family, but many neighbors! They all seem to come over when I make this supper. It's one of those things you throw together after work on a busy day because you know it works.

—**JULIE MAY** HATTIESBURG, MS

START TO FINISH: 30 MIN.
MAKES: 4 SERVINGS

- 3 **cups uncooked egg noodles**
- 1 **tablespoon olive oil**
- 1 **package (12 ounces) frozen fully cooked Italian meatballs, thawed**
- 1½ **cups beef broth**
- 1 **teaspoon dried parsley flakes**
- ¾ **teaspoon dried basil**
- ½ **teaspoon salt**
- ½ **teaspoon dried oregano**
- ¼ **teaspoon pepper**
- 1 **cup heavy whipping cream**
- ¾ **cup sour cream**

1. Cook egg noodles according to package directions for al dente; drain.

2. Meanwhile, in a large skillet, heat oil over medium-high heat. Brown the meatballs; remove from pan. Add broth, stirring to loosen browned bits from pan. Add seasonings. Bring to a boil; cook 5-7 minutes or until liquid is reduced to ½ cup.

3. Add meatballs, noodles and cream. Bring to a boil. Reduce the heat; simmer, covered, 3-5 minutes or until slightly thickened. Stir in sour cream; heat through.

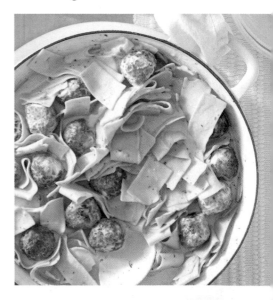

TURKEY CLUB ROULADES

Weeknights turn elegant when these short-prep roulades made with familiar ingredients are on the menu. Not a fan of turkey? You can substitute lightly pounded chicken breasts.

—*TASTE OF HOME* TEST KITCHEN

PREP: 20 MIN. • **COOK:** 15 MIN.
MAKES: 8 SERVINGS

- ¾ pound fresh asparagus, trimmed
- 8 turkey breast cutlets (about 1 pound)
- 1 tablespoon Dijon-mayonnaise blend
- 8 slices deli ham
- 8 slices provolone cheese
- ½ teaspoon poultry seasoning
- ½ teaspoon pepper
- 8 bacon strips

SAUCE
- ⅔ cup Dijon-mayonnaise blend
- 4 teaspoons 2% milk
- ¼ teaspoon poultry seasoning

1. Bring 4 cups water to a boil in a large saucepan. Add asparagus; cook, uncovered, for 3 minutes or until crisp-tender. Drain and immediately place asparagus in ice water. Drain and pat dry; set aside.

2. Spread the turkey cutlets with Dijon-mayonnaise. Layer with ham, cheese and asparagus. Sprinkle with poultry seasoning and pepper. Roll up tightly and wrap with bacon.

3. Cook roulades in a large skillet over medium-high heat for 12-15 minutes, turning occasionally, until bacon is crisp and turkey is no longer pink. Combine the sauce ingredients; serve with roulades.

SPICY BEEF & PEPPER STIR-FRY

Think of this stir-fry as your chance to play with heat and spice. I balance the beef with coconut milk and a spritz of lime.

—**JOY ZACHARIA** CLEARWATER, FL

PREP: 20 MIN. + STANDING • **COOK:** 10 MIN.
MAKES: 4 SERVINGS

- 1 pound beef top sirloin steak, cut into thin strips
- 1 tablespoon minced fresh gingerroot
- 3 garlic cloves, minced, divided
- ¼ teaspoon pepper
- ¾ teaspoon salt, divided
- 1 cup light coconut milk
- 2 tablespoons sugar
- 1 tablespoon Sriracha Asian hot chili sauce
- ½ teaspoon grated lime peel
- 2 tablespoons lime juice
- 2 tablespoons canola oil, divided
- 1 large sweet red pepper, cut into thin strips
- ½ medium red onion, thinly sliced
- 1 jalapeno pepper, seeded and thinly sliced
- 4 cups fresh baby spinach
- 2 green onions, thinly sliced
- 2 tablespoons chopped fresh cilantro

1. In a large bowl, toss the beef with ginger, 2 garlic cloves, pepper and ½ teaspoon salt; let stand 15 minutes. In a small bowl, whisk coconut milk, sugar, chili sauce, lime peel, lime juice and remaining salt until blended.

2. In a large skillet, heat 1 tablespoon oil over medium-high heat. Add beef; stir-fry 2-3 minutes or until no longer pink. Remove from pan.

3. Stir-fry the red pepper, red onion, jalapeno and remaining garlic in remaining oil 2-3 minutes or just until vegetables are crisp-tender. Stir in coconut milk mixture; heat through. Add spinach and beef; cook until spinach is wilted and beef is heated through, stirring occasionally. Sprinkle with green onions and cilantro.

SATURN'S PIZZA RING

My 7-year-old, Sarah, loves pizza. This is a recipe she came up with, and it was a huge success! You can add other pizza toppings if you wish.

—TRICIA RICHARDSON SPRINGDALE, AR

START TO FINISH: 30 MIN.
MAKES: 8 SERVINGS

- 1 pound bulk Italian sausage
- 1 can (15 ounces) pizza sauce, divided
- 1½ cups shredded part-skim mozzarella cheese, divided
- 4 ounces Canadian bacon, chopped
- 2 tubes (8 ounces each) refrigerated crescent rolls

1. Cook sausage in a large skillet over medium heat until no longer pink; drain. Stir in ½ cup pizza sauce, 1 cup cheese and Canadian bacon.
2. Unroll crescent dough and separate into triangles. On an ungreased 14-in. pizza pan, arrange triangles in a ring with points toward the outside and wide ends overlapping at the center, leaving a 4-in. opening. Press the overlapping dough to seal.
3. Spoon filling onto the wide end of triangles. Fold pointed end of triangles over filling, tucking points under to form a ring (filling will be visible).
4. Bake at 375° for 12-15 minutes or until golden brown and heated through. Sprinkle with remaining cheese. Bake 5 minutes longer or until cheese is melted. Serve with remaining pizza sauce.

PECAN-CRUSTED CHICKEN NUGGETS

I loved chicken nuggets as a child. This baked version is healthier than the original, and it's a great meal for kids.

—HAILI CARROLL VALENCIA, CA

START TO FINISH: 30 MIN.
MAKES: 6 SERVINGS

- 1½ cups cornflakes
- 1 tablespoon dried parsley flakes
- 1 teaspoon salt
- ½ teaspoon garlic powder
- ½ teaspoon pepper
- ½ cup panko (Japanese) bread crumbs
- ½ cup finely chopped pecans
- 3 tablespoons 2% milk
- 1½ pounds boneless skinless chicken breasts, cut into 1-inch pieces
  Cooking spray

1. Preheat oven to 400°. Place the cornflakes, parsley, salt, garlic powder and pepper in a blender; cover and pulse until finely ground. Transfer to a shallow bowl; stir in bread crumbs and pecans. Place milk in another shallow bowl. Dip chicken in milk, then roll in crumb mixture to coat.
2. Place on a greased baking sheet; spritz chicken with cooking spray. Bake 12-16 minutes or until chicken is no longer pink, turning once halfway through cooking.

MOM'S MEAT LOAF

Mom made the best meat loaf, and now I do, too. When I first met my husband, he wasn't a fan of meat loaf, but this recipe won him over.

—**MICHELLE BERAN** CLAFLIN, KS

PREP: 15 MIN. • **BAKE:** 1 HOUR + STANDING
MAKES: 6 SERVINGS

- 2 **large eggs, lightly beaten**
- ¾ **cup 2% milk**
- ⅔ **cup finely crushed saltines**
- ½ **cup chopped onion**
- 1 **teaspoon salt**
- ½ **teaspoon rubbed sage**
  Dash pepper
- 1½ **pounds lean ground beef (90% lean)**
- 1 **cup ketchup**
- ½ **cup packed brown sugar**
- 1 **teaspoon Worcestershire sauce**

1. Preheat oven to 350°. In a large bowl, combine first seven ingredients. Add beef; mix lightly but thoroughly. Shape into an 8x4-in. loaf on an ungreased 15x10x1-in. baking pan.
2. In a small bowl, combine remaining ingredients, stirring to dissolve sugar; remove ½ cup for sauce. Spread remaining mixture over meat loaf.
3. Bake 60-65 minutes or until a thermometer reads 160°. Let stand 10 minutes before slicing. Serve with reserved sauce.

TOP TIP

Add Meat Loaf to Grilled Cheese

I use extra slices of meat loaf in grilled cheese sandwiches. Just slip in a thin slice of meat loaf and grill the sandwich as usual.

—**RUTH F.** CROOKSVILLE, OH

CANNELLONI-STYLE LASAGNA

I created this lasagna, combining two favorite dishes, for our family's Christmas celebration. It was extra special because my parents had just come back from a trip to Italy.

—**DEBORAH LOOP** CLINTON TOWNSHIP, MI

PREP: 1 HOUR • **BAKE:** 50 MIN. + STANDING
MAKES: 12 SERVINGS

- 1 tablespoon olive oil
- 1 small onion, finely chopped
- ⅓ cup finely chopped celery
- ¼ cup finely chopped carrot
- 2 garlic cloves, minced
- ¾ pound ground beef
- ¾ pound ground pork
- ⅓ cup white wine or beef stock
- ⅔ cup beef stock
- 1 bay leaf
- ¾ teaspoon Italian seasoning
- ½ teaspoon coarsely ground pepper
- ¼ teaspoon salt
- 2 jars (15 ounces each) Alfredo sauce, divided
- 2 large egg yolks
- 1 jar (24 ounces) marinara sauce
- 1 package (9 ounces) no-cook lasagna noodles

1. In a Dutch oven, heat oil over medium-high heat. Add the onion, celery and carrot; cook and stir 4-6 minutes or until tender. Add the garlic; cook 1 minute longer.

2. Add beef and pork; cook 4-6 minutes or until meat is no longer pink, breaking into crumbles; drain. Stir in wine. Bring to a boil; cook until liquid is almost evaporated, about 1 minute.

3. Stir in stock and seasonings; bring to a boil. Reduce heat; simmer, covered, 15 minutes to allow flavors to blend. Cool slightly. Remove the bay leaf; stir in 1 cup Alfredo sauce and egg yolks.

4. Preheat oven to 350°. To assemble, spread ¾ cup marinara sauce into a greased 13x9-in. baking dish. Layer with four noodles, ¾ cup Alfredo sauce and 2 cups meat mixture. Top with four noodles and ¾ cup marinara sauce. Layer with four noodles, ¾ cup Alfredo sauce and remaining meat mixture. Top with the remaining noodles and marinara sauce. Drizzle remaining Alfredo sauce over top.

5. Bake, covered, 30 minutes. Uncover; bake 20-25 minutes longer or until bubbly. Let lasagna stand 15 minutes before serving.

BARBECUED STRAWBERRY CHICKEN

When it's time to impress family and friends, we serve barbecue chicken garnished with strawberries. It's easier than anyone would ever guess.

—**BONNIE HAWKINS** ELKHORN, WI

PREP: 25 MIN. • **BAKE:** 15 MIN.
MAKES: 4 SERVINGS

- 2 tablespoons canola oil
- 4 boneless skinless chicken breast halves (6 ounces each)
- 2 tablespoons butter
- ¼ cup finely chopped red onion
- 1 cup barbecue sauce
- 2 tablespoons brown sugar
- 2 tablespoons balsamic vinegar
- 2 tablespoons honey
- 1 cup sliced fresh strawberries

1. Preheat oven to 350°. In a large ovenproof skillet, heat the oil over medium-high heat. Brown chicken on both sides. Remove from pan. In same pan, heat butter over medium-high heat. Add onion; cook and stir 1 minute or until tender.

2. Stir in barbecue sauce, brown sugar, vinegar and honey. Bring to a boil. Reduce the heat; simmer, uncovered, 4-6 minutes or until thickened. Return chicken to pan. Bake 12-15 minutes or until a thermometer reads 165°. Stir in the strawberries.

SPICY VEGGIE PASTA BAKE

My dad always cooked with cast-iron skillets, so when I do, I remember his amazing culinary skills.
—SONYA GOERGEN MOORHEAD, MN

START TO FINISH: 30 MIN.
MAKES: 6 SERVINGS

- 3 cups uncooked spiral pasta
- 1 medium yellow summer squash
- 1 small zucchini
- 1 medium sweet red pepper
- 1 medium green pepper
- 1 tablespoon olive oil
- 1 small red onion, halved and sliced
- 1 cup sliced fresh mushrooms
- ½ teaspoon salt
- ¼ teaspoon pepper
- ¼ teaspoon crushed red pepper flakes
- 1 jar (24 ounces) spicy marinara sauce
- 8 ounces fresh mozzarella cheese pearls
   Grated Parmesan cheese and julienned fresh basil, optional

1. Preheat oven to 375°. Cook pasta according to package directions for al dente; drain.
2. Cut squashes and peppers into ¼-in. julienne strips. In a 12-in. cast-iron skillet, heat oil over medium-high heat. Add onion, mushrooms and the julienned vegetables; cook and stir 5-7 minutes or until crisp-tender. Stir in seasonings. Add marinara sauce and pasta; toss to combine. Top with the cheese pearls.
3. Transfer to oven; bake, uncovered, 10-15 minutes or until cheese is melted. If desired, sprinkle with Parmesan cheese and basil before serving.

━━━━━━━━━━ READER REVIEW

"I don't care for marinara sauce from a jar, so I whipped up a batch of my own while the pasta was cooking and used that instead. One of those recipes you'll return to time and again!"

CAST_IRON_KING TASTEOFHOME.COM

QUINOA-STUFFED SQUASH BOATS

My colorful boats—with quinoa, chickpeas and pumpkin seeds—use delicata squash, a winter squash that's cream-colored with green stripes. In a pinch, acorn squash will do.
—LAUREN KNOELKE MILWAUKEE, WI

START TO FINISH: 30 MIN.
MAKES: 8 SERVINGS

- 4 delicata squash (about 12 ounces each)
- 3 teaspoons olive oil, divided
- ⅛ teaspoon pepper
- 1 teaspoon salt, divided
- 1½ cups vegetable broth
- 1 cup quinoa, rinsed
- 1 can (15 ounces) chickpeas, rinsed and drained
- ¼ cup dried cranberries
- 1 green onion, thinly sliced
- 1 teaspoon minced fresh sage
- ½ teaspoon grated lemon peel
- 1 teaspoon lemon juice
- ½ cup crumbled goat cheese
- ¼ cup salted pumpkin seeds or pepitas, toasted

1. Preheat oven to 450°. Cut each squash lengthwise in half; remove and discard seeds. Lightly brush cut sides with 1 teaspoon oil; sprinkle with pepper and ½ teaspoon salt. Place on a baking sheet, cut side down. Bake 15-20 minutes or until tender.
2. Meanwhile, in a large saucepan, combine broth and quinoa; bring to a boil. Reduce heat; simmer, covered, for 12-15 minutes or until the liquid is absorbed.
3. Stir in chickpeas, cranberries, green onion, sage, lemon peel, lemon juice and the remaining oil and salt; spoon into squash. Sprinkle with cheese and pumpkin seeds.

SOUTHWEST KIELBASA BOWLS

Here's our at-home take on restaurant burrito bowls. We start with with rice, kielbasa and black beans, then top 'em with salsa, red onion and cilantro. Use a spicier sausage if you want to crank up the heat.
—**ABBY WILLIAMSON** DUNEDIN, FL

START TO FINISH: 20 MIN.
MAKES: 4 SERVINGS

- 2 **cups uncooked instant brown rice**
- 2 **tablespoons olive oil**
- 1 **package (14 ounces) smoked turkey kielbasa, cut into ¼-inch slices**
- 1 **can (15 ounces) black beans, rinsed and drained**
- 1½ **cups fresh salsa**
- ¼ **cup finely chopped red onion**
  Fresh cilantro leaves, optional

1. Cook rice according to package directions.
2. Meanwhile, in a large skillet, heat oil over medium-high heat. Add kielbasa; cook and stir 4-6 minutes or until browned. Stir in beans and salsa. Divide rice among four bowls. Top with the kielbasa mixture, onion and, if desired, cilantro.

BROWN SUGAR PINEAPPLE HAM

With pineapple, brown sugar, mustard and cloves, this baked ham is straightforward and simple—just what you're looking for in a holiday ham with easy steps.
—**TASTE OF HOME** TEST KITCHEN

PREP: 10 MIN. • **BAKE:** 2 HOURS
MAKES: 12 SERVINGS

- 1 **fully cooked bone-in ham (7 to 9 pounds)**
- 1 **can (20 ounces) crushed pineapple, undrained**
- 1 **cup packed brown sugar**
- 1 **tablespoon Dijon mustard**
- ¼ **teaspoon ground cloves**

1. Preheat oven to 325°. Place ham on a rack in a shallow roasting pan. Using a sharp knife, score surface of ham with ½-in.-deep cuts in a diamond pattern. Cover and bake 1½ hours.
2. In a small bowl, mix remaining ingredients. Spread over ham, pressing the mixture into cuts. Bake ham, uncovered, 30-60 minutes longer or until a thermometer reads 140°.

ZESTY CHICKEN SOFT TACOS

We've made these tacos with corn and flour tortillas, but flatbread is our favorite wrap. Set out toppings and let everyone assemble his or her own taco.
—**JESSIE GREARSON-SAPAT** FALMOUTH, ME

START TO FINISH: 25 MIN.
MAKES: 6 SERVINGS

- 1 **cup (8 ounces) reduced-fat sour cream**
- 2 **tablespoons Sriracha Asian hot chili sauce**
- 2 **tablespoons lime juice**
- 1½ **teaspoons grated lime peel**
- ½ **teaspoon salt**
- ⅛ **teaspoon pepper**
- 6 **naan flatbreads, warmed**
- 1 **rotisserie chicken, skin removed, shredded**
  Minced fresh cilantro, optional

In a small bowl, mix sour cream, chili sauce, lime juice, lime peel, salt and pepper. Spread over flatbreads; top with chicken and, if desired, cilantro.

TERIYAKI PINEAPPLE DRUMSTICKS

We have a large family and throw big parties, so I look for ways to free my husband from the grill. Oven-roasted drumsticks keep everyone happy.

—ERICA ALLEN TUCKERTON, NJ

PREP: 35 MIN. • **BAKE:** 1½ HOURS
MAKES: 12 SERVINGS

- 1 tablespoon garlic salt
- 1 tablespoon minced chives
- 1½ teaspoons paprika
- 1½ teaspoons pepper
- ½ teaspoon salt
- 24 chicken drumsticks
- ½ cup canola oil
- 1 can (8 ounces) crushed pineapple
- ½ cup water
- ¼ cup Worcestershire sauce
- ¼ cup packed brown sugar
- ¼ cup yellow mustard
- 4 teaspoons cornstarch
- 2 tablespoons cold water

1. Preheat oven to 350°. Mix the first five ingredients; sprinkle over chicken. In a large skillet, heat oil over medium-high heat. Brown the drumsticks in batches. Transfer to a roasting pan.

2. Meanwhile, combine the pineapple, ½ cup water, Worcestershire sauce, brown sugar and mustard; pour over chicken. Cover; bake until tender, about 1½ to 2 hours, uncovering during the last 20-30 minutes of baking to let skin crisp.

3. Remove drumsticks to a platter; keep warm. Transfer cooking juices to a small saucepan; skim fat. Bring the juices to a boil. In a small bowl, mix cornstarch and cold water until smooth; stir into cooking juices. Return to a boil; cook and stir 1-2 minutes or until thickened. Serve with drumsticks.

PENNE ALLA VODKA

This impressive pasta is always on the menu when my husband and I invite first-time guests over for dinner. Many friends have asked me to make the recipe again years after they first tried it.

—CARA LANGER OVERLAND PARK, KS

START TO FINISH: 30 MIN.
MAKES: 6 SERVINGS

- 1 package (16 ounces) penne pasta
- 3 tablespoons butter
- 2 garlic cloves, minced
- 4 ounces thinly sliced prosciutto, cut into strips
- 1 can (28 ounces) whole plum tomatoes, drained and chopped
- ¼ cup vodka
- ½ teaspoon salt
- ½ teaspoon crushed red pepper flakes
- ½ cup heavy whipping cream
- ½ cup shredded Parmesan cheese

1. Cook pasta according to package directions.

2. Meanwhile, in a large skillet, heat butter over medium-high heat. Add garlic; cook and stir 1 minute. Add prosciutto; cook 2 minutes longer. Stir in tomatoes, vodka, salt and pepper flakes. Bring to a boil. Reduce heat; simmer, uncovered, 5 minutes. Stir in cream; cook 2-3 minutes longer, stirring occasionally.

3. Drain pasta. Add pasta and cheese to sauce; toss to combine.

CHORIZO PUMPKIN PASTA

I'm a busy student, and this spicy-sweet pasta makes a perfect quick dinner. Even better, it works on a bigger scale to feed a bunch of friends.

—**CHRISTINE YANG** SYRACUSE, NY

START TO FINISH: 30 MIN.
MAKES: 6 SERVINGS

- 3 cups uncooked gemelli or spiral pasta (about 12 ounces)
- 1 package (12 ounces) fully cooked chorizo chicken sausage links or flavor of choice, sliced
- 1 cup canned pumpkin
- 1 cup half-and-half cream
- ¾ teaspoon salt
- ¼ teaspoon pepper
- 1½ cups shredded Manchego or Monterey Jack cheese
  Minced fresh cilantro, optional

1. Cook pasta according to package directions. Drain, reserving ¾ cup pasta water.
2. Meanwhile, in a large skillet, saute sausage over medium heat until lightly browned; reduce heat to medium-low. Add pumpkin, cream, salt and pepper; cook and stir until heated through. Toss with pasta and enough pasta water to moisten; stir in cheese. If desired, sprinkle with cilantro.

PINTO BEAN TOSTADAS

Ready-to-go pinto beans and crispy corn tortillas prove how easy it is to make a healthy meal. Sometimes I add some chopped leftover meat to the tostadas, but they're equally satisfying just as they are.

—**LILY JULOW** LAWRENCEVILLE, GA

START TO FINISH: 30 MIN.
MAKES: 6 SERVINGS

- ¼ cup sour cream
- ¾ teaspoon grated lime peel
- ¼ teaspoon ground cumin
- ½ teaspoon salt, divided
- 2 tablespoons canola oil, divided
- 2 garlic cloves, minced
- 2 cans (15 ounces each) pinto beans, rinsed and drained
- 1 to 2 teaspoons hot pepper sauce
- 1 teaspoon chili powder
- 6 corn tortillas (6 inches)
- 2 cups shredded lettuce
- ½ cup salsa
- ¾ cup crumbled feta cheese or queso fresco
  Lime wedges

1. In a small bowl, mix sour cream, lime peel, cumin and ¼ teaspoon salt. In a large saucepan, heat 1 tablespoon oil over medium heat. Add the garlic; cook and stir just until fragrant, about 45 seconds. Stir in beans, pepper sauce, chili powder and the remaining salt; heat through, stirring occasionally. Keep warm.
2. Brush both sides of tortillas with remaining oil. Place a large skillet over medium-high heat. Add tortillas in two batches; cook 2-3 minutes on each side or until lightly browned and crisp.
3. To serve, arrange beans and lettuce over tostada shells; top with salsa, sour cream mixture and cheese. Serve with lime wedges.

CHICKEN SPINACH DIP BREAD BOWLS

My family loves artichoke spinach dip, so I thought I could turn this popular appetizer into a chicken entree. The sourdough bowl makes a fun presentation. I love that with this recipe I can make one for dinner and wrap one for the freezer!

—MERRY GRAHAM NEWHALL, CA

PREP: 35 MIN. • **BAKE:** 20 MIN. + STANDING
MAKES: 8 SERVINGS

- 1 package (10 ounces) frozen chopped spinach
- 3 tablespoons olive oil
- 2 garlic cloves, minced
- 2 loaves sourdough bread (1 pound each)
- 1 medium sweet red pepper, chopped
- 1 medium onion, chopped
- 1½ pounds boneless skinless chicken breasts, cut into ½-inch pieces
- 1 can (14 ounces) water-packed artichoke hearts, rinsed, drained and chopped
- 1 package (8 ounces) cream cheese, softened
- ½ cup grated Parmesan cheese, divided
- 1½ teaspoons Italian seasoning
- 1 teaspoon salt
- 6 bacon strips, cooked and crumbled, divided

1. Preheat oven to 400°. Thaw spinach, reserving 2 tablespoons of the liquid.

2. In a small microwave-safe bowl, combine oil and garlic. Microwave on high 30-45 seconds or until warmed. Cut a thin slice off top of each bread loaf. Hollow out bottoms, leaving ½-in.-thick shells (save removed bread for another use). Brush 2 tablespoons oil mixture over outside and inside of bread bowls. Place bread bowls on a baking sheet.

3. Strain remaining oil mixture into a large skillet; discard garlic. Heat oil over medium-high heat. Add pepper and onion; cook and stir 5-7 minutes or until tender. Remove from pan.

4. Add chicken to pan; cook and stir over medium-high heat 6-8 minutes or until no longer pink. Reduce heat to medium. Add artichoke hearts, cream cheese, ¼ cup Parmesan cheese, Italian seasoning, salt, spinach, pepper mixture and reserved spinach liquid; cook and stir until cream cheese is melted. Stir in ¼ cup crumbled bacon. Remove from heat.

5. Divide mixture between bread bowls; top with remaining bacon. Sprinkle remaining Parmesan cheese over filling and bowls.

6. Bake, uncovered, 10 minutes. Cover loosely with foil; bake 8-12 minutes

longer or until filling is heated through. Let stand 10 minutes before serving. To serve, cut each bowl into 4 wedges.

FREEZE OPTION *Cool chicken mixture before filling bread bowls. Securely wrap unbaked bowls in foil; place in resealable plastic freezer bags and freeze. To use, partially thaw in refrigerator overnight. Unwrap bowls and place on a baking sheet. Cover loosely with foil and bake in a preheated 350° oven 1 hour. Bake, uncovered, 10-15 minutes longer or until filling is heated through and a thermometer inserted in center reads 165°.*

FAST FIX
SPINACH & GOUDA-STUFFED PORK CUTLETS

I started this dish in an attempt to copy a restaurant entree I liked. Cheese just oozes out of the center, and mustard lends a lot of flavor.

—JOAN OAKLAND TROY, MT

START TO FINISH: 30 MIN.
MAKES: 2 SERVINGS

- 3 tablespoons dry bread crumbs
- 2 tablespoons grated Parmesan cheese
- 2 pork sirloin cutlets (3 ounces each)
- ¼ teaspoon salt
- ⅛ teaspoon pepper
- 2 slices smoked Gouda cheese (about 2 ounces)
- 2 cups fresh baby spinach
- 2 tablespoons horseradish mustard

1. Preheat oven to 400°. In a shallow bowl, mix the bread crumbs and Parmesan cheese.

2. Sprinkle tops of cutlets with salt and pepper. Layer one end of each with Gouda cheese and spinach. Fold the cutlets in half, enclosing filling; secure with toothpicks. Brush the mustard over outsides of pork; dip in bread crumb mixture, patting to help the coating adhere.

3. Place on a greased foil-lined baking sheet. Bake 12-15 minutes or until golden brown and pork is tender. Discard toothpicks before serving.

SEARED SALMON WITH STRAWBERRY BASIL RELISH

Take a sweet new approach to salmon by topping it off with a relish of strawberries, basil, honey and pepper.

—**STACY MULLENS** GRESHAM, OR

START TO FINISH: 20 MIN.
MAKES: 6 SERVINGS

- 6 salmon fillets (4 ounces each)
- 1 tablespoon butter, melted
- ¼ teaspoon salt
- ⅛ teaspoon freshly ground pepper

RELISH
- 1¼ cups finely chopped fresh strawberries
- 1 tablespoon minced fresh basil
- 1 tablespoon honey
  Dash freshly ground pepper

1. Brush fillets with melted butter; sprinkle with salt and pepper. Heat a large skillet over medium-high heat. Add fillets, skin side up, in batches if necessary; cook 2-3 minutes on each side or until fish just begins to flake easily with a fork.

2. In a small bowl, toss strawberries with basil, honey and pepper. Serve salmon with relish.

FONTINA ROLLED CHICKEN

Good food has a way of transporting you to faraway places. My chicken dish with fontina and cream cheese is like a blissful trip overseas.

—**TAMMY REX** NEW TRIPOLI, PA

PREP: 30 MIN. • **BAKE:** 30 MIN.
MAKES: 4 SERVINGS

- 4 ounces cream cheese, softened
- 1 cup shredded fontina cheese
- 5 bacon strips, cooked and crumbled
- 4 green onions, chopped
- ¼ cup chopped fresh Italian parsley
- ¼ cup julienned oil-packed sun-dried tomatoes, drained, chopped and patted dry
- ½ teaspoon salt, divided
- ¾ teaspoon pepper, divided
- 1 large egg
- 1½ cups panko (Japanese) bread crumbs
- 1 teaspoon paprika
- 4 boneless skinless chicken breast halves (6 ounces each)
- 1 tablespoon olive oil

1. Preheat oven to 375°. In a bowl, mix first six ingredients; stir in ¼ teaspoon each salt and pepper. In a shallow bowl, whisk egg and the remaining salt and pepper. In another shallow bowl, toss bread crumbs with paprika.

2. Carefully pound chicken breasts with a meat mallet to ¼-in. thickness. Spread cheese mixture over chicken. Roll up chicken from a short side; secure with toothpicks.

3. Dip chicken in egg, then coat with crumbs. Place in a foil-lined 15x10x1-in. baking pan, seam side down. Drizzle tops with oil.

4. Bake, uncovered, 30-35 minutes or until golden brown and chicken is no longer pink. Let stand 5 minutes; discard toothpicks before serving.

JUST PEACHY PORK TENDERLOIN

I had a pork tenderloin and ripe peaches and decided to put them together. The results couldn't have been more irresistible! It's a fresh entree that tastes like summer any time.

—JULIA GOSLIGA ADDISON, VT

START TO FINISH: 20 MIN.
MAKES: 4 SERVINGS

- 1 **pound pork tenderloin, cut into 12 slices**
- ½ **teaspoon salt**
- ¼ **teaspoon pepper**
- 2 **teaspoons olive oil**
- 4 **medium peaches, peeled and sliced**
- 1 **tablespoon lemon juice**
- ¼ **cup peach preserves**

1. Flatten each tenderloin slice to ¼-in. thickness. Sprinkle with salt and pepper. In a large nonstick skillet over medium heat, cook pork in oil until tender. Remove and keep warm.

2. Add peaches and lemon juice, stirring to loosen browned bits from pan. Cook and stir for 3-4 minutes or until peaches are tender. Stir in the pork and preserves; heat through.

TOP TIP

Find the Sweetest Peaches

Purchase peaches that have an intense fragrance and that give slightly to palm pressure. Avoid those that are too hard or have soft spots. That way, you'll know you only have the sweetest peaches on hand!

BIG JOHN'S CHILI-RUBBED RIBS

When my family thinks of summer grilling, it's ribs all the way. Our recipe is a fun, welcome change from the usual version, with a glaze instead of barbecue sauce .
—GINGER SULLIVAN CUTLER BAY, FL

PREP: 20 MIN. + CHILLING
GRILL: 1½ HOURS
MAKES: 10 SERVINGS

- 3 tablespoons packed brown sugar
- 2 tablespoons paprika
- 2 tablespoons chili powder
- 3 teaspoons ground cumin
- 2 teaspoons garlic powder
- 1 teaspoon salt
- 6 pounds pork baby back ribs

GLAZE
- 1 cup reduced-sodium soy sauce
- 1 cup packed brown sugar
- ⅔ cup ketchup
- ⅓ cup lemon juice
- 1½ teaspoons minced fresh gingerroot

1. Mix first six ingredients; rub over ribs. Refrigerate, covered, 30 minutes.
2. Wrap rib racks in large pieces of heavy-duty foil; seal tightly. Grill, covered, over indirect medium heat 1 to 1½ hours or until tender.
3. In a large saucepan, combine glaze ingredients; cook, uncovered, over medium heat 6-8 minutes or until heated through and sugar is dissolved, stirring occasionally.
4. Carefully remove ribs from foil. Place ribs over direct heat; brush with some of the glaze. Grill, covered, over medium heat 25-30 minutes or until browned, turning and brushing ribs occasionally with remaining glaze.

=== READER REVIEW

"The ribs were tender, sweet and a little different than the norm. Definitely a fun change!"

AUG2295 TASTEOFHOME.COM

FAST FIX
HAM AND PEA PASTA ALFREDO

When I want a filling meal that even the kids enjoy, I toss ham and sugar snap peas with Romano cream sauce and pasta.
—CR MONACHINO KENMORE, NY

START TO FINISH: 25 MIN.
MAKES: 8 SERVINGS

- 1 package (16 ounces) fettuccine
- 2 tablespoons butter
- 1½ pounds sliced fully cooked ham, cut into strips (about 5 cups)
- 2 cups fresh sugar snap peas
- 2 cups heavy whipping cream
- ½ cup grated Romano cheese
- ¼ teaspoon pepper

1. Cook fettuccine according to package directions. Meanwhile, in a large skillet, heat butter over medium heat. Add the ham and peas; cook and stir 5 minutes. Stir in cream, cheese and pepper; bring to a boil. Reduce heat; simmer, uncovered, 1-2 minutes or until sauce is slightly thickened and peas are crisp-tender.
2. Drain fettuccine; add to skillet and toss to coat. Serve immediately.

FAST FIX
GREEK FISH BAKE

As a military spouse living overseas, I got the chance to try many styles of cooking. Here's a Mediterranean-inspired recipe that we still love today.
—STACEY BOYD SPRINGFIELD, VA

START TO FINISH: 30 MIN.
MAKES: 4 SERVINGS

- 4 cod fillets (6 ounces each)
- 2 tablespoons olive oil
- ¼ teaspoon salt
- ⅛ teaspoon pepper
- 1 small green pepper, cut into thin strips
- ½ small red onion, thinly sliced
- ¼ cup pitted Greek olives, sliced
- 1 can (8 ounces) tomato sauce
- ¼ cup crumbled feta cheese

1. Preheat oven to 400°. Place cod in a greased 13x9-in. baking dish. Brush with oil; sprinkle with the salt and pepper. Top with green pepper, onion and olives.
2. Pour tomato sauce over top; sprinkle with cheese. Bake until fish just begins to flake easily with a fork, 15-20 minutes.

PERSONAL MARGHERITA PIZZAS

This family-friendly supper is simplicity at its finest. Delectable fresh mozzarella and a sprinkling of basil give these little pies Italian flair.

—**JERRY GULLEY** PLEASANT PRAIRIE, WI

START TO FINISH: 25 MIN.
MAKES: 3 SERVINGS

- 1 package (6½ ounces) pizza crust mix
- ½ teaspoon dried oregano
- ¾ cup pizza sauce
- 6 ounces fresh mozzarella cheese, thinly sliced
- ¼ cup thinly sliced fresh basil leaves

1. Preheat oven to 425°. Prepare pizza dough according to package directions, adding oregano before mixing. Divide into three portions.

2. Pat each portion of dough into an 8-in. circle on greased baking sheets. Bake 8-10 minutes or until edges are lightly browned.

3. Spread each crust with ¼ cup pizza sauce to within ½ in. of edge. Top with cheese. Bake 5-10 minutes longer or until crust is golden and cheese is melted. Sprinkle with basil.

ANDOUILLE-STUFFED PEPPERS

I was inspired by the important role of green peppers in Cajun dishes when I created my spiced-up recipe. For a healthy choice, substitute chicken sausage or cubed cooked chicken breast for the andouille sausage.

—**SARAH LARSON** CARLSBAD, CA

PREP: 40 MIN. • **BAKE:** 40 MIN.
MAKES: 4 SERVINGS

- 1 package (8 ounces) jambalaya mix
- 4 small green peppers
- ¾ pound fully cooked andouille sausage links, chopped
- 1 jalapeno pepper, seeded and minced
- 1 can (16 ounces) tomato juice Louisiana-style hot sauce, optional

1. Prepare the jambalaya mix according to the package directions. Meanwhile, cut peppers lengthwise in half; remove seeds.

2. In a skillet, cook and stir sausage over medium-high heat until browned. Add jalapeno; cook 1 minute longer.

3. Stir sausage mixture into the prepared jambalaya. Spoon into pepper halves. Place in a greased 13x9-in. baking dish; pour tomato juice over and around peppers.

4. Bake, uncovered, at 350° for 40-45 minutes or until peppers are tender. Serve with hot sauce if desired.

NOTES *This recipe was prepared with Zatarain's New Orleans-style Jambalaya mix. Wear disposable gloves when cutting hot peppers; the oils can burn skin. Avoid touching your face.*

ARTICHOKE & LEMON PASTA

While sailing in the Mediterranean, I tasted a lemony pasta and fell in love with it. I developed my own version that our guests now love. Try it with shrimp and kalamata olives, too.

—**PETER HALFERTY** CORPUS CHRISTI, TX

PREP: 20 MIN. • **COOK:** 20 MIN.
MAKES: 6 SERVINGS

- 2½ teaspoons salt, divided
- ½ pound fresh asparagus, trimmed and cut into 1½-inch pieces
- 4 cups uncooked bow tie pasta (about 12 ounces)
- 3 tablespoons olive oil, divided
- 1 can (14 ounces) water-packed quartered artichoke hearts, well drained
- 2 garlic cloves, minced
- 1 cup crumbled goat cheese
- 2 tablespoons minced fresh parsley
- 1 tablespoon grated lemon peel
- 2 to 3 tablespoons lemon juice
- ⅓ cup grated Parmesan cheese

1. Fill a 6-qt. stockpot three-fourths full with water; add 2 teaspoons salt and bring to a boil. Add asparagus; cook, uncovered, 1-2 minutes or just until crisp-tender. Remove asparagus and immediately drop into ice water. Drain and pat dry.

2. In the same pot of water, cook the pasta according to package directions for al dente. Drain, reserving 1 cup pasta water. Return pasta to pot.

3. Meanwhile, in a large skillet, heat 1 tablespoon oil over medium-high heat. Add artichoke hearts; cook and stir for 3-4 minutes or until lightly browned. Add garlic; cook 1 minute longer. Add to pasta.

4. Add the asparagus, goat cheese, parsley, lemon peel, lemon juice and remaining salt and oil; toss to combine, adding enough reserved pasta water to coat. Heat through. Serve pasta with Parmesan cheese.

SPICY ROASTED SAUSAGE, POTATOES AND PEPPERS

I enjoy sharing my cooking, and this hearty meal-in-one has gotten a tasty reputation. People have actually approached me in public to ask for the recipe!

—**LAURIE SLEDGE** BRANDON, MS

PREP: 20 MIN. • **BAKE:** 30 MIN.
MAKES: 4 SERVINGS

- 1 pound potatoes (about 2 medium), peeled and cut into ½-inch cubes
- 1 package (12 ounces) fully cooked andouille chicken sausage links or flavor of your choice, cut into 1-inch pieces
- 1 medium red onion, cut into wedges
- 1 medium sweet red pepper, cut into 1-inch pieces
- 1 medium green pepper, cut into 1-inch pieces
- ½ cup pickled pepper rings
- 1 tablespoon olive oil
- ½ to 1 teaspoon Creole seasoning
- ¼ teaspoon pepper

1. Preheat oven to 400°. In a large bowl, combine potatoes, sausage, onion, red pepper, green pepper and pepper rings. Mix oil, Creole seasoning and pepper; drizzle over the potato mixture and toss to coat.

2. Transfer to a 15x10x1-in. baking pan coated with cooking spray. Roast 30-35 minutes or until vegetables are tender, stirring occasionally.

CASSEROLE ENTREES

Comfort in one convenient pan—yes, we're talking casseroles! Whether you want to spice up the usual dinner rotation or you're looking for a new awe-inspiring potluck offering, these family favorites are ready to impress at breakfast, lunch or dinner.

PIZZA NOODLE BAKE

You can throw this yummy casserole together in a snap. It's perfect for a weeknight meal. Double the recipe and freeze one for later!

—BERNICE KNUTSON SOLDIER, IA

PREP: 25 MIN. • **BAKE:** 15 MIN.
MAKES: 6 SERVINGS

- 10 **ounces uncooked egg noodles**
- 1½ **pounds ground beef**
- ½ **cup finely chopped onion**
- ¼ **cup chopped green pepper**
- 1 **jar (14 ounces) pizza sauce**
- 1 **can (4 ounces) mushroom stems and pieces, drained**
- 1 **cup shredded cheddar cheese**
- 1 **cup shredded part-skim mozzarella cheese**
- 1 **package (3½ ounces) sliced pepperoni**

1. Cook noodles according to package directions. Meanwhile, in a large skillet, cook the beef, onion and green pepper over medium heat until meat is no longer pink; drain. Add pizza sauce and mushrooms; heat through.

2. Drain the noodles. In a greased 13x9-in. baking dish, layer half each of the noodles, beef mixture, cheeses and pepperoni. Repeat layers. Cover and bake at 350° for 15-20 minutes or until heated through.

FREEZE OPTION *Cover and freeze unbaked casserole for up to 3 months. Remove from freezer 30 minutes before baking (do not thaw). Cover and bake at 350° for 45-50 minutes. Uncover; bake 15-20 minutes longer or until heated through.*

SAUERKRAUT CASSEROLE

Mom fermented her own sauerkraut, and the cabbage was from our big farm garden. Blending the kraut with spicy sausage and apples was Mom's favorite way to fix it, and I still love this country dish.

—**ROSEMARY PRYOR** PASADENA, MD

PREP: 20 MIN. • **BAKE:** 1 HOUR
MAKES: 6-8 SERVINGS

- 1 **pound mild Italian sausage links, cut into 1-inch slices**
- 1 **large onion, chopped**
- 2 **medium apples, peeled and quartered**
- 1 **can (27 ounces) sauerkraut, rinsed and well drained**
- 1 **cup water**
- ½ **cup packed brown sugar**
- 2 **teaspoons caraway seeds**

1. In a large skillet, cook sausage and onion over medium heat until sausage is no longer pink and onion is tender; drain. Stir in the apples, sauerkraut, water, brown sugar and caraway seeds.
2. Transfer to a 2½-qt. baking dish. Cover and bake at 350° for 1 hour.

CHICKEN CORDON BLEU BAKE

Many years ago, a friend gave me the recipe for this treasured dish. I freeze several in disposable pans so that I can share with neighbors on a whim.

—**REA NEWELL** DECATUR, IL

PREP: 20 MIN. • **BAKE:** 40 MIN.
MAKES: 2 CASSEROLES (6 SERVINGS EACH)

- 2 **packages (6 ounces each) reduced-sodium stuffing mix**
- 1 **can (10¾ ounces) condensed cream of chicken soup, undiluted**
- 1 **cup 2% milk**
- 8 **cups cubed cooked chicken**
- ½ **teaspoon pepper**
- ¾ **pound sliced deli ham, cut into 1-inch strips**
- 1 **cup shredded Swiss cheese**
- 3 **cups shredded cheddar cheese**

1. Preheat oven to 350°. Prepare stuffing mixes according to package directions. Meanwhile, whisk together soup and milk.
2. Toss chicken with pepper; divide between two greased 13x9-in. baking dishes. Layer with the ham, Swiss cheese, 1 cup cheddar cheese, soup mixture and stuffing. Sprinkle with remaining cheddar cheese.
3. Bake, covered, 30 minutes. Uncover; bake until cheese is melted, 10-15 minutes.

FREEZE OPTION *Cover and freeze unbaked casseroles. To use, partially thaw in refrigerator overnight. Remove from refrigerator 30 minutes before baking. Preheat oven to 350°. Bake, covered, until heated through and a thermometer inserted in center reads 165°, about 45 minutes. Uncover; bake until cheese is melted, 10-15 minutes.*

CRAB-SPINACH EGG CASSEROLE

My love of cooking has evolved over the years. I came up with this casserole as a special breakfast for our daughter when she was home for a visit.
—**STEVE HEATON** DELTONA, FL

PREP: 10 MIN. • **BAKE:** 30 MIN. + STANDING
MAKES: 12-16 SERVINGS

- 8 **large eggs**
- 2 **cups half-and-half cream**
- 2 **cans (6 ounces each) crabmeat, drained**
- 1 **package (10 ounces) frozen chopped spinach, thawed and squeezed dry**
- 1 **cup dry bread crumbs**
- 1 **cup shredded Swiss cheese**
- ½ **teaspoon salt**
- ¼ **teaspoon pepper**
- ¼ **teaspoon ground nutmeg**
- 2 **celery ribs, chopped**
- ½ **cup chopped onion**
- ½ **cup chopped sweet red pepper**
- 3 **medium fresh mushrooms, chopped**
- 2 **tablespoons butter**

1. In a large bowl, beat eggs and cream. Stir in the crab, spinach, bread crumbs, cheese, salt, pepper and nutmeg; set aside. In a skillet, saute celery, onion, red pepper and mushrooms in butter until tender. Add to spinach mixture.
2. Transfer to a greased shallow 2½-qt. baking dish. Bake, uncovered, at 375° for 30-35 minutes or until a thermometer reads 160°. Let stand for 10 minutes before serving.

BEST-EVER BEANS AND SAUSAGE

My wife came up with this dish, which is extremely popular now with our friends and family.
—**ROBERT SAULNIER** CLARKSBURG, MA

PREP: 15 MIN. • **BAKE:** 1 HOUR 20 MIN.
MAKES: 12-16 SERVINGS

- 1½ **pounds bulk spicy pork sausage**
- 1 **medium green pepper, chopped**
- 1 **medium onion, chopped**
- 1 **can (31 ounces) pork and beans**
- 1 **can (16 ounces) kidney beans, rinsed and drained**
- 1 **can (15½ ounces) great northern beans, rinsed and drained**
- 1 **can (15½ ounces) black-eyed peas, rinsed and drained**
- 1 **can (15 ounces) pinto beans, rinsed and drained**
- 1 **can (15 ounces) chickpeas, rinsed and drained**
- 1½ **cups ketchup**
- ¾ **cup packed brown sugar**
- 2 **teaspoons ground mustard**

1. In a large skillet, cook sausage over medium heat until no longer pink; drain. Add green pepper and onion; saute until tender. Drain. Add the remaining ingredients.
2. Pour into a greased 13x9-in. baking dish. Cover and bake at 325° for 1 hour. Uncover; bake 20-30 minutes longer or until bubbly.

SWEET POTATO CHILI BAKE

I'm a vegetarian and wanted to develop dishes that would be a little heartier than traditional meatless fare. This one's great!

—JILLIAN TOURNOUX MASSILLON, OH

PREP: 30 MIN. • **BAKE:** 20 MIN.
MAKES: 7 SERVINGS

- 2 **cups cubed peeled sweet potato**
- 1 **medium sweet red pepper, chopped**
- 1 **tablespoon olive oil**
- 1 **garlic clove, minced**
- 1 **can (28 ounces) diced tomatoes, undrained**
- 2 **cups vegetable broth**
- 1 **can (15 ounces) black beans, rinsed and drained**
- 4½ **teaspoons brown sugar**
- 3 **teaspoons chili powder**
- 1 **teaspoon salt**
- ½ **teaspoon pepper**
- 1 **package (6½ ounces) corn bread/ muffin mix**
- ½ **cup shredded cheddar cheese**
 Optional toppings: sour cream, shredded cheddar cheese and chopped seeded jalapeno pepper

1. In a Dutch oven, saute sweet potato and red pepper in oil until crisp-tender. Add garlic; cook 1 minute longer. Add tomatoes, broth, beans, brown sugar, chili powder, salt and pepper. Bring to a boil. Reduce heat and simmer, uncovered, 15-20 minutes or until the potatoes are tender.

2. Meanwhile, preheat oven to 400°. Prepare corn bread batter according to package directions; stir in cheese. Drop by tablespoonfuls over chili.

3. Cover and bake 18-20 minutes or until a toothpick inserted in center comes out clean. Serve with toppings of your choice.

NOTE *Wear disposable gloves when cutting hot peppers; the oils can burn skin. Avoid touching your face.*

CHICKEN AMANDINE

With colorful green beans and pimientos, this attractive casserole is terrific for the holidays or family dinners. This is true comfort food at its finest.

—KAT WOOLBRIGHT WICHITA FALLS, TX

PREP: 35 MIN. • **BAKE:** 30 MIN.
MAKES: 8 SERVINGS

- ¼ **cup chopped onion**
- 1 **tablespoon butter**
- 1 **package (6 ounces) long grain and wild rice**
- 2¼ **cups chicken broth**
- 3 **cups cubed cooked chicken**
- 2 **cups frozen french-style green beans, thawed**
- 1 **can (10¾ ounces) condensed cream of chicken soup, undiluted**
- ¾ **cup sliced almonds, divided**
- 1 **jar (4 ounces) diced pimientos, drained**
- 1 **teaspoon pepper**
- ½ **teaspoon garlic powder**
- 1 **bacon strip, cooked and crumbled**

1. In a large saucepan, saute onion in butter until tender. Add rice with contents of seasoning packet and broth. Bring to a boil. Reduce heat; cover and simmer for 25 minutes or until liquid is absorbed. Uncover; set aside to cool.

2. In a large bowl, combine chicken, green beans, soup, ½ cup of almonds, pimientos, pepper and garlic powder. Stir in rice.

3. Transfer to a greased 2½-qt. baking dish. Sprinkle with bacon and the remaining almonds. Cover and bake at 350° for 30-35 minutes or until heated through.

LOADED TATER TOT BAKE

I keep frozen Tater Tots on hand for meals like this. It's a super brunch, breakfast or side dish for kids of all ages.

—**NANCY HEISHMAN** LAS VEGAS, NV

PREP: 15 MIN. • **BAKE:** 35 MIN.
MAKES: 6 SERVINGS

- **1 tablespoon canola oil**
- **1 medium onion, finely chopped**
- **6 ounces Canadian bacon, cut into ½-inch strips**
- **4 cups frozen Tater Tots, thawed**
- **6 large eggs, lightly beaten**
- **½ cup reduced-fat sour cream**
- **½ cup half-and-half cream**
- **1 tablespoon dried parsley flakes**
- **¾ teaspoon garlic powder**
- **½ teaspoon pepper**
- **1½ cups shredded cheddar cheese**

1. Preheat oven to 350°. In a large skillet, heat oil over medium heat. Add onion; cook and stir 2-3 minutes or until tender. Add Canadian bacon; cook 1-2 minutes or until lightly browned, stirring occasionally. Remove from heat.

2. Line bottom of a greased 11x7-in. baking dish with Tater Tots; top with Canadian bacon mixture. In a large bowl, whisk eggs, sour cream, cream and seasonings until blended. Stir in cheese; pour over top. Bake, uncovered, 35-40 minutes or until golden brown.

SHEPHERD'S INN BREAKFAST PIE
Substitute 1½ pounds of bulk pork sausage, cooked and drained, for onion and Canadian bacon. Substitute ¾ cup of milk for sour cream and cream; omit pepper. Assemble and bake as directed. Top with 2 chopped tomatoes.

POTLUCK SPECIAL

I often take this hearty meal-in-one dish to potlucks for the community seniors group my husband and I help organize. Sometimes I double it for a larger crowd.

—**RETA CHRISTENSEN** NEW DENMARK, NB

PREP: 10 MIN. • **BAKE:** 1 HOUR
MAKES: 6-8 SERVINGS

- **1 pound ground beef**
- **1 medium onion, chopped**
- **1 can (28 ounces) diced tomatoes, undrained**
- **1 can (16 ounces) sauerkraut, rinsed and drained**
- **1½ cups cooked rice**
- **1 medium green pepper, chopped**

In a skillet, brown ground beef and onion; drain. Add the remaining ingredients; transfer to a 2-qt. baking dish. Cover and bake at 350° for 1 hour.

SOUTHWEST VEGETARIAN BAKE

This veggie-packed casserole hits the spot on chilly nights, and it's great anytime I'm in the mood for Mexican food with all the fixings.

—TRISH GALE MONTICELLO, IL

PREP: 40 MIN. • **BAKE:** 35 MIN. + STANDING
MAKES: 8 SERVINGS

- ¾ cup uncooked brown rice
- 1½ cups water
- 1 can (15 ounces) black beans, rinsed and drained
- 1 can (11 ounces) Mexicorn, drained
- 1 can (10 ounces) diced tomatoes and green chilies
- 1 cup salsa
- 1 cup (8 ounces) reduced-fat sour cream
- 1 cup shredded reduced-fat cheddar cheese
- ¼ teaspoon pepper
- ½ cup chopped red onion
- 1 can (2¼ ounces) sliced ripe olives, drained
- 1 cup shredded reduced-fat Mexican cheese blend

1. In a large saucepan, bring rice and water to a boil. Reduce the heat; cover and simmer 35-40 minutes or until tender. Preheat oven to 350°. In a large bowl, combine the beans, Mexicorn, tomatoes, salsa, sour cream, cheddar cheese, pepper and rice. Transfer to a shallow 2½-qt. baking dish coated with cooking spray. Sprinkle with onion and olives.

2. Bake, uncovered, 30 minutes. Sprinkle with Mexican cheese. Bake 5-10 minutes longer or until heated through and the cheese is melted. Let stand 10 minutes before serving.

═══════ **READER REVIEW**

"Added extra corn and beans, used sliced green onion, and served the dish with fresh tomatoes and chopped lettuce on tortillas. Yum!"

ROBBINTHORNTON TASTEOFHOME.COM

SHRIMP AND FONTINA CASEROLE

Looking for a seafood casserole that tastes gourmet? Try this Cajun-inspired one! The confetti of green onions and red peppers makes it pretty enough for a dinner party.
—**EMORY DOTY** JASPER, GA

PREP: 35 MIN. • **BAKE:** 15 MIN. + STANDING
MAKES: 8 SERVINGS

- ½ cup all-purpose flour
- 1 tablespoon Cajun seasoning
- ½ teaspoon pepper
- 2 pounds uncooked large shrimp, peeled and deveined
- 2 tablespoons olive oil
- 4 thin slices prosciutto or deli ham, cut into thin strips
- ½ pound medium fresh mushrooms, quartered
- 2 tablespoons butter
- 4 green onions, chopped
- 2 garlic cloves, minced
- 1 cup heavy whipping cream
- 8 ounces fontina cheese, cubed
- 1 jar (7 ounces) roasted sweet red peppers, drained and chopped
- ¼ cup grated Parmigiano-Reggiano cheese
- ¼ cup grated Romano cheese

1. Preheat oven to 350°. In a large resealable plastic bag, combine flour, Cajun seasoning and pepper. Add shrimp, a few at a time, and shake bag to coat.
2. In a large skillet over medium heat, cook shrimp in oil in batches until golden brown. Drain on paper towels. Transfer to an ungreased 13x9-in. baking dish; top with the prosciutto. Set aside.
3. In same skillet, saute mushrooms in butter until tender. Add onions and garlic; cook 1 minute longer. Add cream and fontina cheese; cook and stir until cheese is melted. Remove from heat; stir in peppers. Pour over prosciutto. Sprinkle with remaining cheeses.
4. Bake, uncovered, 15-20 minutes or until bubbly and cheese is melted. Let stand 10 minutes before serving.

CHICKEN AND SWISS STUFFING BAKE

I love to cook but usually don't have much time to spend in the kitchen. This casserole is both good and fast, which makes it my favorite kind of recipe. I serve it with a green salad.
—**JENA COFFEY** SUNSET HILLS, MO

PREP: 20 MIN. • **BAKE:** 25 MIN.
MAKES: 8 SERVINGS

- 1 can (10¾ ounces) condensed cream of mushroom soup, undiluted
- 1 cup whole milk
- 1 package (6 ounces) stuffing mix
- 2 cups cubed cooked chicken breast
- 2 cups fresh broccoli florets, cooked
- 2 celery ribs, finely chopped
- 1½ cups shredded Swiss cheese, divided

1. In a large bowl, combine soup and milk until blended. Add the stuffing mix with contents of seasoning packet, chicken, broccoli, celery and 1 cup of cheese. Transfer to a greased 13x9-in. baking dish.
2. Bake casserole, uncovered, at 375° for 20 minutes or until heated through. Sprinkle with the remaining cheese; bake 5 minutes longer or until the cheese is melted.
FREEZE OPTION *Sprinkle remaining cheese over unbaked casserole. Cover and freeze. To use, partially thaw in refrigerator overnight. Remove from refrigerator 30 minutes before baking. Preheat oven to 375°. Bake casserole as directed, increasing time as necessary to heat through and for a thermometer inserted in center to read 165°.*

TURKEY SPAGHETTI CASSEROLE

My mom made this creamy spaghetti when I was growing up. Whenever I have any leftover chicken or turkey, I look forward to preparing this simple, tasty dinner.
—**CASANDRA HETRICK** LINDSEY, OH

PREP: 30 MIN. • **BAKE:** 1¼ HOURS
MAKES: 6 SERVINGS

- 1 **medium onion, chopped**
- 1 **medium carrot, chopped**
- 1 **celery rib, chopped**
- ⅓ **cup sliced fresh mushrooms**
- 1 **tablespoon butter**
- 2½ **cups reduced-sodium chicken broth**
- 1 **can (10¾ ounces) reduced-fat reduced-sodium condensed cream of mushroom soup, undiluted**
- ¼ **teaspoon salt**
- ¼ **teaspoon pepper**
- 2½ **cups cubed cooked turkey breast**
- 6 **ounces uncooked spaghetti, broken into 2-inch pieces**
- ½ **cup shredded reduced-fat Colby-Monterey Jack cheese**
- ½ **teaspoon paprika**

1. In a small skillet, saute vegetables in butter until tender. In a large bowl, combine broth, soup, salt and pepper.
2. In a 2½-qt. baking dish coated with cooking spray, layer turkey, spaghetti and vegetable mixture. Pour broth mixture over the top.
3. Cover and bake at 350° for 70-80 minutes or until spaghetti is tender, stirring once. Uncover; sprinkle with cheese and paprika. Bake 5-10 minutes longer or until cheese is melted.

TOP TIP

Quickly Sliced Mushrooms

My husband and I love fresh mushrooms, but slicing them always seemed to take a lot of time. One day I decided to try out an egg slicer for the task—and now I use this method all the time!
—**JENNIFER I.** BROOKHAVEN, PA

CHICKEN NOODLE CASSEROLE

Everyone who tries my casserole asks for the recipe. It's so simple to make that sometimes I feel like I'm cheating!
—**KAY PEDERSON** YELLVILLE, AR

PREP: 15 MIN. • **BAKE:** 40 MIN.
MAKES: 6 SERVINGS

- 1 **can (10¾ ounces) condensed cream of chicken soup, undiluted**
- ½ **cup mayonnaise**
- 2 **tablespoons lemon juice**
- 2 **cups cubed cooked chicken**
- 1 **small onion, chopped**
- ¼ **cup chopped green pepper**
- ¼ **cup chopped sweet red pepper**
- 1 **cup shredded Monterey Jack cheese, divided**
- 1 **cup shredded sharp cheddar cheese, divided**
- 12 **ounces egg noodles, cooked and drained**

1. In a large bowl, combine the soup, mayonnaise and lemon juice. Stir in the chicken, onion, peppers, ½ cup Monterey Jack cheese and ½ cup cheddar cheese. Add noodles and toss to coat.
2. Transfer to a greased 2-qt. baking dish. Bake, uncovered, at 350° for 30-35 minutes. Sprinkle with the remaining cheeses. Bake 10 minutes longer or until cheese is melted.
FREEZE OPTION *Sprinkle remaining cheeses over unbaked casserole. Cover and freeze. To use, partially thaw in refrigerator overnight. Remove from refrigerator 30 minutes before baking. Preheat oven to 350°. Bake casserole as directed, increasing time as necessary to heat through and for a thermometer inserted in center to read 165°.*

DELUXE BAKED MACARONI AND CHEESE

By adding diced ham, tomatoes and a crumb topping, I turned mac and cheese into a comforting dinner.
—KATHY YAROSH APOPKA, FL

PREP: 30 MIN. • **BAKE:** 25 MIN.
MAKES: 12 SERVINGS

- 1 package (16 ounces) elbow macaroni
- ¼ cup all-purpose flour
- 2 cups 2% milk
- ½ cup heavy whipping cream
- 1 package (8 ounces) process cheese (Velveeta), cubed
- 1 cup shredded cheddar cheese
- ⅔ cup whipped cream cheese
- ¼ cup grated Parmesan cheese
- 1 can (14½ ounces) diced tomatoes, drained
- 1½ cups cubed fully cooked ham
- 1 cup (8 ounces) sour cream
- 1 teaspoon Dijon mustard

TOPPING

- 1½ cups soft bread crumbs
- ¼ cup grated Parmesan cheese
- 2 tablespoons butter, melted

1. Preheat oven to 350°. Cook macaroni according to package directions. In a Dutch oven, whisk flour, milk and cream until smooth. Bring to a boil; cook and stir 2 minutes or until thickened.

2. Stir in cheeses until melted. Add the tomatoes, ham, sour cream and mustard. Drain macaroni; add to cheese mixture and toss to coat.

3. Transfer to a greased 13x9-in. baking dish. In a small bowl, mix topping ingredients; sprinkle over top. Bake, uncovered, 25-30 minutes or until bubbly and bread crumbs are lightly browned.

NOTE *To make soft bread crumbs, tear bread into pieces and place in a food processor or blender. Cover and pulse until crumbs form. One slice of bread yields ½ to ¾ cup crumbs.*

CHURCH SUPPER SPAGHETTI

Because this recipe feeds so many, I often take it to church dinners and potlucks. It also comes in handy when we have lots of folks helping out on our farm.
—VERLYN WILSON WILKINSON, IN

PREP: 50 MIN. • **BAKE:** 20 MIN.
MAKES: 12 SERVINGS

- 1 pound ground beef
- 1 large onion, chopped
- 1 medium green pepper, chopped
- 1 can (14½ ounces) diced tomatoes, undrained
- 1 cup water
- 2 tablespoons chili powder
- 1 package (10 ounces) frozen corn, thawed
- 1 package (10 ounces) frozen peas, thawed
- 1 can (4 ounces) mushroom stems and pieces, drained
  Salt and pepper to taste
- 1 package (12 ounces) spaghetti, cooked and drained
- 2 cups shredded cheddar cheese, divided

1. In a large skillet, cook beef, onion and green pepper over medium heat until meat is no longer pink. Add the tomatoes, water and chili powder. Cover and simmer 30 minutes. Add the corn, peas, mushrooms, salt and pepper. Stir in spaghetti.

2. Layer half of mixture in a greased 4-qt. baking dish. Sprinkle with 1 cup cheese; repeat layers.

3. Bake, uncovered, at 350° for 20 minutes or until heated through.

TACO CASSEROLE

My family always devours this casserole, which tastes like a taco salad. I like that it's a breeze to prepare.

—RHONDA MCKEE GREENSBURG, KS

PREP: 25 MIN. • **BAKE:** 15 MIN.
MAKES: 4 SERVINGS

- 1 pound ground beef
- ¼ cup chopped onion
- ¼ cup chopped green pepper
- 1 envelope taco seasoning
- ½ cup water
- 1 cup crushed tortilla chips
- 1 can (16 ounces) refried beans
- 1 cup shredded cheddar cheese
    Toppings: chopped lettuce and tomatoes, sliced ripe olives, sour cream and picante sauce

1. In a large skillet, cook beef, onion and green pepper over medium heat until meat is no longer pink; drain. Stir in taco seasoning and water. Cook and stir until thickened, about 3 minutes; set aside.

2. Place chips in a greased 8-in. square baking dish. In a small bowl, stir refried beans; spread over chips. Top with beef mixture and cheese.

3. Bake, uncovered, at 375° for 15-20 minutes or until heated through. Top with chopped lettuce, tomatoes and olives. Serve with sour cream and picante sauce.

CHICKEN POTPIE CASSEROLE

I always have leftover chicken broth on hand and use it for many things, including this family-favorite bake. You can make your own biscuits, like I do, or buy them at the store. I like to bake extra biscuits to eat with butter and jam.

—LILIANE JAHNKE CYPRESS, TX

PREP: 40 MIN. • **BAKE:** 15 MIN.
MAKES: 8 SERVINGS

- ⅓ cup butter, cubed
- 1½ cups sliced fresh mushrooms
- 2 medium carrots, sliced
- ½ medium onion, chopped
- ¼ cup all-purpose flour
- 1 cup chicken broth
- 1 cup 2% milk
- 4 cups cubed cooked chicken
- 1 cup frozen peas
- 1 jar (2 ounces) diced pimientos, drained
- ½ teaspoon salt

BISCUIT TOPPING

- 2 cups all-purpose flour
- 4 teaspoons baking powder
- 2 teaspoons sugar
- ½ teaspoon salt
- ½ teaspoon cream of tartar
- ½ cup cold butter, cubed
- ⅔ cup 2% milk

1. Preheat oven to 400°. In a large saucepan, heat butter over medium heat. Add mushrooms, carrots and onion; cook and stir until tender.

2. Stir in the flour until blended; gradually stir in broth and milk. Bring to a boil, stirring constantly; cook and stir 2 minutes or until thickened. Stir in chicken, peas, pimientos and salt; heat through. Transfer to a greased 11x7-in. baking dish.

3. For topping, in a large bowl, whisk flour, baking powder, sugar, salt and cream of tartar. Cut in butter until mixture resembles coarse crumbs. Add milk; stir just until moistened.

4. Turn onto a lightly floured surface; knead gently 8-10 times. Pat or roll dough to ½-in. thickness; cut with a floured 2½-in. biscuit cutter. Place over the chicken mixture. Bake, uncovered, 15-20 minutes or until biscuits are golden brown.

CORDON BLEU CASSEROLE

I often roast a turkey just to have leftovers for this creamy casserole.

—JOYCE PAUL QU'APPELLE, SK

PREP: 25 MIN. • **BAKE:** 25 MIN.
MAKES: 6 SERVINGS

- 2 cups cubed fully cooked ham
- 4 cups cubed cooked turkey
- 1 cup shredded Swiss cheese
- 1 large onion, chopped
- ⅓ cup butter, cubed
- ⅓ cup all-purpose flour
- ⅛ teaspoon ground mustard
- ⅛ teaspoon ground nutmeg
- 1¾ cups whole milk

TOPPING

- 1½ cups soft bread crumbs
- ½ cup shredded Swiss cheese
- ¼ cup butter, melted

1. In a large nonstick skillet, cook ham for 4-5 minutes or until browned; drain and pat dry. In a greased 2-qt. baking dish, layer the turkey, cheese and ham; set aside.

2. In a large saucepan, saute onion in butter until tender. Stir in the flour, mustard and nutmeg until blended. Gradually stir in milk. Bring to a boil; cook and stir for 2 minutes or until thickened. Pour over ham.

3. Combine topping ingredients; sprinkle over the top. Bake, uncovered, at 350° for 25-30 minutes or until golden brown and bubbly.

ITALIAN CASSEROLE

I come from a huge family, and it seems there is always an occasion for a potluck. I turn to this reliable recipe often.

—RITA GOSHAW SOUTH MILWAUKEE, WI

PREP: 40 MIN. • **BAKE:** 25 MIN.
MAKES: 16-20 SERVINGS

- 1½ pounds bulk Italian sausage
- 1½ pounds ground beef
- 1 cup chopped onion
- 1 cup chopped green pepper
- 2 cans (15 ounces each) tomato sauce
- 2 cans (6 ounces each) tomato paste
- ½ cup water
- 1 teaspoon dried basil
- 1 teaspoon dried oregano
- 1 teaspoon salt
- 1 teaspoon pepper
- ⅛ teaspoon garlic powder
- 2 cans (8¾ ounces each) whole kernel corn, drained
- 2 cans (2¼ ounces each) sliced ripe olives, drained
- 1 package (16 ounces) wide noodles, cooked and drained
- 8 ounces cheddar cheese, cut into strips

1. In a Dutch oven over medium heat, cook sausage, beef, onion and green pepper until meat is no longer pink; drain. Add the tomato sauce, tomato paste, water and seasonings; bring to a boil. Reduce heat; cover and simmer for 15 minutes. Add corn and olives. Cover and simmer for 5 minutes. Stir in the noodles.

2. Pour into two greased 13x9-in. baking dishes. Top with cheese. Cover and bake at 350° for 25-30 minutes or until heated through.

SOUTHWESTERN CASSEROLE

I've made this family-pleasing casserole for years. It's bold, budget-friendly and, best of all, you get a second casserole to freeze.

—JOAN HALLFORD NORTH RICHLAND HILLS, TX

PREP: 15 MIN. • **BAKE:** 40 MIN.
MAKES: 2 CASSEROLES (6 SERVINGS EACH)

- 2 cups (8 ounces) uncooked elbow macaroni
- 2 pounds ground beef
- 1 large onion, chopped
- 2 garlic cloves, minced
- 2 cans (14½ ounces each) diced tomatoes, undrained
- 1 can (16 ounces) kidney beans, rinsed and drained
- 1 can (6 ounces) tomato paste
- 1 can (4 ounces) chopped green chilies, drained
- 1½ teaspoons salt
- 1 teaspoon chili powder
- ½ teaspoon ground cumin
- ½ teaspoon pepper
- 2 cups shredded Monterey Jack cheese
- 2 jalapeno peppers, seeded and chopped

1. Cook macaroni according to package directions. Meanwhile, in a large saucepan, cook beef and onion over medium heat, crumbling beef, until meat is no longer pink. Add garlic; cook 1 minute longer. Drain. Stir in next eight ingredients. Bring to a boil. Reduce heat; simmer, uncovered, for 10 minutes. Drain macaroni; stir into beef mixture.

2. Preheat oven to 375°. Transfer the macaroni mixture to two greased 2-qt. baking dishes. Top with cheese and jalapenos. Cover and bake at 375° for 30 minutes. Uncover; bake until bubbly and heated through, about 10 minutes longer. Serve one casserole. Cool the second casserole; cover and freeze for up to 3 months.

TO USE FROZEN CASSEROLE *Thaw casserole in the refrigerator 8 hours. Preheat oven to 375°. Remove from refrigerator 30 minutes before baking. Cover and bake, increasing time as necessary to heat through and for a thermometer inserted in center to read 165°, 20-25 minutes.*

NOTE *Wear disposable gloves when cutting hot peppers; the oils can burn skin. Avoid touching your face.*

ROAST BEEF WITH CHIVE ROASTED POTATOES

It's hard to believe that last night's beef roast could get any better, but it shines in this heartwarming dish.

—*TASTE OF HOME* TEST KITCHEN

PREP: 20 MIN. • **BAKE:** 25 MIN.
MAKES: 6 SERVINGS

- 2 pounds red potatoes, cut into 1-inch cubes
- 2 tablespoons olive oil
- 2 teaspoons minced chives
- ¾ teaspoon salt, divided
- 2 medium onions, halved and thinly sliced
- 1 pound sliced fresh mushrooms
- ¼ cup butter, cubed
- 1 garlic clove, minced
- 1 teaspoon dried rosemary, crushed
- ¼ teaspoon pepper
- ⅓ cup dry red wine or beef broth
- 2 cups cubed cooked roast beef
- 1 cup beef gravy

1. Place the potatoes in a greased 15x10x1-in. baking pan. Drizzle potatoes with oil and sprinkle with chives and ¼ teaspoon salt; toss to coat. Bake, uncovered, at 425° for 25-30 minutes or until tender, stirring occasionally.

2. Meanwhile, in a large skillet, saute onions and mushrooms in butter until tender. Add garlic, rosemary, pepper and remaining salt; cook 1 minute longer. Stir in wine. Add beef and gravy; heat through. Serve with potatoes.

BROCCOLI SCALLOPED POTATOES

The combination of ham and Swiss creates a wonderfully rich, smoky flavor. I also love that I can cook an entire standout meal—veggies and all—in one dish.
—**DENELL SYSLO** FULLERTON, NE

PREP: 25 MIN. • **BAKE:** 1 HOUR
MAKES: 8 SERVINGS

- ¼ cup butter, cubed
- 2 tablespoons chopped onion
- 4 garlic cloves, minced
- 5 tablespoons all-purpose flour
- ¼ teaspoon white pepper
- ⅛ teaspoon salt
- 2½ cups whole milk
- 2 cups shredded Swiss cheese, divided
- 2 pounds potatoes, peeled and thinly sliced (about 4 cups)
- 2 cups julienned fully cooked ham
- 2 cups frozen broccoli florets, thawed and patted dry

1. Preheat oven to 350°. In a Dutch oven, heat butter over medium-high heat. Add onion and garlic; cook and stir 2-3 minutes or until tender. Stir in the flour, white pepper and salt until blended; gradually whisk in milk. Bring to a boil, stirring constantly; cook and stir 2 minutes or until thickened.
2. Stir in 1 cup cheese. Reduce heat; cook 1-2 minutes or until cheese is melted (sauce will be thick). Remove from the heat.
3. Add potatoes, ham and broccoli to sauce; stir gently to coat. Transfer to eight greased 8-oz. ramekins.
4. Bake, covered, for 40 minutes. Sprinkle with the remaining cheese. Bake, uncovered, 20-25 minutes longer or until the potatoes are tender and cheese is melted.

TOP TIP
Corn Chowder Boost
Whenever I have leftover scalloped potatoes, I add them to corn chowder. It thickens the soup and makes it extra hearty!
—**JEAN J.** CHULA VISTA, CA

CHICKEN TAMALE BAKE

When I serve this Mexican-style casserole, everyone scrapes their plates clean. Offer fresh toppings like green onions, tomatoes and avocado.
—**JENNIFER STOWELL** MONTEZUMA, IA

PREP: 10 MIN. • **BAKE:** 25 MIN. + STANDING
MAKES: 8 SERVINGS

- 1 large egg, lightly beaten
- 1 can (14¾ ounces) cream-style corn
- 1 package (8½ ounces) corn bread/muffin mix
- 1 can (4 ounces) chopped green chilies
- ⅓ cup 2% milk
- ¼ cup shredded Mexican cheese blend

TOPPING
- 2 cups coarsely shredded cooked chicken
- 1 can (10 ounces) enchilada sauce
- 1 teaspoon ground cumin
- ½ teaspoon onion powder
- 1¾ cups shredded Mexican cheese blend
- Chopped green onions, tomatoes and avocado, optional

1. Preheat oven to 400°. In a large bowl, combine the first six ingredients; stir just until dry ingredients are moistened. Transfer to a greased 13x9-in. baking dish. Bake 15-18 minutes or until light golden brown and a toothpick inserted in the center comes out clean.
2. In a large skillet, combine chicken, enchilada sauce, cumin and onion powder; bring to a boil, stirring occasionally. Reduce heat; simmer, uncovered, 5 minutes. Spread over corn bread layer; sprinkle with cheese.
3. Bake 10-12 minutes longer or until cheese is melted. Let stand 10 minutes before serving. If desired, top with green onions, tomatoes and avocado.

PENNE AND SMOKED SAUSAGE

My sausage and pasta dish is a must-try. It just tastes so good when it's hot and bubbly from the oven. The cheddar french-fried onions lend a cheesy, crunchy touch.

—**MARGARET WILSON** SAN BERNARDINO, CA

PREP: 15 MIN. • **BAKE:** 30 MIN.
MAKES: 6 SERVINGS

- 2 cups uncooked penne pasta
- 1 pound smoked sausage, cut into ¼-inch slices
- 1½ cups 2% milk
- 1 can (10¾ ounces) condensed cream of celery soup, undiluted
- 1½ cups cheddar french-fried onions, divided
- 1 cup shredded part-skim mozzarella cheese, divided
- 1 cup frozen peas

1. Preheat oven to 375°. Cook pasta according to package directions.
2. Meanwhile, in a large skillet, brown sausage over medium heat 5 minutes; drain. In a large bowl, combine milk and soup. Stir in ½ cup onions, ½ cup cheese, peas and sausage. Drain pasta; stir into sausage mixture.
3. Transfer to a greased 13x9-in. baking dish. Cover and bake casserole for 25-30 minutes or until bubbly. Sprinkle with remaining onions and cheese. Bake, uncovered, 3-5 minutes longer or until cheese is melted.

FREEZE OPTION *Sprinkle the remaining onions and cheese over unbaked casserole. Cover and freeze. To use, partially thaw in refrigerator overnight. Remove from refrigerator 30 minutes before baking. Preheat oven to 375°. Bake casserole as directed, increasing time as necessary to heat through and for a thermometer inserted in center to read 165°.*

CHILI TORTILLA BAKE

A home-style Tex-Mex casserole is all it takes to gather my whole family around the dinner table. There's never a need to worry about leftovers.

—CELINE WELDY CAVE CREEK, AZ

PREP: 20 MIN. • **BAKE:** 25 MIN.
MAKES: 6 SERVINGS

- 1 **pound extra-lean ground beef (95% lean)**
- 2 **cans (8 ounces each) no-salt-added tomato sauce**
- 1 **can (15 ounces) black beans, rinsed and drained**
- 1 **cup frozen corn**
- 1 **can (4 ounces) chopped green chilies**
- 2 **tablespoons dried minced onion**
- 2 **tablespoons chili powder**
- 1 **teaspoon ground cumin**
- ½ **teaspoon garlic powder**
- ½ **teaspoon dried oregano**
- 6 **whole wheat tortillas (8 inches)**
- 1 **cup shredded reduced-fat cheddar cheese**

1. In a large skillet, cook beef over medium heat until no longer pink. Stir in tomato sauce, beans, corn, green chilies, onion, chili powder, cumin, garlic powder and oregano; heat through.

2. In an 11x7-in. baking dish coated with cooking spray, layer half of the tortillas, beef mixture and cheese. Repeat the layers. Bake, uncovered, at 350° for 25-30 minutes or until bubbly.

FREEZE OPTION *Cool unbaked casserole; cover and freeze. To use, partially thaw in the refrigerator overnight. Remove from refrigerator 30 minutes before baking. Preheat oven to 350°. Bake casserole as directed, increasing time as necessary to heat through and for a thermometer inserted in center to read 165°.*

BISCUIT PIZZA BAKE

You'll get all the flavor of traditional pizza in this easy casserole. It's got everything you could want: ground beef, pepperoni, veggies and two kinds of cheese!

—EMMA HAGEMAN WAUCOMA, IA

PREP: 15 MIN. • **BAKE:** 30 MIN.
MAKES: 6-8 SERVINGS

- 1 **pound ground beef**
- 2 **tubes (12 ounces each) refrigerated buttermilk biscuits**
- 1 **package (3½ ounces) sliced pepperoni**
- 1 **can (4 ounces) mushroom stems and pieces, drained**
- 1 **can (15 ounces) pizza sauce**
- 1 **cup chopped green pepper**
- ½ **cup chopped onion**
- 1 **cup shredded cheddar cheese**
- 1 **cup shredded part-skim mozzarella cheese**

1. Preheat oven to 350°. In a large skillet, cook the beef over medium heat 6-8 minutes or until no longer pink, breaking into crumbles. Meanwhile, cut biscuits into quarters; place in a greased 13x9-in. baking dish. Drain beef; sprinkle over biscuits.

2. Layer with pepperoni, mushrooms, pizza sauce, green pepper and onion. Bake, uncovered, 15 minutes. Sprinkle with cheeses. Bake 15-20 minutes longer or until cheese is melted. Let stand 5-10 minutes before serving.

CURRIED CHICKEN AND GRITS CASSEROLE

I moved to the South about seven years ago from Ohio. I've been creating recipes with grits recently and feel like I'm finally getting the Southern vibe! This recipe turns out beautifully every time. I love the mix of veggies, golden sauce and cheese-crusted grits.

—**LORI SHAMSZADEH** POINT CLEAR, AL

PREP: 25 MIN. • **BAKE:** 50 MIN.
MAKES: 8 SERVINGS

- 1 **cup water**
- 1½ **cups chicken broth, divided**
- ¼ **teaspoon salt**
- ½ **cup quick-cooking grits**
- 2 **large eggs, beaten**
- 2 **cups shredded cheddar cheese, divided**
- 3 **tablespoons butter, cubed**
- 1 **can (10¾ ounces) condensed cream of chicken and mushroom soup, undiluted**
- 1½ **cups mayonnaise**
- 2 **teaspoons curry powder**
- 1 **package (16 ounces) frozen broccoli-cauliflower blend**
- 2 **cups cubed cooked chicken**
- 2 **cups refrigerated diced potatoes with onion**

1. Bring water, 1 cup broth and salt to a boil in a large saucepan. Slowly stir in grits. Reduce heat; cook and stir 5-6 minutes or until thickened. Remove from heat; stir a small amount of grits into eggs. Return all to pan, stirring constantly. Add 1½ cups cheese and the butter; stir until melted.
2. Preheat oven to 350°. In a large bowl, combine soup, mayonnaise, curry powder and remaining broth. Add vegetable blend, chicken and potatoes; toss to coat. Transfer to a greased 13x9-in. baking dish. Top with grits; sprinkle with remaining cheese.
3. Bake, uncovered, 50-55 minutes or until heated through.

REUBEN BREAD PUDDING

My Aunt Renee always brought this casserole to our family picnics in Chicago. It became so popular that she started bringing two or three! I have also used dark rye bread or marbled rye, and ham instead of corned beef.

—**JOHNNA JOHNSON** SCOTTSDALE, AZ

PREP: 20 MIN. • **BAKE:** 35 MIN.
MAKES: 6 SERVINGS

- 4 **cups cubed rye bread (about 6 slices)**
- 2 **tablespoons butter, melted**
- 2 **cups cubed or shredded cooked corned beef (about ½ pound)**
- 1 **can (14 ounces) sauerkraut, rinsed and well drained**
- 1 **cup shredded Swiss cheese, divided**
- 3 **large eggs**
- 1 **cup 2% milk**
- ⅓ **cup prepared Thousand Island salad dressing**
- 1½ **teaspoons prepared mustard**
- ¼ **teaspoon pepper**

1. Preheat oven to 350°. In a large bowl, toss bread cubes with butter. Stir in corned beef, sauerkraut and ½ cup cheese; transfer to a greased 11x7-in. baking dish.
2. In the same bowl, whisk the eggs, milk, salad dressing, mustard and pepper; pour over top. Bake casserole, uncovered, 30 minutes. Sprinkle with remaining cheese. Bake 5-7 minutes longer or until golden and a knife inserted in center comes out clean.

TUNA 'N' PEA CASSEROLE

Turn to this recipe when you want a tuna casserole with a twist. In this case, the extra flavor comes from horseradish. This dish is an old favorite in our family, and it never fails to win folks over.
—JACKIE SMULSKI LYONS, IL

PREP: 20 MIN. • **BAKE:** 40 MIN.
MAKES: 6 SERVINGS

- 8 ounces uncooked egg noodles
- 2 cans (10¾ ounces each) condensed cream of mushroom soup, undiluted
- ½ cup mayonnaise
- ½ cup 2% milk
- 2 to 3 teaspoons prepared horseradish
- ½ teaspoon dill weed
- ⅛ teaspoon pepper
- 1 cup frozen peas, thawed
- 1 can (4 ounces) mushroom stems and pieces, drained
- 1 small onion, chopped
- 1 jar (2 ounces) diced pimientos, drained
- 2 cans (6 ounces each) tuna, drained and flaked
- ¼ cup dry bread crumbs
- 1 tablespoon butter, melted

1. Cook the noodles according to package directions. Meanwhile, in a large bowl, combine soup, mayonnaise, milk, horseradish, dill and pepper. Stir in peas, mushrooms, onion, pimientos and tuna.
2. Drain noodles; stir into the soup mixture. Transfer to a greased 2-qt. baking dish. Toss bread crumbs and butter together; sprinkle over the top.
3. Bake casserole, uncovered, at 375° for 40-45 minutes or until bubbly.

=== READER REVIEW

"Excellent. I added ½ teaspoon of curry and 1 teaspoon of hot mustard, and substituted a small can of mild chilies for the pimientos. "
TYANSIA TASTEOFHOME.COM

SAUSAGE HASH BROWN BAKE

Pork sausage is sandwiched here between layers of hash browns and topped with cream of chicken soup and French onion dip. Cheddar cheese tops this all-in-one, anytime casserole.
—ESTHER WRINKLES VANZANT, MO

PREP: 15 MIN. • **BAKE:** 55 MIN.
MAKES: 10-12 SERVINGS

- 2 pounds bulk pork sausage
- 2 cups shredded cheddar cheese, divided
- 1 can (10¾ ounces) condensed cream of chicken soup, undiluted
- 1 cup (8 ounces) sour cream
- 1 carton (8 ounces) French onion dip
- 1 cup chopped onion
- ¼ cup chopped green pepper
- ¼ cup chopped sweet red pepper
- ⅛ teaspoon pepper
- 1 package (30 ounces) frozen shredded hash brown potatoes, thawed

1. In a large skillet, cook sausage over medium heat until no longer pink; drain on paper towels. In a large bowl, combine 1¾ cups cheese and the next seven ingredients; fold in potatoes.
2. Spread half into a greased shallow 3-qt. baking dish. Top with sausage and remaining potato mixture. Sprinkle with the remaining cheese. Cover and bake at 350° for 45 minutes. Uncover; bake casserole 10 minutes longer or until heated through.

SLOW COOKER DINNERS

What's on the menu tonight? Maximum deliciousness with very little effort! Choose any of the entrees inside to feed your home crowd—all with the ease of flipping a switch in the morning and coming home to a ready-made meal. Whether you're in the mood for a stew, main dish or sandwich, you'll find just what you need here.

SWEET & SPICY PULLED PORK SANDWICHES

I threw some always-available condiments into my slow cooker with a roast to create this fantastic pulled pork. It has become a staple sandwich filler for large get-togethers. Serve with rolls, on top of toasted crostini, or as a filling for empanadas.

—LORI TERRY CHICAGO, IL

PREP: 30 MIN. • **COOK:** 8 HOURS
MAKES: 10 SERVINGS

- 2 **medium onions, sliced (about 2 cups)**
- 2 **tablespoons brown sugar**
- 1 **tablespoon smoked paprika**
- 1½ **teaspoons salt**
- ½ **teaspoon pepper**
- 1 **boneless pork shoulder roast (4 to 5 pounds)**
- ½ **cup chicken or vegetable broth**
- ¼ **cup cider vinegar**
- 3 **tablespoons reduced-sodium soy sauce**
- 3 **tablespoons Worcestershire sauce**
- 2 **tablespoons Sriracha Asian hot chili sauce**
- 1 **tablespoon molasses**
- 2 **garlic cloves, minced**
- 2 **teaspoons Dijon mustard**
- 3 **cups coleslaw mix**
- 3 **tablespoons lime juice**
- 10 **kaiser or onion rolls, split**

1. Place onions in a 4- or 5-qt. slow cooker. Mix brown sugar, paprika, salt and pepper; rub over roast. Place over the onions.

2. In a small bowl, mix broth, vinegar, soy sauce, Worcestershire sauce, chili sauce, molasses, garlic and mustard; pour over roast. Cook, covered, on low 8-10 hours or until meat is tender.

3. Remove roast; cool slightly. Skim fat from cooking juices. In a small bowl, toss coleslaw mix with lime juice. Shred pork with two forks. Return pork to slow cooker; heat through. Serve on rolls with coleslaw.

SPICED LAMB STEW WITH APRICOTS

My son claimed to be a vegetarian during college. When he came home, I had a pot of this stew simmering. When my husband and I went to eat dinner, there were only a few shreds of meat left—turns out my son was the culprit!

—ARLENE ERLBACH MORTON GROVE, IL

PREP: 30 MIN. • **COOK:** 5 HOURS
MAKES: 5 SERVINGS

- 2 pounds lamb stew meat, cut into ¾-inch cubes
- 3 tablespoons butter
- 1½ cups chopped sweet onion
- ¾ cup dried apricots
- ½ cup orange juice
- ½ cup chicken broth
- 2 teaspoons paprika
- 2 teaspoons ground allspice
- 2 teaspoons ground cinnamon
- 1½ teaspoons salt
- 1 teaspoon ground cardamom
  Hot cooked couscous
  Chopped dried apricots, optional

1. In a large skillet, brown lamb in butter in batches. With a slotted spoon, transfer to a 3-qt. slow cooker. In the same skillet, saute onion in drippings until tender. Stir in the apricots, orange juice, broth and seasonings; pour over the lamb.

2. Cover and cook on high for 5-6 hours or until meat is tender. Serve with couscous. Sprinkle with chopped apricots if desired.

ITALIAN SAUSAGE & KALE SOUP

The first time I made this colorful soup, our home smelled wonderful. We knew it was a keeper to see us through winter days.

—SARAH STOMBAUGH CHICAGO, IL

PREP: 20 MIN. • **COOK:** 8 HOURS
MAKES: 8 SERVINGS (3½ QUARTS)

- 1 pound bulk hot Italian sausage
- 6 cups chopped fresh kale
- 2 cans (15½ ounces each) great northern beans, rinsed and drained
- 1 can (28 ounces) crushed tomatoes
- 4 large carrots, finely chopped (about 3 cups)
- 1 medium onion, chopped
- 3 garlic cloves, minced
- 1 teaspoon dried oregano
- ¼ teaspoon salt
- ⅛ teaspoon pepper
- 5 cups chicken stock
  Grated Parmesan cheese

1. In a large skillet, cook sausage over medium heat 6-8 minutes or until no longer pink, breaking into crumbles; drain. Transfer to a 5-qt. slow cooker.

2. Add kale, beans, tomatoes, carrots, onion, garlic, seasonings and stock to the slow cooker. Cook, covered, on low 8-10 hours or until vegetables are tender. Top each serving with cheese.

UPSIDE-DOWN FRITO PIE

Using ground turkey is a smart way to lighten up this hearty family-pleaser.
—**MARY BERG** LAKE ELMO, MN

PREP: 15 MIN. • **COOK:** 2 HOURS
MAKES: 6 SERVINGS

- 2 pounds ground turkey or beef
- 1 medium onion, chopped
- 2 envelopes chili seasoning mix
- 1 can (10 ounces) diced tomatoes and green chilies, undrained
- 1 can (8 ounces) tomato sauce
- 1 can (15 ounces) pinto beans, rinsed and drained
- 1 cup shredded cheddar cheese
- 3 cups corn chips
  Sour cream, minced fresh cilantro and additional chopped onion, optional

1. In a large skillet, cook turkey and onion over medium heat 8-10 minutes or until no longer pink, breaking into crumbles; stir in chili seasoning. Transfer to a 3- or 4-qt. slow cooker. Pour tomatoes and tomato sauce over the turkey.
2. Cook, covered, on low 2-3 hours or until heated through. Stir turkey mixture to combine. Top with beans. Sprinkle with cheese. Cook, covered, 5-10 minutes or until cheese is melted. Top with chips. If desired, serve with sour cream, minced cilantro and additional onion.

SLOW COOKER SPLIT PEA SOUP

When I have leftover ham in the fridge, I always like to make this soup. Just throw the ingredients in the slow cooker, turn it on and dinner is done.
—**PAMELA CHAMBERS** WEST COLUMBIA, SC

PREP: 15 MIN. • **COOK:** 8 HOURS
MAKES: 8 SERVINGS

- 1 package (16 ounces) dried green split peas, rinsed
- 2 cups cubed fully cooked ham
- 1 large onion, chopped
- 1 cup julienned or chopped carrots
- 3 garlic cloves, minced
- ½ teaspoon dried rosemary, crushed
- ½ teaspoon dried thyme
- 1 carton (32 ounces) reduced-sodium chicken broth
- 2 cups water

In a 4- or 5-qt. slow cooker, combine all ingredients. Cover and cook on low for 8-10 hours or until peas are tender.
FREEZE OPTION *Freeze cooled soup in freezer containers. To use, thaw overnight in the refrigerator. Heat through in a saucepan over medium heat, stirring occasionally.*

SPICY LENTIL SOUP

I've finally found a lentil soup my husband enjoys. Adjust the spice level to your taste, and present this yummy soup with warm pita bread.
—**EVA BARKER** LEBANON, NH

PREP: 25 MIN. • **COOK:** 9 HOURS
MAKES: 14 SERVINGS (3½ QUARTS)

- 1½ pounds potatoes, peeled and cubed (about 5 cups)
- 1 large onion, chopped
- 2 large carrots, chopped
- 2 celery ribs, chopped
- ¼ cup olive oil
- 4 teaspoons ground cumin
- 2 teaspoons chili powder
- 1 teaspoon salt
- 1 teaspoon ground coriander
- 1 teaspoon coarsely ground pepper
- ½ teaspoon ground turmeric
- ½ teaspoon cayenne pepper
- 5 garlic cloves, minced
- 2 cartons (32 ounces each) reduced-sodium chicken broth
- 2 cans (15 ounces each) tomato sauce
- 1 package (16 ounces) dried lentils, rinsed
- ¼ cup lemon juice

1. Place potatoes, onion, carrots and celery in a 6-qt. slow cooker. In a small skillet, heat oil over medium heat. Add seasonings; cook and stir 2 minutes. Add garlic; cook 1-2 minutes longer. Transfer to slow cooker.
2. Stir in broth, tomato sauce and lentils. Cook, covered, on low 9-11 hours or until lentils are tender. Stir in lemon juice.

VEGETARIAN CHILI OLE!

I combine ingredients for this chili the night before, start my trusty slow cooker in the morning and come home to a rich, spicy meal at night!

—**MARJORIE AU** HONOLULU, HI

PREP: 35 MIN. • **COOK:** 6 HOURS
MAKES: 7 SERVINGS

- 1 can (16 ounces) kidney beans, rinsed and drained
- 1 can (15 ounces) black beans, rinsed and drained
- 1 can (14½ ounces) diced tomatoes, undrained
- 1½ cups frozen corn
- 1 large onion, chopped
- 1 medium zucchini, chopped
- 1 medium sweet red pepper, chopped
- 1 can (4 ounces) chopped green chilies
- 1 ounce Mexican chocolate, chopped
- 1 cup water
- 1 can (6 ounces) tomato paste
- 1 tablespoon cornmeal
- 1 tablespoon chili powder
- ½ teaspoon salt
- ½ teaspoon dried oregano
- ½ teaspoon ground cumin
- ¼ teaspoon hot pepper sauce, optional
  Optional toppings: diced tomatoes, chopped green onions and crumbled queso fresco

1. In a 4-qt. slow cooker, combine the first nine ingredients. Combine the water, tomato paste, cornmeal, chili powder, salt, oregano, cumin and pepper sauce if desired until smooth; stir into slow cooker. Cover and cook on low for 6-8 hours or until vegetables are tender.
2. Serve with toppings of your choice.

━━━━━ **READER REVIEW**

"I made this instead of going out to our favorite Mexican restaurant one Friday night. Very satisfying!"

MMHILLL TASTEOFHOME.COM

FESTIVE SLOW-COOKED BEEF TIPS

We once owned an organic greenhouse and produce business. Weekends were hectic, so I made no-fuss meals like yummy beef tips to fortify us at day's end.

—**SUE GRONHOLZ** BEAVER DAM, WI

PREP: 45 MIN. • **COOK:** 6 HOURS
MAKES: 8 SERVINGS

- 1 boneless beef chuck roast (about 2 pounds), cut into 2-inch pieces
- 1 teaspoon salt
- ¼ teaspoon pepper
- 2 tablespoons canola oil
- 1 medium onion, coarsely chopped
- 1 celery rib, coarsely chopped
- 6 garlic cloves, halved
- 2 cups beef broth
- 1½ cups dry red wine
- 1 fresh rosemary sprig
- 1 bay leaf
- 2 cans (4 ounces each) sliced mushrooms
- 2 tablespoons cornstarch
- ½ cup water
- 1 tablespoon balsamic vinegar
  Hot cooked egg noodles

1. Sprinkle beef with salt and pepper. In a large skillet, heat oil over medium-high heat. Brown the beef in batches. Remove with a slotted spoon to a 3- or 4-qt. slow cooker.
2. In the same pan, add onion and celery; cook and stir 6-8 minutes or until tender. Add garlic; cook 1 minute longer. Add the broth, wine, rosemary and bay leaf. Bring to a boil; cook 8-10 minutes or until liquid is reduced to about 2 cups.
3. Pour over the beef in slow cooker; stir in mushrooms. Cook, covered, on low 6-8 hours or until meat is tender. Remove rosemary and bay leaf.
4. In a small bowl, mix cornstarch, water and vinegar until smooth; gradually stir into the beef mixture. Serve with noodles.

BARBECUE PORK TACOS WITH APPLE SLAW

We celebrate taco Tuesdays, so I keep things interesting by switching up the varieties. These pork tacos are super simple to make.

—**JENN TIDWELL** FAIR OAKS, CA

PREP: 15 MIN. • **COOK:** 2¼ HOURS
MAKES: 8 SERVINGS

- 2 **pork tenderloins (1 pound each)**
- 1 **can (12 ounces) root beer**
SLAW
- 6 **cups shredded red cabbage (about 12 ounces)**
- 2 **medium Granny Smith apples, julienned**
- ⅓ **cup cider vinegar**
- ¼ **cup minced fresh cilantro**
- ¼ **cup lime juice**
- 2 **tablespoons sugar**
- ½ **teaspoon salt**
- ½ **teaspoon pepper**
ASSEMBLY
- 1 **bottle (18 ounces) barbecue sauce**
- 16 **taco shells**

1. Place pork in a 3-qt. slow cooker. Pour root beer over top. Cook, covered, on low 2 to 2½ hours or just until tender (a thermometer inserted in pork should read at least 145°).
2. Meanwhile, in a large bowl, toss slaw ingredients. Refrigerate, covered, until serving.
3. Remove tenderloins to a cutting board; let stand, covered, 5 minutes. Discard cooking juices.
4. Coarsely chop pork; return to slow cooker. Stir in barbecue sauce; heat through. Serve in taco shells; top with some of the slaw. Serve remaining slaw on the side.

GERMAN-STYLE BEEF ROAST

I serve this popular German entree with potato pancakes and vegetables. Crushed gingersnaps, lemon and vinegar give the marinated slow-cooked beef and gravy their appetizing sweet-sour flavor.

—**SUSAN GAROUTTE** GEORGETOWN, TX

PREP: 10 MIN. + MARINATING
COOK: 6 HOURS 10 MIN.
MAKES: 12 SERVINGS

- 1½ **cups water, divided**
- 1¼ **cups cider vinegar, divided**
- 2 **large onions, sliced, divided**
- 1 **medium lemon, sliced**
- 15 **whole cloves, divided**
- 6 **bay leaves, divided**
- 6 **whole peppercorns**
- 2 **tablespoons sugar**
- 2 **teaspoons salt**
- 1 **beef sirloin tip roast (3 pounds), cut in half**
- ¼ **teaspoon pepper**
- 12 **gingersnap cookies, crumbled**

1. In a large resealable plastic bag, combine 1 cup water, 1 cup vinegar, half of the onions, lemon, 10 cloves, four bay leaves, peppercorns, sugar and salt; mix well. Add roast. Seal bag and turn to coat; refrigerate overnight, turning occasionally.
2. Drain and discard marinade. Place roast in a 5-qt. slow cooker; add pepper and remaining water, vinegar, onions, cloves and bay leaves. Cover and cook on low until meat is tender, 6-8 hours.
3. Remove the roast and keep warm. Discard the bay leaves. Stir in the gingersnaps. Cover and cook on high for 10-15 minutes or until gravy is thickened. Slice roast; serve with gravy.

SLOW-COOKED PORK STEW

Try this comforting stew that's easy to put together but tastes like you've been working hard in the kitchen all day. It's even better served over polenta, egg noodles or mashed potatoes.

—**NANCY ELLIOTT** HOUSTON, TX

PREP: 15 MIN. • **COOK:** 5 HOURS
MAKES: 8 SERVINGS

- 2 pork tenderloins (1 pound each), cut into 2-inch pieces
- 1 teaspoon salt
- ½ teaspoon pepper
- 2 large carrots, cut into ½-inch slices
- 2 celery ribs, coarsely chopped
- 1 medium onion, coarsely chopped
- 3 cups beef broth
- 2 tablespoons tomato paste
- ⅓ cup pitted dried plums, chopped
- 4 garlic cloves, minced
- 2 bay leaves
- 1 fresh rosemary sprig
- 1 fresh thyme sprig
- ⅓ cup Greek olives, optional
  Chopped fresh parsley, optional
  Hot cooked mashed potatoes, optional

1. Sprinkle pork with salt and pepper; transfer to a 4-qt. slow cooker. Add carrots, celery and onion. In a small bowl, whisk broth and tomato paste; pour over vegetables. Add the plums, garlic, bay leaves, rosemary, thyme and, if desired, olives. Cook, covered, on low 5-6 hours or until meat and vegetables are tender.

2. Discard bay leaves, rosemary and thyme. If desired, sprinkle stew with parsley and serve with potatoes.

TOP TIP

Be Patient—Don't Peek

Although it's tempting to lift the lid and check on your meal while it slow-cooks, resist the urge! The lid seals in steam that helps to cook the food, so don't peek unless the recipe instructs you to stir in or add ingredients.

Sprinkle with remaining cheeses. Cover and cook on low for 4-5 hours or until pasta is tender.

BAKE OPTION *Spread half of the sauce mixture into a greased 13x9-in. baking dish. Arrange stuffed manicotti shells in a single layer over sauce. Top with remaining sauce. Cover and bake at 375° for 45-55 minutes or until pasta is tender. Uncover; sprinkle with the remaining cheeses. Bake 10-15 minutes longer or until cheese is melted. Let stand 5 minutes before serving.*

LOUISIANA ROUND STEAK

After simmering in a slow cooker, the steak in this dish takes on a robust taste, and the filling portions will keep you satisfied.

—**MEGAN ROHLCK** VERMILLION, SD

PREP: 20 MIN. • **COOK:** 7 HOURS
MAKES: 6 SERVINGS

- 2 **pounds sweet potatoes, peeled and cut into 1-inch pieces**
- 1 **large onion, chopped**
- 1 **medium green pepper, sliced**
- 2 **beef top round steaks (¾-inch thick and 1 pound each)**
- 1 **teaspoon salt, divided**
- 2 **tablespoons olive oil**
- 1 **garlic clove, minced**
- 3 **tablespoons all-purpose flour**
- 1 **can (28 ounces) diced tomatoes, undrained**
- ½ **cup beef broth**
- 1 **teaspoon sugar**
- ½ **teaspoon dried thyme**
- ½ **teaspoon pepper**
- ¼ **teaspoon hot pepper sauce**

1. Place the sweet potatoes, onion and the green pepper in a 6-qt. slow cooker. Cut each steak into three serving-size pieces; sprinkle with ½ teaspoon salt. In a large skillet over medium heat, brown steaks in oil in batches on both sides. Place steaks over vegetables in slow cooker, reserving the drippings in the pan.

2. Add garlic to drippings; cook and stir for 1 minute. Stir in flour until blended. Stir in remaining ingredients and the remaining salt. Bring to a boil, stirring constantly. Cook and stir for 4-5 minutes or until thickened. Pour over meat. Cover and cook on low for 7-9 hours or until beef is tender.

TWO-MEAT MANICOTTI

I wanted to create my ideal version of a stuffed manicotti, which requires a fantastic filling and a meat sauce to die for. This recipe is the final result, and I don't mind saying it's a huge success!

—**SHALIMAR WIECH** GLASSPORT, PA

PREP: 45 MIN. • **COOK:** 4 HOURS
MAKES: 7 SERVINGS

- ½ **pound medium fresh mushrooms, chopped**
- 2 **small green peppers, chopped**
- 1 **medium onion, chopped**
- 1½ **teaspoons canola oil**
- 4 **garlic cloves, minced**
- ¾ **pound ground sirloin**
- ¾ **pound bulk Italian sausage**
- 2 **jars (23½ ounces each) Italian sausage and garlic spaghetti sauce**
- 1 **carton (15 ounces) ricotta cheese**
- 1 **cup minced fresh parsley**
- ½ **cup shredded part-skim mozzarella cheese, divided**
- ½ **cup grated Parmesan cheese, divided**
- 2 **large eggs, lightly beaten**
- ½ **teaspoon salt**
- ¼ **teaspoon pepper**
- ⅛ **teaspoon ground nutmeg**
- 1 **package (8 ounces) manicotti shells**

1. In a large skillet over medium-high heat, saute the mushrooms, peppers and onion in oil until tender. Add garlic; cook 1 minute longer. Remove from the pan.

2. In the same skillet, cook beef and sausage over medium heat until no longer pink; drain. Stir in mushroom mixture and spaghetti sauce; set aside.

3. In a small bowl, combine the ricotta cheese, parsley, ¼ cup mozzarella cheese, ¼ cup Parmesan cheese, eggs and seasonings. Stuff into uncooked manicotti shells.

4. Spread 2¼ cups sauce onto the bottom of a 6-qt. slow cooker. Arrange five stuffed manicotti shells over sauce; repeat two times, using four shells on top layer. Top with remaining sauce.

BEEF 'N' BEAN TORTA

Boosting a big, bold Southwestern taste, this slow-cooked torta is a cinch to prepare. I serve it on nights when we have only a few minutes to eat before running off to meetings or sports events.

—**JOAN HALLFORD** NORTH RICHLAND HILLS, TX

PREP: 30 MIN. • **COOK:** 4 HOURS
MAKES: 4 SERVINGS

- 1 pound ground beef
- 1 small onion, chopped
- 1 can (15 ounces) pinto or black beans, rinsed and drained
- 1 can (10 ounces) diced tomatoes and green chilies, undrained
- 1 can (2¼ ounces) sliced ripe olives, drained
- 1½ teaspoons chili powder
- ½ teaspoon salt
- ⅛ teaspoon pepper
- 3 drops hot pepper sauce
- 4 flour tortillas (8 inches)
- 1 cup shredded cheddar cheese
   Minced fresh cilantro, optional
   Salsa, sour cream, shredded lettuce and chopped tomatoes, optional

1. Cut four 20x3-in. strips of heavy-duty foil; crisscross so they resemble spokes of a wheel. Place strips on the bottom and up the sides of a 5-qt. slow cooker. Coat strips with cooking spray.
2. In a large skillet, cook beef and onion over medium heat until meat is no longer pink; drain. Stir in beans, tomatoes, olives, chili powder, salt, pepper and hot pepper sauce. Spoon about 1⅔ cups into prepared slow cooker; top with one tortilla and ¼ cup cheese. Repeat layers three times.
3. Cover and cook on low for 4-5 hours or until heated through. Using foil strips as handles, remove the tortilla stack to a platter. Sprinkle with the cilantro. Serve with salsa, sour cream, lettuce and tomatoes if desired.

CHIPOTLE PULLED CHICKEN

I love chicken that has a chipotle kick to it. This is a go-to meal when I'm looking for something extra tasty.

—**TAMRA PARKER** MANLIUS, NY

PREP: 15 MIN. • **COOK:** 3 HOURS
MAKES: 12 SERVINGS

- 2 cups ketchup
- 1 small onion, finely chopped
- ¼ cup Worcestershire sauce
- 3 tablespoons reduced-sodium soy sauce
- 2 tablespoons brown sugar
- 2 tablespoons cider vinegar
- 3 garlic cloves, minced
- 1 tablespoon molasses
- 2 teaspoons dried oregano
- 2 teaspoons minced chipotle pepper in adobo sauce plus 1 teaspoon sauce
- 1 teaspoon ground cumin
- 1 teaspoon smoked paprika
- ¼ teaspoon salt
- ¼ teaspoon crushed red pepper flakes
- 2½ pounds boneless skinless chicken breasts
- 12 sesame seed hamburger buns, split and toasted

1. In a 3-qt. slow cooker, combine the first 14 ingredients; add chicken. Cook, covered, on low 3-4 hours or until the chicken is tender (a thermometer should read at least 165°).
2. Remove chicken from slow cooker. Shred with two forks; return to slow cooker. Using tongs, place chicken mixture on bun bottoms. Replace tops.
FREEZE OPTION *Freeze the cooled meat mixture and sauce in the freezer containers. To use, partially thaw in refrigerator overnight. Heat through in a saucepan, stirring occasionally.*

ISLAND PORK ROAST

This fork-tender roast is a nice mixture of sweet and tang. It is especially good when served over rice. The leftovers make wonderful sandwiches.
—**HEATHER CAMPBELL** LAWRENCE, KS

PREP: 25 MIN. • **COOK:** 5 HOURS
MAKES: 10 SERVINGS

- 1 boneless pork loin roast (about 4 pounds)
- 1 large onion, sliced
- 2 cans (8 ounces each) unsweetened pineapple chunks, undrained
- ½ cup sugar
- ½ cup lime juice
- ½ cup soy sauce
- ¼ cup packed brown sugar
- 2 tablespoons teriyaki sauce
- 2 garlic cloves, minced
- 1 teaspoon ground ginger
- 1 teaspoon curry powder
- ¼ teaspoon salt
- ¼ teaspoon pepper
- 1 bay leaf
- ¼ cup cornstarch
- ½ cup cold water

1. Cut roast in half. Place onion in a 4- or 5-qt. slow cooker. Add pork. Drain pineapple, reserving juice; set pineapple aside. In a small bowl, combine the sugar, lime juice, soy sauce, brown sugar, teriyaki sauce, garlic, ginger, curry, salt, pepper, bay leaf and reserved juice. Pour over roast.
2. Cover and cook on low for 5-6 hours or until a thermometer reads 160°. Add pineapple during last hour of cooking.
3. Remove the meat, onion and pineapple to a serving platter; keep warm. Discard bay leaf. Skim fat from cooking juices; transfer juice to a small saucepan and bring to a boil. Combine cornstarch and water until smooth; gradually stir into the pan. Bring to a boil; cook and stir for 2 minutes or until thickened. Serve with pork.

SLOW-COOKED CHICKEN ENCHILADA SOUP

This soup delivers a big bowl of summery comfort. Toppings like avocado, sour cream and tortilla strips are a must.
—**HEATHER SEWELL** HARRISONVILLE, MO

PREP: 25 MIN. • **COOK:** 6 HOURS
MAKES: 8 SERVINGS (3¼ QUARTS)

- 1 tablespoon canola oil
- 2 Anaheim or poblano peppers, finely chopped
- 1 medium onion, chopped
- 3 garlic cloves, minced
- 1 pound boneless skinless chicken breasts
- 1 carton (48 ounces) chicken broth
- 1 can (14½ ounces) Mexican diced tomatoes, undrained
- 1 can (10 ounces) enchilada sauce
- 2 tablespoons tomato paste
- 1 tablespoon chili powder
- 2 teaspoons ground cumin
- ½ teaspoon pepper
- ½ to 1 teaspoon chipotle hot pepper sauce, optional
- ⅓ cup minced fresh cilantro

Optional toppings: shredded cheddar cheese, cubed avocado, sour cream and crispy tortilla strips

1. In a large skillet, heat oil over medium heat. Add peppers and onion; cook and stir 6-8 minutes or until tender. Add garlic; cook 1 minute longer. Transfer pepper mixture and chicken to a 5- or 6-qt. slow cooker. Stir in broth, tomatoes, enchilada sauce, tomato paste, seasonings and, if desired, pepper sauce. Cook, covered, on low 6-8 hours or until chicken is tender (a thermometer should read at least 165°).
2. Remove chicken from slow cooker. Shred with two forks; return to slow cooker. Stir in cilantro. Serve with toppings as desired.
FREEZE OPTION *Freeze cooled soup in freezer containers. To use, partially thaw in refrigerator overnight. Heat through in a saucepan, stirring occasionally and adding a little water if necessary.*

SLOW COOKER PORK POZOLE

When the snow begins falling, I know it's time to make my heartwarming stew with pork ribs and hominy.

—**GENIE GUNN** ASHEVILLE, NC

PREP: 10 MIN. • **COOK:** 3 HOURS
MAKES: 6 SERVINGS

- 1 can (15½ ounces) hominy, rinsed and drained
- 1 can (14½ ounces) diced tomatoes, undrained
- 1 can (14½ ounces) diced tomatoes with mild green chilies, undrained
- 1 can (10 ounces) green enchilada sauce
- 2 medium carrots, finely chopped
- 1 medium onion, finely chopped
- 3 garlic cloves, minced
- 2 teaspoons ground cumin
- ¼ teaspoon salt
- 1 pound boneless country-style pork ribs
  Lime wedges and minced fresh cilantro
  Corn tortillas, optional

1. In a 3- or 4-qt. slow cooker, combine the first nine ingredients; add pork. Cook, covered, on low 3-4 hours or until pork is tender.

2. Remove the pork from slow cooker. Cut pork into bite-size pieces; return to the slow cooker. Serve with lime wedges and cilantro and, if desired, corn tortillas.

BROCCOLI-CAULIFLOWER CHICKEN CASSEROLE

A chicken, broccoli and rice casserole is one of our favorite comfort foods. I make my easy variation in the slow cooker, with no rice. You can easily swap in whatever cheese you prefer. I sometimes use dairy-free cheese to create a more paleo-friendly dinner. The dish is also delicious sprinkled with a simple bread crumb topping.

—**COURTNEY STULTZ** WEIR, KS

PREP: 20 MIN. • **COOK:** 4 HOURS
MAKES: 8 SERVINGS

- 2 pounds boneless skinless chicken breasts, cut into 1-inch pieces
- 1 small head cauliflower, chopped (about 4 cups)
- 1 bunch broccoli, chopped (about 4 cups)
- ½ pound medium fresh mushrooms, chopped
- 1 large onion, chopped
- 2 medium carrots, finely chopped
- 1 cup reduced-sodium chicken broth
- 4 ounces cream cheese, softened
- 2 tablespoons olive oil
- 2 teaspoons dried sage leaves
- 1 teaspoon salt
- ½ teaspoon pepper
- 1 cup shredded cheddar cheese
  Hot cooked brown rice

In a 6-qt. slow cooker, combine the first six ingredients. In a small bowl, whisk broth, cream cheese, oil, sage, salt and pepper; pour over chicken mixture. Sprinkle with cheese. Cook, covered, on low 4-5 hours or until chicken and vegetables are tender. Serve with rice.

RED PEPPER CHICKEN

Chicken breasts are treated to black beans, red peppers and juicy tomatoes in this supper. We love it served with rice cooked in chicken broth.

—PIPER SPIWAK VIENNA, VA

PREP: 15 MIN. • **COOK:** 6 HOURS
MAKES: 4 SERVINGS

- 4 boneless skinless chicken breast halves (4 ounces each)
- 1 can (15 ounces) black beans, rinsed and drained
- 1 can (14½ ounces) Mexican stewed tomatoes, undrained
- 1 jar (12 ounces) roasted sweet red peppers, drained and cut into strips
- 1 large onion, chopped
- ½ teaspoon salt
  Pepper to taste
  Hot cooked rice

Place the chicken in a 3-qt. slow cooker. In a bowl, combine beans, tomatoes, red peppers, onion, salt and pepper. Pour over the chicken. Cover and cook on low for 6 hours or until chicken is tender. Serve with rice.

LIME-CHIPOTLE CARNITAS TOSTADAS

When I serve these at a party, I set out various toppings and garnishes so guests can custom-make their own tostadas with the lime-kissed shredded pork.

—JAN VALDEZ CHICAGO, IL

PREP: 20 MIN. • **COOK:** 8 HOURS
MAKES: 16 SERVINGS

- ½ cup chicken broth
- 4 teaspoons ground chipotle pepper
- 4 teaspoons ground cumin
- 1 teaspoon salt
- 1 boneless pork shoulder roast (4 to 5 pounds), halved
- 1 large onion, peeled and halved
- 8 garlic cloves, peeled
- 1 to 2 limes, halved
- 16 tostada shells
  Optional toppings: warmed refried beans, salsa, sour cream, shredded lettuce, chopped avocado, crumbled queso fresco and minced fresh cilantro
  Lime wedges

1. Add broth to a 5-qt. slow cooker. Mix seasonings; rub over all sides of pork. Place in slow cooker. Add onion and garlic cloves. Cook, covered, on low 8-10 hours or until meat is tender.

2. Remove pork; cool slightly. Strain cooking juices, reserving garlic cloves; discard onion. Skim fat from cooking juices. Mash garlic with a fork. Shred pork with two forks.

3. Return cooking juices, garlic and pork to slow cooker. Squeeze lime juice over pork; heat through, stirring to combine. Layer tostada shells with pork mixture and toppings as desired. Serve with lime wedges.

═══ READER REVIEW

"This meat was so tender and scrumptious! I even loved eating just the meat with some fresh pico de gallo on it. Yum!"

QUEENLALISA TASTEOFHOME.COM

HARVEST TIME CHICKEN WITH COUSCOUS

Even on busy days, I can start this chicken in a slow cooker and still get to work on time. When I come home, I throw together a spinach salad and bake crescent rolls.

—**HEIDI RUDOLPH** OREGON, IL

PREP: 30 MIN. • **COOK:** 3 HOURS
MAKES: 6 SERVINGS

- 2 medium sweet potatoes (about 1¼ pounds), peeled and cut into ½-inch pieces
- 1 medium sweet red pepper, coarsely chopped
- 1½ pounds boneless skinless chicken breasts
- 1 can (14½ ounces) stewed tomatoes, undrained
- ½ cup peach or mango salsa
- ¼ cup golden raisins
- ½ teaspoon salt
- ¼ teaspoon ground cumin
- ¼ teaspoon ground cinnamon
- ¼ teaspoon pepper

COUSCOUS

- 1 cup water
- ½ teaspoon salt
- 1 cup uncooked whole wheat couscous

1. In a 4-qt. slow cooker, layer sweet potatoes, red pepper and the chicken breasts. In a small bowl, mix tomatoes, salsa, raisins and seasonings; pour over the chicken. Cook, covered, on low 3-4 hours or until sweet potatoes and chicken are tender.

2. About 10 minutes before serving, prepare couscous. In a small saucepan, bring water and salt to a boil. Stir in couscous. Remove from heat; let stand, covered, 5 minutes or until water is absorbed. Fluff with a fork.

3. Remove chicken from slow cooker; coarsely shred with two forks. Return chicken to slow cooker, stirring gently to combine. Serve with couscous.

FREEZE OPTION *Place the cooled chicken mixture in freezer containers. To use, partially thaw in refrigerator overnight. Microwave, covered, on high in a microwave-safe dish until heated through, stirring gently and adding a little broth or water if necessary.*

ITALIAN SAUSAGES WITH PROVOLONE

These sausages with their pepper and onion topping will go quickly, so I personally recommend making a second batch for backup.

—**SHELLY BEVINGTON** HERMISTON, OR

PREP: 15 MIN. • **COOK:** 4 HOURS
MAKES: 10 SERVINGS

- 10 Italian sausage links (4 ounces each)
- 1 tablespoon canola oil
- 1 each small sweet red, yellow and orange peppers, cut into strips
- 2 medium onions, halved and sliced
- 2 cups Italian salad dressing
- 10 slices provolone cheese
- 10 brat buns, split

1. In a large skillet, brown sausages in batches in oil. Drain. Transfer to a 5-qt. slow cooker. Add the peppers, onions and salad dressing. Cover and cook on low for 4-5 hours or until a thermometer reads 160° and the vegetables are tender.

2. Place sausages and cheese in buns; using a slotted spoon, top with the pepper mixture.

CRAZY DELICIOUS BABY BACK RIBS

My husband craves baby back ribs, so we cook them multiple ways. This low and slow method with a tangy sauce is the best we've found.

—JAN WHITWORTH ROEBUCK, SC

PREP: 15 MIN. • **COOK:** 5¼ HOURS
MAKES: 8 SERVINGS

- 2 tablespoons smoked paprika
- 2 teaspoons chili powder
- 2 teaspoons garlic salt
- 1 teaspoon onion powder
- 1 teaspoon pepper
- ½ teaspoon cayenne pepper
- 4 pounds pork baby back ribs

SAUCE

- ½ cup Worcestershire sauce
- ½ cup mayonnaise
- ½ cup yellow mustard
- ¼ cup reduced-sodium soy sauce
- 3 tablespoons hot pepper sauce

1. In a small bowl, combine the first six ingredients. Cut ribs into serving-size pieces; rub with seasoning mixture. Place ribs in a 6-qt. slow cooker. Cook, covered, on low 5-6 hours or until meat is tender.

2. Preheat oven to 375°. In a small bowl, whisk the sauce ingredients. Transfer ribs to a foil-lined 15x10x1-in. baking pan; brush with some of the sauce. Bake 15-20 minutes or until browned, turning once and brushing occasionally with sauce. Serve with remaining sauce.

BEAN & BEEF CHILI

This chili may be full of great ingredients, but we love to build it up even more with toppings like pico de gallo, red onion, cilantro and cheese.

—MALLORY LYNCH MADISON, WI

PREP: 20 MIN. • **COOK:** 6 HOURS
MAKES: 6 SERVINGS (2¼ QUARTS)

- 1 pound lean ground beef (90% lean)
- 1 large sweet onion, chopped
- 3 garlic cloves, minced
- 2 cans (14½ ounces each) diced tomatoes with mild green chilies
- 2 cans (15 ounces each) pinto beans, rinsed and drained
- 2 cans (15 ounces each) black beans, rinsed and drained
- 2 to 3 tablespoons chili powder
- 2 teaspoons ground cumin
- ½ teaspoon salt
  Optional toppings: sour cream, chopped red onion and minced fresh cilantro

1. In a large skillet, cook the beef, onion and the garlic over medium heat 6-8 minutes or until beef is no longer pink, breaking up beef into crumbles; drain.

2. Transfer beef mixture to a 5-qt. slow cooker. Drain one can tomatoes, discarding liquid; add to slow cooker. Stir in beans, chili powder, cumin, salt and the remaining tomatoes. Cook, covered, on low 6-8 hours to allow flavors to blend.

3. Mash beans to desired consistency. Serve with toppings as desired.

FREEZE OPTION *Freeze cooled chili in freezer containers. To use, partially thaw in refrigerator overnight. Heat chili through in a saucepan, stirring occasionally and adding a little water if necessary.*

CHICKEN SLIDERS WITH SESAME SLAW

At our potlucks, these chicken sliders vanish quickly. The sesame slaw really takes these little sandwiches over the top!

—**PRISCILLA YEE** CONCORD, CA

PREP: 25 MIN. • **COOK:** 6 HOURS
MAKES: 20 SERVINGS

- 1 **medium onion, coarsely chopped**
- 3 **pounds boneless skinless chicken thighs**
- ½ **cup ketchup**
- ¼ **cup reduced-sodium teriyaki sauce**
- 2 **tablespoons dry sherry or reduced-sodium chicken broth**
- 2 **tablespoons minced fresh gingerroot**
- ½ **teaspoon salt**

SESAME SLAW

- ¼ **cup mayonnaise**
- 1 **tablespoon rice wine vinegar**
- 1 **tablespoon sesame oil**
- 1 **teaspoon Sriracha Asian hot chili sauce**
- 3 **cups coleslaw mix**
- ⅓ **cup dried cherries or cranberries**
- 2 **tablespoons minced fresh cilantro**
- 20 **slider buns or dinner rolls, split**

1. Place the onion and chicken in a 4-qt. slow cooker. In a small bowl, mix ketchup, teriyaki sauce, sherry, ginger and salt. Pour over chicken. Cook, covered, on low 6-7 hours or until a thermometer reads 170°.

2. Remove chicken; cool slightly. Skim fat from cooking juices. Shred chicken with two forks. Return chicken to slow cooker. Meanwhile, in a small bowl, whisk mayonnaise, vinegar, sesame oil and Sriracha sauce until blended. Stir in coleslaw mix, cherries and cilantro. Using a slotted spoon, place ¼ cup chicken mixture on each bun bottom; top with about 2 tablespoons slaw. Replace tops.

SLOW COOKER BOEUF BOURGUIGNON

I've wanted to make boeuf bourguignon ever since I got one of Julia Child's cookbooks, but I wanted to find a way to fix it in a slow cooker. My version of the popular beef stew is still rich, hearty and delicious, but without the need to watch on the stovetop or in the oven.

—CRYSTAL JO BRUNS ILIFF, CO

PREP: 30 MIN. + MARINATING
COOK: 8 HOURS
MAKES: 12 SERVINGS (⅔ CUP EACH)

- 3 pounds beef stew meat
- 1¾ cups dry red wine
- 3 tablespoons olive oil
- 3 tablespoons dried minced onion
- 2 tablespoons dried parsley flakes
- 1 bay leaf
- 1 teaspoon dried thyme
- ¼ teaspoon pepper
- 8 bacon strips, chopped
- 1 pound whole fresh mushrooms, quartered
- 24 pearl onions, peeled (about 2 cups)
- 2 garlic cloves, minced
- ⅓ cup all-purpose flour
- 1 teaspoon salt
  Hot cooked whole wheat egg noodles, optional

1. Place beef in a large resealable plastic bag; add the wine, oil and seasonings. Seal the bag and turn to coat. Refrigerate overnight.

2. In a large skillet, cook bacon over medium heat until crisp, stirring occasionally. Remove with a slotted spoon; drain on paper towels. Discard the drippings, reserving 1 tablespoon in the pan.

3. Add mushrooms and onions to drippings; cook and stir over medium-high heat until tender. Add garlic; cook 1 minute longer.

4. Drain beef, reserving marinade; transfer beef to a 4- or 5-qt. slow cooker. Sprinkle beef with flour and salt; toss to coat. Top with bacon and mushroom mixture. Add reserved marinade.

5. Cook, covered, on low 8-10 hours or until beef is tender. Remove bay leaf. If desired, serve stew with noodles.

STUFFED FLANK STEAK

I'll serve this stuffed steak on special occasions, but it's also simple enough to enjoy any evening. The tender steak cuts into appetizing spirals, and extra stuffing cooks in a foil packet on top of the steak.

—DIANE HIXON NICEVILLE, FL

PREP: 25 MIN. • **COOK:** 6 HOURS
MAKES: 6 SERVINGS

- 1 package (8 ounces) crushed corn bread stuffing
- 1 cup chopped onion
- 1 cup chopped celery
- ¼ cup minced fresh parsley
- ½ cup egg substitute
- 1¼ cups beef broth
- ⅓ cup butter, melted
- ½ teaspoon seasoned salt
- ½ teaspoon pepper
- 1 beef flank steak (1½ pounds)

1. In a large bowl, combine stuffing, onion, celery and parsley. In a small bowl, beat the egg substitute; stir in broth and butter. Pour over stuffing mixture. Sprinkle with seasoned salt and pepper; stir well.

2. Pound steak to ½-in. thickness. Spread 1½ cups stuffing mixture over steak. Roll up, starting with a short side; tie with string. Place in a 5-qt. slow cooker. Wrap remaining stuffing in foil and placed over the rolled steak.

3. Cover and cook on low for 6-8 hours or until a thermometer inserted in the stuffing reads 160° and meat is tender. Remove string before slicing.

NOTE *No liquid is added to the slow cooker for this recipe. The moisture comes from the meat.*

CHEESY HAM & CORN CHOWDER

When the day calls for a warm bowl of chunky soup, we make a big pot of the goods—potatoes, corn, ham and cheese.

—ANDREA LAIDLAW SHADY SIDE, MD

PREP: 25 MIN. • **COOK:** 8½ HOURS
MAKES: 12 SERVINGS (3¾ QUARTS)

- 1½ **pounds potatoes (about 3 medium), peeled and cut into ½-inch cubes**
- 4 **cups fresh or frozen corn, thawed (about 20 ounces)**
- 4 **cups cubed deli ham**
- 2 **small onions, chopped**
- 4 **celery ribs, chopped**
- 4 **garlic cloves, minced**
- ¼ **teaspoon pepper**
- 3 **cups chicken broth**
- 2 **tablespoons cornstarch**
- 2 **cups whole milk**
- 2 **cups shredded sharp cheddar cheese**
- 1 **cup sour cream**
- 3 **tablespoons minced fresh parsley**

1. Place the first eight ingredients in a 6-qt. slow cooker. Cook, covered, on low 8-10 hours or until the potatoes are tender.
2. In a small bowl, mix cornstarch and milk until smooth; stir into soup. Cook, covered, on high 20-30 minutes or until thickened, stirring occasionally. Stir in cheese, sour cream and parsley until cheese is melted.

CAROLINA SHRIMP & CHEDDAR GRITS

Shrimp and grits are a house favorite, if only we could agree on a recipe. I stirred things up with cheddar and Cajun seasoning to find a true winner!

—CHARLOTTE PRICE RALEIGH, NC

PREP: 15 MIN. • **COOK:** 2¾ HOURS
MAKES: 6 SERVINGS

- 1 **cup uncooked stone-ground grits**
- 1 **large garlic clove, minced**
- ½ **teaspoon salt**
- ¼ **teaspoon pepper**
- 4 **cups water**
- 2 **cups shredded cheddar cheese**
- ¼ **cup butter, cubed**
- 1 **pound peeled and deveined cooked shrimp (31–40 per pound)**
- 2 **medium tomatoes, seeded and finely chopped**
- 4 **green onions, finely chopped**
- 2 **tablespoons chopped fresh parsley**
- 4 **teaspoons lemon juice**
- 2 **to 3 teaspoons Cajun seasoning**

1. Place the first five ingredients in a 3-qt. slow cooker; stir to combine. Cook, covered, on high 2½ to 3 hours or until water is absorbed and grits are tender, stirring every 45 minutes.
2. Stir in the cheese and butter until melted. Stir in remaining ingredients; cook, covered, on high 15-30 minutes or until heated through.

COUNTRY RIBS DINNER

Ribs with carrots, celery, onions and red potatoes are pure comfort food for us. To add a little zip, we'll sprinkle in cayenne.

—**ROSE INGALL** MANISTEE, MI

PREP: 10 MIN. • **COOK:** 6¼ HOURS
MAKES: 4 SERVINGS

- 2 **pounds boneless country-style pork ribs**
- ½ **teaspoon salt**
- ¼ **teaspoon pepper**
- 8 **small red potatoes (about 1 pound), halved**
- 4 **medium carrots, cut into 1-inch pieces**
- 3 **celery ribs, cut into ½-inch pieces**
- 1 **medium onion, coarsely chopped**
- ¾ **cup water**
- 1 **garlic clove, crushed**
- 1 **can (10¾ ounces) condensed cream of mushroom soup, undiluted**

1. Sprinkle ribs with salt and pepper; transfer to a 4-qt. slow cooker. Add potatoes, carrots, celery, onion, water and the garlic. Cook, covered, on low 6-8 hours or until meat and vegetables are tender.

2. Remove meat and vegetables; skim fat from cooking juices. Whisk soup into cooking juices; return the meat and vegetables to slow cooker. Cook, covered, 15-30 minutes longer or until heated through.

SASSY POT ROAST

We lost this recipe for several years, so it's even more special to us now that we found it again. I love walking into my home after a long day at the office and smelling this lovely pot roast.

—**SUSAN BURKETT** MONROEVILLE, PA

PREP: 15 MIN. • **COOK:** 8 HOURS
MAKES: 8 SERVINGS

- 1 **boneless beef chuck roast (2 pounds)**
- ½ **teaspoon salt**
- ½ **teaspoon pepper**
- 2 **teaspoons olive oil**
- 1 **large onion, chopped**
- 1 **can (8 ounces) tomato sauce**
- ¼ **cup water**
- ¼ **cup lemon juice**
- ¼ **cup cider vinegar**
- ¼ **cup ketchup**
- 2 **tablespoons brown sugar**
- 1 **tablespoon Worcestershire sauce**
- ½ **teaspoon ground mustard**
- ½ **teaspoon paprika**

1. Sprinkle beef with salt and pepper. In a large skillet, brown beef in oil on all sides; drain.

2. Transfer to a 4-qt. slow cooker. Sprinkle with onion. Combine the remaining ingredients; pour over meat. Cover and cook on low for 8-10 hours or until meat is tender. Skim fat. If desired, thicken cooking liquid.

HAM WITH CHERRY SAUCE

I often make my cherry ham for church breakfasts. It's such a favorite that I've even served it at Easter dinners and at a friend's wedding brunch.

—**CAROL LEE JONES** TAYLORS, SC

PREP: 20 MIN. • **COOK:** 4 HOURS
MAKES: 10-12 SERVINGS

- 1 **boneless fully cooked ham (3 to 4 pounds)**
- ½ **cup apple jelly**
- 2 **teaspoons prepared mustard**
- ⅔ **cup ginger ale, divided**
- 1 **can (21 ounces) cherry pie filling**
- 2 **tablespoons cornstarch**

1. Score surface of ham, making diamond shapes ½ in. deep. In a small bowl, combine the jelly, mustard and 1 tablespoon ginger ale; rub over scored surface of ham. Cut the ham in half; place in a 5-qt. slow cooker. Cover and cook on low for 4-5 hours or until a thermometer reads 140°, basting with the cooking juices near the end of cooking time.

2. For the sauce, place pie filling in a saucepan. Combine cornstarch and remaining ginger ale; stir into pie filling until blended. Bring to a boil; cook and stir for 2 minutes or until thickened. Serve over ham.

BREADS & ROLLS

"Please pass the bread...and pass the recipe, too!" That's what friends and family will say when they try any of the golden specialties found here. Not only were the breads in this chapter tested and approved in the *Taste of Home* Test Kitchen, but these loaves, biscuits, muffins and scones have all received high praise from families across the country. Shared by home bakers, these buttery bites are sure to turn out right.

APPLE & CHEDDAR MINI SCONES

Cheese and sage go well with apples, so why not put them all in scones? These mini bites make a brunch, tailgate or any other party that much more fun.

—SUE GRONHOLZ BEAVER DAM, WI

PREP: 25 MIN. • **BAKE:** 10 MIN.
MAKES: 32 SCONES

- 3 cups all-purpose flour
- 3 teaspoons baking powder
- ½ teaspoon salt
- ½ teaspoon baking soda
- 1 cup cold butter, cubed
- 1 large egg
- ¾ cup (6 ounces) vanilla yogurt
- 3 tablespoons 2% milk, divided
- ⅓ cup shredded peeled apple
- ⅓ cup shredded sharp cheddar cheese
- 1 tablespoon minced fresh sage
- 1 tablespoon sugar

1. Preheat oven to 425°. In a large bowl, whisk flour, baking powder, salt and baking soda. Cut in butter until mixture resembles coarse crumbs. In another bowl, whisk egg, yogurt and 2 tablespoons milk; stir into crumb mixture just until moistened. Stir in apple, cheese and sage.

2. Turn onto a lightly floured surface; knead gently 10 times. Divide dough in half; pat each portion into a 6-in. circle. Cut each circle into eight wedges; cut each wedge in half.

3. Transfer to parchment paper-lined baking sheets. Brush the tops with the remaining milk; sprinkle with sugar. Bake 10-12 minutes or until golden brown. Serve warm.

FOR REGULAR-SIZE SCONES
Do not cut wedges in half. Bake as directed, increasing baking time to 12-14 minutes. Makes 16 scones.

CHIMICHURRI MONKEY BREAD

The herby goodness of my favorite sauce shines in this nostalgic bread recipe. It comes together quickly thanks to the refrigerated biscuits. Serve warm as an appetizer with marinara for dipping, or as a side to an Italian entree.

—EDEN DRANGER LOS ANGELES, CA

PREP: 20 MIN. • **BAKE:** 20 MIN.
MAKES: 12 SERVINGS

- ¼ cup minced fresh parsley
- ¼ cup olive oil
- 2 tablespoons minced fresh oregano
- 1 tablespoon white wine vinegar
- 2 garlic cloves
- ¾ teaspoon kosher salt
- ¼ teaspoon ground cumin
- ¼ teaspoon pepper
- ⅛ teaspoon crushed red pepper flakes
- 2 tubes (12 ounces each) refrigerated buttermilk biscuits

1. In a shallow bowl, combine the first nine ingredients. Cut each biscuit in half and shape into a ball. Roll in the herb mixture.

2. Place biscuit pieces in a greased 10-in. fluted tube pan. Bake at 375° for 18-22 minutes or until golden brown. Cool for 5 minutes before inverting onto a serving plate.

PUMPKIN CHOCOLATE LOAF

This no-fuss recipe bakes into three moist chocolate loaves. Featuring a tasty hint of pumpkin and spice, they've been a favorite of mine for years. The loaves can be sliced to serve as a snack or dessert.

—KATHY GARDNER ROCKVILLE, MD

PREP: 15 MIN.
BAKE: 55 MIN. + COOLING
MAKES: 3 LOAVES

- 3¾ cups all-purpose flour
- 3½ cups sugar
- 1½ teaspoons salt
- 1½ teaspoons baking powder
- 1¼ teaspoons baking soda
- 1¼ teaspoons ground cinnamon
- 1 to 1¼ teaspoons ground cloves
- ½ teaspoon ground nutmeg
- 3 large eggs
- 1 can (29 ounces) solid-pack pumpkin
- 1¼ cups canola oil
- 3 ounces unsweetened chocolate, melted and cooled
- 1½ teaspoons vanilla extract
- 2 cups (12 ounces) semisweet chocolate chips

1. In a large bowl, combine the flour, sugar, salt, baking powder, baking soda, cinnamon, cloves and nutmeg. In another large bowl, whisk the eggs, pumpkin, oil, chocolate and vanilla. Stir into dry ingredients just until moistened. Fold in chips.

2. Transfer to three greased 9x5-in. loaf pans. Bake loaves at 350° for 55-65 minutes or until a toothpick inserted in the center comes out clean.

3. Cool 10 minutes before removing from pans to wire racks. Loaves can be wrapped and frozen for up to 6 months.

HONEY-SQUASH DINNER ROLLS

These puffy dinner rolls take on rich color when you add squash to the dough. Any squash variety works. I've even used cooked carrots with great results.

—**MARCIA WHITNEY** GAINESVILLE, FL

PREP: 40 MIN. + RISING • **BAKE:** 20 MIN.
MAKES: 2 DOZEN

- 2 packages (¼ ounce each) active dry yeast
- 2 teaspoons salt
- ¼ teaspoon ground nutmeg
- 6 to 6½ cups all-purpose flour
- 1¼ cups 2% milk
- ½ cup butter, cubed
- ½ cup honey
- 1 package (12 ounces) frozen mashed winter squash, thawed (about 1⅓ cups)
- 1 large egg, lightly beaten
  Poppy seeds, salted pepitas or sesame seeds

1. In a large bowl, mix yeast, salt, nutmeg and 3 cups flour. In a small saucepan, heat milk, butter and honey to 120°-130°. Add to dry ingredients; beat on medium speed 2 minutes. Add squash; beat on high 2 minutes. Stir in enough remaining flour to form a soft dough (dough will be sticky).

2. Turn dough onto a floured surface; knead until smooth and elastic, 6-8 minutes. Place into a greased bowl, turning once to grease the top. Cover with plastic wrap and let rise in a warm place until doubled, about 1 hour.

3. Punch down the dough. Turn onto a lightly floured surface; divide and shape into 24 balls. Divide between two greased 9-in. round baking pans. Cover with kitchen towels; let rise in a warm place until doubled, about 45 minutes.

4. Preheat oven to 375°. Brush tops with beaten egg; sprinkle with seeds. Bake for 20-25 minutes or until dark golden brown. Cover loosely with foil during the last 5-7 minutes if needed to prevent overbrowning. Remove from pans to wire racks; serve warm.

BANANA MOCHA-CHIP MUFFINS

These moist muffins combine my two favorite things—chocolate and coffee. The banana is just an added bonus.

—**MELISSA WILLIAMS** TAYLORVILLE, IL

PREP: 20 MIN. • **BAKE:** 20 MIN.
MAKES: 2 DOZEN

- 5 teaspoons instant coffee granules
- 5 teaspoons hot water
- ¾ cup butter, softened
- 1¼ cups sugar
- 1 large egg
- 1⅓ cups mashed ripe bananas
- 1 teaspoon vanilla extract
- 2¼ cups all-purpose flour
- 1½ teaspoons baking powder
- ½ teaspoon baking soda
- ½ teaspoon salt
- 1½ cups semisweet chocolate chips

1. Preheat oven to 350°. In a small bowl, dissolve coffee granules in hot water. In a large bowl, cream butter and sugar until light and fluffy. Add egg; beat well. Beat in bananas, vanilla and coffee mixture. Combine flour, baking powder, baking soda and salt; add to creamed mixture just until moistened. Fold in chocolate chips.

2. Fill 24 paper-lined muffin cups two-thirds full. Bake 18-20 minutes or until a toothpick inserted in muffin comes out clean. Cool 5 minutes before removing from pans to wire racks. Serve warm.

HONEY WHEAT ROLLS

Two things really stand out about these rolls: they're easy to make, and they have the most wonderful honey flavor.

—**SANDY KLOCINSKI** SUMMERVILLE, SC

PREP: 40 MIN. + RISING • **BAKE:** 10 MIN.
MAKES: 2 DOZEN

- 2 packages (¼ ounce each) active dry yeast
- 1¾ cups warm fat-free milk (110° to 115°)
- 2 large eggs, divided use
- ½ cup honey
- ¼ cup mashed potatoes (without added milk and butter)
- ¼ cup butter, melted
- 1 teaspoon salt
- 3 cups whole wheat flour
- 2¼ to 2¾ cups all-purpose flour

1. In a small bowl, dissolve yeast in warm milk. In a large bowl, combine 1 egg, honey, mashed potatoes, butter, salt, whole wheat flour, yeast mixture and 1½ cups all-purpose flour; beat on medium speed for 3 minutes. Stir in enough remaining flour to form a soft dough (dough will be sticky).

2. Turn onto a floured surface; knead until smooth and elastic, 6-8 minutes. Place in a bowl coated with cooking spray, turning once to coat the top. Cover with plastic wrap and let rise in a warm place until doubled, about 1 hour.

3. Turn onto a floured surface; divide into 24 balls. Roll each into a 7-in. rope. Holding one end of rope, loosely wrap dough around, forming a coil. Tuck end under; pinch to seal. Place in 24 muffin cups coated with cooking spray. Cover and let dough rise until doubled, about 30 minutes.

4. Beat remaining egg; brush over rolls. Bake at 400° for 9-11 minutes or until golden brown. Remove from pans to wire racks to cool.

APPLE-RHUBARB BREAD

Rhubarb is such a jewel that I freeze it to have all year. Here's how my mother used rhubarb—in an apple bread spiced with cinnamon. I hope you enjoy it, too!

—**LINDA TOM** SIOUX FALLS, SD

PREP: 15 MIN. • **BAKE:** 50 MIN. + COOLING
MAKES: 2 LOAVES (12 SLICES EACH)

- 4 large eggs
- 1½ cups sugar
- ½ cup canola oil
- 1 teaspoon vanilla extract
- 3 cups all-purpose flour
- 4½ teaspoons baking powder
- 1 teaspoon salt
- 1 teaspoon ground cinnamon
- 1½ cups chopped peeled apple
- 1½ cups finely chopped fresh or frozen rhubarb, thawed
- 1 cup chopped walnuts

1. Preheat oven to 350°. In a large bowl, whisk eggs, sugar, oil and vanilla extract until blended. In another bowl, whisk flour, baking powder, salt and cinnamon. Add to egg mixture; stir just until moistened. Fold in apples, rhubarb and walnuts.

2. Transfer to two greased 8x4-in. loaf pans. Bake 50-60 minutes or until a toothpick inserted in center comes out clean. Cool in pans for 10 minutes before removing to wire racks to cool.

FREEZE OPTION *Securely wrap and freeze cooled loaves in plastic and foil. To use, thaw at room temperature.*

NOTE *If using frozen rhubarb, measure rhubarb while still frozen, then thaw completely. Drain in a colander, but do not press liquid out.*

room temperature until the dough expands to a 7½-in. loaf, about 1¼ hours.

5. Preheat oven to 500°. Using a sharp knife, make a slash (¼ in. deep) across top of loaf. Cover pan tightly with foil. Bake on lowest oven rack 25 minutes.

6. Reduce the oven setting to 450°. Remove foil; bake 25-30 minutes more or until bread is a deep golden brown. Remove loaf to a wire rack to cool.

FOR CHEDDAR CHEESE BREAD
Prepare the dough as directed. After refrigerating dough overnight, knead in 4 ounces diced sharp cheddar cheese before shaping.

FOR RUSTIC CRANBERRY & ORANGE BREAD
Prepare the dough as directed. After refrigerating dough overnight, knead in 1 cup dried cranberries and 4 teaspoons grated orange peel before shaping.

FOR GARLIC & OREGANO BREAD
Prepare the dough as directed. After refrigerating overnight, microwave ½ cup peeled and quartered garlic cloves with ¼ cup of 2% milk on high for 45 seconds. Drain garlic, discarding milk; knead garlic and 2 tablespoons of minced fresh oregano into dough before shaping.

⑤ INGREDIENTS FAST FIX ▶

CHOCOLATE BISCUIT PUFFS

I know my favorite snack is fun for kids to make and eat because I dreamed it up at age 9! The puffs are shaped to hide the chocolate inside for a tasty surprise.
—**JOY CLARK** SEABECK, WA

START TO FINISH: 20 MIN.
MAKES: 10 SERVINGS

- 1 **tube (12 ounces) refrigerated buttermilk biscuits**
- 1 **milk chocolate candy bar (1.55 ounces)**
- 2 **teaspoons cinnamon sugar**

1. Preheat oven to 450°. Flatten each biscuit into a 3-in. circle. Break candy bar into 10 pieces; place a piece on each biscuit. Bring up edges to enclose the candy and pinch to seal.

2. Place biscuits seam side down on an ungreased baking sheet. Sprinkle with cinnamon sugar. Bake 8-10 minutes or until golden brown.

⑤ INGREDIENTS

CRUSTY HOMEMADE BREAD

Crackling homemade bread makes an average day extraordinary. Enjoy this beautiful loaf as is, or stir in a few favorites like cheese, garlic, herbs or dried fruits.
—**MEGUMI GARCIA** MILWAUKEE, WI

PREP: 20 MIN. + RISING
BAKE: 50 MIN. + COOLING
MAKES: 1 LOAF (16 SLICES)

- 1½ **teaspoons active dry yeast**
- 1¾ **cups water (70° to 75°)**
- 3½ **cups plus 1 tablespoon all-purpose flour, divided**
- 2 **teaspoons salt**
- 1 **tablespoon cornmeal or additional flour**

1. In a small bowl, dissolve yeast in water. In a large bowl, mix 3½ cups of flour and salt. Using a rubber spatula, stir in yeast mixture to form a soft, sticky dough. Do not knead. Cover with plastic wrap; let rise at room temperature 1 hour.

2. Punch down dough. Turn onto a lightly floured surface; pat into a 9-in. square. Fold the square into thirds, forming a 9x3-in. rectangle. Fold rectangle into thirds, forming a 3-in. square. Turn dough over and place in a greased bowl. Cover with plastic wrap; let rise at room temperature until almost doubled, about 1 hour.

3. Punch down the dough and repeat folding process. Return dough to bowl; refrigerate, covered, overnight.

4. Dust bottom of a disposable foil roasting pan with cornmeal. Turn dough onto a floured surface. Knead gently 6-8 times; shape into a 6-in. round loaf. Place in prepared pan; dust top with remaining 1 tablespoon flour. Cover pan with plastic wrap; let rise at

WALNUT ZUCCHINI MUFFINS

Shredded zucchini adds moisture to these tender muffins dotted with raisins and chopped walnuts. If you have a surplus of zucchini in summer, as many of us do, this is a good way to use some of it.

—**HARRIET STICHTER** MILFORD, IN

PREP: 20 MIN. • **BAKE:** 20 MIN.
MAKES: 1 DOZEN

- 1 **cup all-purpose flour**
- ¾ **cup whole wheat flour**
- ⅔ **cup packed brown sugar**
- 2 **teaspoons baking powder**
- ¾ **teaspoon ground cinnamon**
- ½ **teaspoon salt**
- 2 **large eggs**
- ¾ **cup 2% milk**
- ½ **cup butter, melted**
- 1 **cup shredded zucchini**
- 1 **cup chopped walnuts**
- ½ **cup raisins**

1. Preheat oven to 375°. In a large bowl, whisk the first six ingredients. In another bowl, whisk eggs, milk and melted butter until blended. Add to flour mixture; stir just until moistened. Fold in zucchini, walnuts and raisins.
2. Fill 12 greased muffin cups three-fourths full. Bake for 18-20 minutes or until a toothpick inserted in center comes out clean. Cool for 5 minutes before removing from pan to a wire rack. Serve warm.
FREEZE OPTION *Freeze cooled muffins in resealable plastic freezer bags. To use, thaw at room temperature or, if desired, microwave each muffin on high for 20-30 seconds or until heated through.*

ORANGE CRANBERRY BREAD

The beauty of this festive quick bread is that it makes a delicious post-dinner snack as well as breakfast the next day. I like to toast leftover slices and spread them with cream cheese or butter for breakfast.

—**RON GARDNER** GRAND HAVEN, MI

PREP: 20 MIN. • **BAKE:** 50 MIN. + COOLING
MAKES: 2 LOAVES (16 SLICES EACH)

- 2¾ **cups all-purpose flour**
- ⅔ **cup sugar**
- ⅔ **cup packed brown sugar**
- 3½ **teaspoons baking powder**
- 1 **teaspoon salt**
- ½ **teaspoon ground cinnamon**
- ¼ **teaspoon ground nutmeg**
- 1 **large egg**
- 1 **cup 2% milk**
- ½ **cup orange juice**
- 3 **tablespoons canola oil**
- 2 to 3 **teaspoons grated orange peel**
- 2 **cups coarsely chopped fresh or frozen cranberries**
- 1 **large apple, peeled and chopped**

1. In a large bowl, combine the flour, sugars, baking powder, salt, cinnamon and nutmeg. Whisk the egg, milk, orange juice, oil and orange peel; stir into dry ingredients just until blended. Fold in the cranberries and apple.
2. Pour into two greased 8x4-in. loaf pans. Bake at 350° for 50-55 minutes or until a toothpick inserted in the center comes out clean. Cool for 10 minutes before removing loaves from pans to wire racks.
FREEZE OPTION *Securely wrap and freeze cooled loaves in plastic and foil. To use, thaw at room temperature.*

AUSTRIAN APPLE TWISTS

The addition of apples makes these sweet butterhorns stand out. The recipe is easy to prepare because you don't have to wait for the dough to rise.

—**KATHY BLESS** FAYETTEVILLE, PA

PREP: 30 MIN. + CHILLING • **BAKE:** 20 MIN.
MAKES: 64 TWISTS

- 1 package (¼ ounce) active dry yeast
- 3 cups all-purpose flour
- 1 cup butter, softened
- 3 large egg yolks, beaten
- 1 cup (8 ounces) sour cream
- ½ cup sugar
- ½ cup finely chopped pecans
- ¾ teaspoon ground cinnamon
- 1 medium tart apple, peeled and finely chopped

ICING
- 1 cup confectioners' sugar
- 4 teaspoons whole milk
- ¼ teaspoon vanilla extract
  Finely chopped pecans

1. In a large bowl, combine the yeast and flour; add butter and mix well. Add the egg yolks and sour cream; mix well. Shape into four balls. Place in separate resealable plastic bags or wrap in plastic; refrigerate overnight.

2. Combine the sugar, pecans and cinnamon; set aside. On a floured surface, roll each ball of dough into a 9-in. circle. Sprinkle with the sugar mixture and apple. Cut each circle into 16 wedges; roll up from wide edge and pinch to seal. Place with point side down on greased baking sheets.

3. Bake at 350° for 16-20 minutes or until lightly browned. Immediately remove to wire racks to cool. For icing, combine sugar, milk and vanilla until smooth; drizzle over twists. Sprinkle with pecans.

NOTE *The yeast does not need to be dissolved in liquid, and no rising time is necessary before baking.*

BLUEBERRY BRUNCH LOAF

I like to make special breakfasts on the weekend for my husband and children. This recipe's sweet frosting really makes the already-delicious blueberry bread even more memorable.

—JEAN NIETERT CLAREMONT, SD

PREP: 15 MIN. • **BAKE:** 50 MIN. + COOLING
MAKES: 1 LOAF

- ¼ cup butter, softened
- ¾ cup packed brown sugar
- 1 large egg
- 1 tablespoon grated orange peel
- 2¼ cups all-purpose flour
- 1 tablespoon baking powder
- ½ teaspoon salt
- ½ cup whole milk
- ¼ cup orange juice
- 1 cup fresh or frozen blueberries

GLAZE
- ½ cup confectioners' sugar
- 2 teaspoons butter, softened
- ½ teaspoon grated orange peel
- 1 to 1½ tablespoons whole milk

1. In a bowl, cream butter and brown sugar. Stir in the egg and orange peel. Combine flour, baking powder and salt; add to creamed mixture alternately with milk and juice, mixing thoroughly after each addition. Fold in blueberries. Pour into a greased 9x5-in. loaf pan.

2. Bake at 350° for 50-55 minutes or until bread tests done. Cool in the pan for 10 minutes before removing to a wire rack.

3. For glaze, combine confectioners' sugar, butter and orange peel. Add milk gradually until glaze is of spreading consistency; drizzle over warm bread.

TOP TIP

Baking with Berries

Frozen blueberries are perfect for many baked items, including breads. For the best results, do not defrost them before adding them to breads, muffins or other baked items.

SOFT BUTTERMILK DINNER ROLLS

Warm, buttery dinner rolls are absolutely irresistible. I save time by using a stand mixer to make my dough.

—JENNIFER PATTERSON SHOSHONE, ID

PREP: 40 MIN. + RISING
BAKE: 20 MIN. + COOLING
MAKES: 20 SERVINGS

- 1 package (¼ ounce) active dry yeast
- ¼ cup warm water (110° to 115°)
- 1 cup plus 2 tablespoons warm buttermilk (110° to 115°), divided
- ½ cup plus 1 teaspoon softened butter, divided
- 1 large egg
- ⅓ cup sugar
- 1 teaspoon salt
- 4 cups bread flour

1. Dissolve yeast in warm water until foamy. In a large bowl, combine 1 cup buttermilk, ½ cup butter, egg, sugar, salt and yeast mixture. Add 3 cups of flour and beat on medium speed until smooth, 1 minute. Add remaining flour, ¼ cup at a time, to form a soft dough.

2. Turn dough onto a lightly floured surface; knead until smooth and elastic, 6-8 minutes. Place in a greased bowl, turning once to grease the top. Cover with plastic wrap and let rise in a warm place until doubled, about 1 hour.

3. Punch down dough. Turn onto a lightly floured surface; divide and shape into 20 balls. Place in a greased 13x9-in. pan. Cover with a kitchen towel; let rise in a warm place until almost doubled, about 45 minutes.

4. Preheat oven to 350°. Brush rolls lightly with remaining buttermilk and butter. Bake until rolls are golden brown, 20-25 minutes. Cool in pan for 20 minutes. Remove to a wire rack; serve warm.

EVELYN'S SOUR CREAM TWISTS

Keep some of these flaky twists in your freezer to serve in a pinch at breakfast, lunch or dinner.

—**LINDA WELCH** NORTH PLATTE, NE

PREP: 40 MIN. + CHILLING • **BAKE:** 15 MIN.
MAKES: 4 DOZEN

- 1 package (¼ ounce) active dry yeast
- ¼ cup warm water (110° to 115°)
- 3 cups all-purpose flour
- 1½ teaspoons salt
- ½ cup cold butter
- ½ cup shortening
- 2 large eggs
- ½ cup sour cream
- 3 teaspoons vanilla extract, divided
- 1½ cups sugar

1. In a small bowl, dissolve yeast in water. In a bowl, combine flour and salt. Cut in butter and shortening until the mixture resembles coarse crumbs. Stir in the eggs, sour cream, 1 teaspoon of vanilla and the yeast mixture; mix thoroughly. Cover and refrigerate overnight.

2. Combine sugar and remaining vanilla; lightly sprinkle ½ cup over a pastry cloth or counter top surface. On the sugared surface, roll half the dough into a 12x8-in. rectangle; refrigerate remaining dough. Sprinkle the rolled dough with about 1 tablespoon of sugar mixture. Fold rectangle into thirds.

3. Give the dough a quarter turn and repeat rolling, sugaring and folding two more times. Roll into a 12x8-in. rectangle. Cut into 4x1-in. strips; twist each strip two or three times. Place on chilled ungreased baking sheets. Repeat with remaining sugar mixture and dough.

4. Bake at 375° for 12-14 minutes or until lightly browned. Immediately remove twists from pan and cool on wire racks.

MONKEY BREAD BISCUITS

Classic monkey bread is a sweetly spiced breakfast treat. I came up with an easy dinner version that features garlic and Italian seasoning. Your crowd will love it.

—**DANA JOHNSON** SCOTTSDALE, AZ

START TO FINISH: 20 MIN.
MAKES: 1 DOZEN

- 1 tube (16.3 ounces) large refrigerated flaky biscuits
- 3 tablespoons butter, melted
- 1 garlic clove, minced
- ½ teaspoon Italian seasoning
- ¼ cup grated Parmesan cheese
  Additional Italian seasoning

1. Preheat oven to 425°. Separate biscuits; cut each into six pieces. In a large bowl, combine butter, garlic and Italian seasoning; add biscuit pieces and toss to coat.

2. Place four biscuit pieces in each of 12 greased muffin cups. Sprinkle with cheese and additional Italian seasoning. Bake 8-10 minutes or until golden brown. Serve warm.

SUN-DRIED TOMATO GARLIC BREAD

My fast bread recipe tastes terrific with a variety of main courses. It comes together in minutes, and it's simple enough for weekdays but special enough for weekend meals with guests.

—**NADINE MESCH** MOUNT HEALTHY, OH

START TO FINISH: 10 MIN.
MAKES: 6 SERVINGS

- ¼ cup butter, softened
- ¼ cup grated Parmesan cheese
- 2 tablespoons chopped oil-packed sun-dried tomatoes
- 1 to 2 garlic cloves, minced
- ½ loaf Italian bread, halved lengthwise

1. In a small bowl, combine the butter, cheese, tomatoes and garlic. Spread over cut sides of bread. Transfer to an ungreased baking sheet.

2. Broil 4 in. from heat for 3-4 minutes or until golden brown. Cut into slices and serve warm.

VEGETABLE & CHEESE FOCACCIA

My family eats up this flavorful bread as fast as I can make it. Sometimes I add different herbs, red onion or crumbled bacon. It's one of my best recipes, and my bread machine makes it a snap!

—MARY CASS BALTIMORE, MD

PREP: 20 MIN. + RISING • **BAKE:** 30 MIN.
MAKES: 15 SERVINGS

- 1 cup water (70° to 80°)
- 4½ teaspoons olive oil
- 4½ teaspoons sugar
- 2 teaspoons dried oregano
- 1¼ teaspoons salt
- 3¾ cups bread flour
- 1½ teaspoons active dry yeast

TOPPING

- 1 tablespoon olive oil
- 1 tablespoon dried basil
- 2 medium tomatoes, thinly sliced
- 1 medium onion, thinly sliced
- 1 cup frozen chopped broccoli, thawed
- ¼ teaspoon salt
- ¼ teaspoon pepper
- ¾ cup grated Parmesan cheese
- 1 cup shredded part-skim mozzarella cheese

1. In bread machine pan, place first seven ingredients in order suggested by manufacturer. Select the dough setting (check dough after 5 minutes of mixing; add 1-2 tablespoons water or flour if needed).

2. When cycle is completed, turn dough onto a lightly floured surface. Punch dough down. Roll into a 13x9-in. rectangle; transfer to a 13x9-in. baking dish coated with cooking spray.

3. For topping, brush dough with olive oil; sprinkle with basil. Layer with the tomatoes, onion and broccoli; sprinkle with salt, pepper and Parmesan cheese. Cover and let rise in a warm place until doubled, about 30 minutes.

4. Bake bread at 350° for 20 minutes. Sprinkle with mozzarella cheese; bake 10-15 minutes longer or until golden brown and cheese is melted.

SKILLET HERB BREAD

My grandmother, aunts and mom were all good bakers, and each had her own specialty when it came to bread. Mom's was my favorite—she started making this skillet bread 40 years ago. The flavors call to mind the taste of corn bread stuffing.

—SHIRLEY SMITH YORBA LINDA, CA

PREP: 10 MIN. • **BAKE:** 35 MIN.
MAKES: 10 SERVINGS

- 1½ cups all-purpose flour
- 2 tablespoons sugar
- 4 teaspoons baking powder
- 1½ teaspoons salt
- 1 teaspoon rubbed sage
- 1 teaspoon dried thyme
- 1½ cups yellow cornmeal
- 1½ cups chopped celery
- 1 cup chopped onion
- 1 jar (2 ounces) chopped pimientos, drained
- 3 large eggs, beaten
- 1½ cups fat-free milk
- ⅓ cup vegetable oil

In a large bowl, combine the flour, sugar, baking powder, salt, sage and thyme. Combine cornmeal, celery, onion and pimientos; add to the dry ingredients and mix well. Add eggs, milk and oil; stir just until moistened. Pour batter into a greased 10- or 11-in. ovenproof skillet. Bake at 400° for 35-45 minutes or until bread tests done. Serve warm.

MINI SWISS CHEESE LOAVES

I usually make these tender little loaves in the morning, so they're ready to eat at lunchtime. There's nothing better than a sandwich prepared with homemade bread.

—HELEN WANAMAKER VAIL GLENSIDE, PA

PREP: 25 MIN. + RISING
BAKE: 25 MIN. + COOLING
MAKES: 4 MINI LOAVES

- 1 package (¼ ounce) active dry yeast
- ½ cup warm water (110° to 115°)
- 1 cup (8 ounces) sour cream
- 2 tablespoons sugar
- 1 teaspoon salt
- ¼ teaspoon baking soda
- 1 large egg
- 2⅓ cups all-purpose flour
- 1 cup shredded Swiss cheese
- 2 teaspoons sesame seeds

1. In a large bowl, dissolve yeast in warm water. Add sour cream, sugar, salt, baking soda, egg and 1⅓ cups flour. Beat on medium for 3 minutes. Stir in Swiss cheese and remaining flour. Do not knead.

2. Spread batter into four greased 5¾x3x2-in. loaf pans. Sprinkle with sesame seeds. Cover and let rise in a warm place until doubled, about 45 minutes.

3. Bake at 350° for 25-30 minutes or until golden brown. Remove from pans to wire racks to cool.

DILLY ROLLS

These versatile rolls are great served warm alongside any dinner. I always make a big batch since my family enjoys the rolls after they're cool, too, stuffed with sandwich fillings like egg salad or ham salad.

—MARY BICKEL TERRE HAUTE, IN

PREP: 25 MIN. + RISING • BAKE: 20 MIN.
MAKES: 2 DOZEN

- 2 cups 4% cottage cheese
- 2 tablespoons butter
- 2 packages (¼ ounce each) active dry yeast
- ½ cup warm water (110° to 115°)
- 2 large eggs
- ¼ cup sugar
- 2 tablespoons dried minced onion
- 1 to 2 tablespoons dill weed
- 1 tablespoon salt
- ½ teaspoon baking soda
- 4½ to 5 cups all-purpose flour

1. In a large saucepan over medium heat, cook cottage cheese and butter until the butter is melted. Cool to 110°-115°. In a large bowl, dissolve yeast in water. Add the eggs, sugar, onion, dill, salt, baking soda and cottage cheese mixture. Add 3 cups of flour; beat until smooth. Add enough remaining flour to form a soft dough.
2. Turn onto a floured surface; knead until smooth and elastic, 6-8 minutes. Place in a greased bowl, turning once to grease top. Cover and let rise in a warm place until doubled, about 1 hour.
3. Punch the dough down. Form into 24 balls; place in a 13x9-in. baking pan that has been sprayed with cooking spray. Cover and let rise until doubled, about 45 minutes.
4. Bake at 350° for 20-25 minutes.

CHOCOLATE CHIP- CRANBERRY SCONES

My daughter started making these as a healthier alternative to cookies, since we seem to like cookies of any kind. For a more citrusy flavor, use cranberries flavored with orange.

—NICHOLE JONES IDAHO FALLS, ID

START TO FINISH: 30 MIN.
MAKES: 1 DOZEN

- 2 cups all-purpose flour
- 3 tablespoons brown sugar
- 2 teaspoons baking powder
- 1 teaspoon grated orange peel
- ½ teaspoon salt
- ½ teaspoon baking soda
- ¼ cup cold butter
- 1 cup plain yogurt
- 1 large egg yolk
- ½ cup dried cranberries
- ½ cup semisweet chocolate chips

1. Preheat oven to 400°. In a large bowl, whisk the first six ingredients. Cut in butter until mixture resembles coarse crumbs. In another bowl, whisk yogurt and egg yolk; stir into crumb mixture just until moistened. Stir in cranberries and chocolate chips.
2. Turn onto a floured surface; knead gently 10 times. Pat dough into an 8-in. circle. Cut into 12 wedges. Place dough wedges on a baking sheet coated with cooking spray. Bake 10-12 minutes or until golden brown. Serve warm.

FREEZE OPTION *Freeze cooled scones in resealable plastic freezer bags. To use, thaw at room temperature or, if desired, microwave each scone on high for 20-30 seconds or until heated through.*

LOUISIANA PECAN BACON BREAD

One Christmas, the babysitter brought us a gift basket of goodies that included pecan bread. Whenever I make this full-flavored bread, I remember that kind soul.

—MARINA CASTLE KELLEY CANYON COUNTRY, CA

PREP: 20 MIN. • **BAKE:** 50 MIN. + COOLING
MAKES: 1 LOAF (16 SLICES)

- 6 bacon strips, chopped
- 6 ounces cream cheese, softened
- ⅓ cup sugar
- 1 large egg
- 2 cups all-purpose flour
- 2½ teaspoons baking powder
- ½ teaspoon salt
- ¾ cup 2% milk
- 1 cup chopped pecans
- ¼ cup finely chopped onion
- ¼ cup chopped green pepper

1. Preheat oven to 350°. In a large skillet, cook bacon over medium-low heat until crisp, stirring occasionally. Remove with a slotted spoon; drain on paper towels. Reserve drippings (about 2 tablespoons); cool slightly.

2. In a large bowl, beat cream cheese, sugar and reserved drippings until smooth. Beat in egg. In another bowl, whisk flour, baking powder and salt; add to the cream cheese mixture alternately with milk, beating well after each addition. Fold in pecans, onion, pepper and bacon. Transfer to a greased 9x5-in. loaf pan.

3. Bake for 50-60 minutes or until a toothpick inserted in center comes out clean. Cool in pan 10 minutes before removing to a wire rack to cool.

FREEZE OPTION *Securely wrap cooled loaves in plastic and foil, then freeze. To use, thaw in the refrigerator.*

TENDER CRESCENT ROLLS

My family's holiday meal consists of different soups and breads. This is among our favorites during that special dinner.

—BONNIE MYERS CALLAWAY, NE

PREP: 45 MIN. + RISING
BAKE: 10 MIN./BATCH
MAKES: 4 DOZEN

- 2 envelopes (¼ ounce each) active dry yeast
- 1 cup warm water (110° to 115°)
- 1 cup warm 2% milk (110° to 115°)
- 3 large eggs
- ½ cup sugar
- 6 tablespoons shortening
- 1 teaspoon salt
- 6½ to 7 cups all-purpose flour

1. In a small bowl, dissolve yeast in warm water. In a large bowl, combine milk, eggs, sugar, shortening, salt, yeast mixture and 3 cups of the flour; beat on medium speed 3 minutes until smooth. Stir in enough remaining flour to form a soft dough (dough will be sticky).

2. Turn onto a floured surface; knead until smooth and elastic, 6-8 minutes. Place in a greased bowl, turning once to grease the top. Cover with plastic wrap and let rise in a warm place until dough has doubled, about 1 hour.

3. Punch down dough. Turn onto a lightly floured surface; divide into four portions. Roll each portion into a 12-in. circle; cut each into 12 wedges. Roll up wedges from the wide ends. Place 2 in. apart on greased baking sheets, point side down; curve to form crescents.

4. Cover with kitchen towels; let rise in a warm place until doubled, about 30 minutes. Preheat oven to 350°.

5. Bake 8-10 minutes or until golden brown. Remove from pans to wire racks; serve warm.

HERB CRESCENTS *Add 1 tablespoon Italian seasoning with the sugar.*

CINNAMON-GLAZED CRESCENTS *Prepare and bake as directed. Heat 6 tablespoons butter in a saucepan until golden brown. In a large bowl, whisk 2 cups confectioners' sugar, 1½ teaspoons ground cinnamon, 2 teaspoons vanilla and browned butter until smooth. Whisk in 2-4 tablespoons hot water to achieve a good spreading consistency. Brush over warm rolls.*

ORANGE CRESCENTS *Prepare dough as directed. Combine 1 cup sugar and ¼ cup grated orange peel; sprinkle over dough circles. Cut, roll up and bake as directed. In a saucepan, bring 1½ cups sugar, 1 cup sour cream, ½ cup butter and ¼ cup orange juice to a boil; cook and stir for 3 minutes. Pour over warm rolls. Refrigerate leftovers.*

HONEY WHOLE WHEAT ROLLS

Most of the farmers in our area grow wheat, so this recipe represents my region well. I bake these rolls often, especially when I'm making soup or stew.

—CELECIA STOUP HOBART, OK

PREP: 20 MIN. + RISING • **BAKE:** 20 MIN.
MAKES: 15 ROLLS

- 2 packages (¼ ounce each) active dry yeast
- 1 cup warm water (110° to 115°)
- ¼ cup butter, melted
- ¼ cup honey
- 1 large egg
- ¾ cup whole wheat flour
- ½ cup old-fashioned oats
- 1 teaspoon salt
- 2½ to 3 cups all-purpose flour
  Additional melted butter, optional

1. In a small bowl, dissolve yeast in warm water. In a large bowl, combine butter, honey, egg, whole wheat flour, oats, salt, yeast mixture and 1 cup of all-purpose flour; beat on medium speed until smooth. Stir in enough remaining flour to form a soft dough.
2. Turn the dough onto a floured surface; knead until it's smooth and elastic, 6-8 minutes. Place in a greased bowl, turning once to grease the top. Cover with plastic wrap and let rise in a warm place until doubled, about 1 hour.
3. Punch down the dough; shape into 15 balls. Place in a greased 13x9-in. pan. Cover with a kitchen towel; let dough rise in warm place until doubled, about 45 minutes. Preheat oven to 375°.
4. Bake until golden brown, about 20 minutes. If desired, brush with additional butter. Serve warm.

READER REVIEW

"What delicious rolls! They were not difficult to make for this first-time wheat bread baker. This recipe will be one I use again and again."

EVELYNDEVRIES TASTEOFHOME.COM

FLAKY WHOLE WHEAT BISCUITS

Whole wheat flour gives these biscuits a nutty flavor. Ever since I started making these, white flour biscuits just don't taste as good! Pair them with soup, or dollop on whipped cream and sweetened berries for an easy dessert.

—TRISHA KRUSE EAGLE, ID

START TO FINISH: 25 MIN.
MAKES: 10 BISCUITS

- 1 **cup all-purpose flour**
- 1 **cup whole wheat flour**
- 3 **teaspoons baking powder**
- 1 **tablespoon brown sugar**
- 1 **teaspoon baking soda**
- ½ **teaspoon salt**
- ¼ **cup cold butter**
- 1 **cup 2% milk**

1. In a large bowl, combine the first six ingredients. Cut in butter until the mixture resembles coarse crumbs. Stir in the milk just until moistened. Turn onto a lightly floured surface; knead 8-10 times.
2. Pat or roll out to ½-in. thickness; cut with a floured 2½-in. biscuit cutter. Place 2 in. apart on an ungreased baking sheet. Bake biscuits at 425° for 8-10 minutes or until golden brown.

CARAWAY SEED RYE BREAD

It was probably 45 years ago when my mother first served this bread. Today, every time I bake it, I get nostalgic for those days and all of that delicious food!

—MILLIE FEATHER BARODA, MI

PREP: 20 MIN. + RISING
BAKE: 25 MIN.
MAKES: 2 LOAVES

- 2 **packages (¼ ounce each) active dry yeast**
- 2 **cups warm water (110° to 115°), divided**
- ¼ **cup packed brown sugar**
- 1 **tablespoon caraway seeds**
- 1 **tablespoon canola oil**
- 2 **teaspoons salt**
- 2½ **cups rye flour**
- 2¾ **to 3¼ cups all-purpose flour, divided**

1. In a large bowl, dissolve yeast in ½ cup warm water. Add brown sugar, caraway, oil, salt and remaining water; mix well. Stir in rye flour and 1 cup all-purpose flour; beat until smooth. Add enough remaining all-purpose flour to form a soft dough.
2. Turn onto a floured surface; knead until smooth and elastic, 6-8 minutes. Place in a greased bowl, turning once to grease top. Cover and let rise in a warm place until doubled, about 1 hour.
3. Punch dough down; divide in half. Shape each half into a ball; place into two greased 8-in. round baking pans or ovenproof skillets. Flatten balls to a 6-in. diameter. Cover; let rise until nearly doubled, about 30 minutes.
4. Bake at 375° for 25-30 minutes or until golden brown.

BUTTONS AND BOWS

Biscuit mix hurries along these nutmeg-spiced buttons and bows. This recipe remains a Saturday morning favorite at our house. Serve the sugar-coated treats with hot coffee for dunking.

—MARCIE HOLLADAY IRVING, TX

PREP: 20 MIN. • **BAKE:** 10 MIN.
MAKES: 1 DOZEN BUTTONS AND BOWS

- 2 **cups biscuit/baking mix**
- 2 **tablespoons plus ¼ cup sugar, divided**
- 1 **teaspoon ground nutmeg**
- ⅛ **teaspoon ground cinnamon**
- 1 **large egg, beaten**
- ⅓ **cup 2% milk**
- ¼ **cup butter, melted**

1. In a large bowl, combine the biscuit mix, 2 tablespoons sugar, nutmeg and cinnamon. Combine egg and milk; stir into the dry ingredients just until moistened.

2. Turn dough onto a heavily floured surface; knead 5-6 times. Roll out to ¼-in. thickness. Cut with a floured 2½-in. doughnut cutter; set centers aside for buttons.

3. For bows, twist each circle to form a figure eight; place on a greased baking sheet. Bake at 400° for 8-10 minutes or until golden brown. Place buttons on another greased baking sheet. Bake for 6-7 minutes.

4. Brush tops of buttons and bows with butter; sprinkle with remaining sugar. Remove from pans to wire racks. Serve warm.

FREEZE OPTION *Freeze cooled biscuits in resealable plastic freezer bags, putting the bows in one bag and buttons in another. To use, place bows on one baking sheet and buttons on another. Heat in a preheated 350° oven 6-8 minutes for bows and 2-4 minutes for buttons or until heated through.*

HAM & GREEN ONION BISCUITS

I added a bit of my personality to my grandmother's biscuit recipe. When I make them with my kids, it feels like she's with us.

—AMY CHASE VANDERHOOF, BC

PREP: 20 MIN. • **BAKE:** 10 MIN.
MAKES: ABOUT 1 DOZEN

- 2 **cups all-purpose flour**
- 3 **teaspoons baking powder**
- 1 **teaspoon sugar**
- ¼ **teaspoon garlic salt**
  Dash pepper
- 6 **tablespoons cold butter, cubed**
- 1 **cup finely chopped fully cooked ham**
- 2 **green onions, chopped**
- ¾ **cup 2% milk**

1. Preheat oven to 450°. In a large bowl, whisk the first five ingredients. Cut in butter until mixture resembles coarse crumbs. Stir in ham and green onions. Add the milk; stir just until moistened.

2. Turn dough onto a lightly floured surface; knead gently 8-10 times. Pat or roll dough to ½-in. thickness; cut with a floured 2½-in. biscuit cutter. Place 2 in. apart on an ungreased baking sheet. Bake 10-12 minutes or until golden brown. Serve warm.

A BIT NUTTY BOSTON BROWN BREAD

Hearty and dense, my homemade Boston brown bread features hazelnuts for a delightfully nutty taste. Thick slices pair well with just about anything, from soups and stews to roasts and casseroles.

—**LORRAINE CALAND** SHUNIAH, ON

PREP: 30 MIN. • **BAKE:** 45 MIN. + COOLING
MAKES: 2 LOAVES (12 SLICES EACH)

- 3 cups whole wheat flour
- 1 cup all-purpose flour
- 2½ teaspoons baking soda
- 1 teaspoon salt
- 2½ cups buttermilk
- 1 cup molasses
- 1 cup golden raisins
- ¾ cup chopped hazelnuts

1. In a large bowl, combine the flours, baking soda and salt. In a small bowl, whisk buttermilk and molasses. Stir into the dry ingredients just until moistened. Fold in raisins and nuts. Transfer mixture to two greased 8x4-in. loaf pans.
2. Bake at 350° for 45-50 minutes or until a toothpick inserted in the center comes out clean. Cool for 10 minutes before removing loaves from pans to wire racks.
NOTE *To toast nuts, bake in a shallow pan in a 350° oven for 5-10 minutes or cook in a skillet over low heat until lightly browned, stirring occasionally.*

ARIZONA CORN BREAD

Unlike other corn breads, this one uses yeast. The oil and sour cream make the loaf tender, and it has a bit of a bite to it from the two jalapenos.

—**MARGARET PACHE** MESA, AZ

PREP: 20 MIN. + RISING • **BAKE:** 30 MIN.
MAKES: 2 LOAVES (16 SLICES EACH)

- 1 cup cornmeal
- 2 tablespoons sugar
- 2 packages (¼ ounce each) active dry yeast
- 1 teaspoon salt
- ½ teaspoon baking soda
- ¼ teaspoon pepper
- 1 cup sour cream
- ½ cup canola oil
- ½ cup chopped green onions
- 2 large eggs
- 1¼ cups shredded pepper jack cheese
- 1 cup cream-style corn
- 2 jalapeno peppers, seeded and chopped
- 5 to 6 cups all-purpose flour
  Additional cornmeal
  Melted butter

1. In a large bowl, combine first six ingredients; set aside. In a saucepan, heat the sour cream, oil and onions to 120°-130°. Add to cornmeal mixture; beat until blended. Beat in eggs, cheese, corn and jalapenos. Stir in enough flour to form a stiff dough.
2. Turn onto a floured surface; knead until smooth and elastic, 6-8 minutes. Place in a greased bowl, turning once to grease top. Cover and let rise in a warm place until doubled, about 1 hour.
3. Punch dough down. Turn onto a lightly floured surface; divide in half. Shape into two loaves. Grease two 9x5-in. loaf pans; dust with additional cornmeal. Place loaves seam side down in prepared pans. Cover and let rise until doubled, about 30 minutes.
4. Brush butter over loaves. Bake at 375° for 30-35 minutes or until golden brown; cover loosely with foil if top browns too quickly. Remove from pans to wire racks to cool.
NOTE *Wear disposable gloves when cutting hot peppers; the oils can burn skin. Avoid touching your face.*

CAKES, PIES & DESSERTS

Dinner is done and the table is cleared, so you know what time it is—dessert! It doesn't get any better than pies and cakes made with love right at home. But the delicious goodness doesn't have to end there! Flip through to discover decadent ice cream, sweet cheesecake, rich brownies, frozen treats, piled-high trifles...and so much more! You know you want a slice of perfection!

TOFFEE BROWNIE TRIFLE

Dress up a brownie mix in a whole new way! Try this trifle with other flavors of pudding or substitute your favorite candy bar. If you prefer, it also tastes great with low-fat and sugar-free products.

—**WENDY BENNETT** SIOUX FALLS, SD

PREP: 20 MIN. • **BAKE:** 25 MIN. + COOLING
MAKES: 16 SERVINGS

- 1 package fudge brownie mix (13x9-inch pan size)
- 2½ cups cold milk
- 1 package (3.4 ounces) instant cheesecake or vanilla pudding mix
- 1 package (3.3 ounces) instant white chocolate pudding mix
- 1 carton (8 ounces) frozen whipped topping, thawed
- 2 to 3 Heath candy bars (1.4 ounces each), chopped

1. Prepare and bake the brownies according to package directions for cake-like brownies, using a greased 13x9-in. baking pan. Cool completely on a wire rack.

2. In a large bowl, beat milk and pudding mixes on low speed for 2 minutes. Let stand for 2 minutes or until soft-set. Fold in whipped topping.

3. Cut brownies into 1-in. cubes; place half in a 3-qt. glass trifle bowl or serving dish. Cover with half of the pudding. Repeat layers. Sprinkle with chopped candy bars. Refrigerate leftovers.

=========== READER REVIEW

"I made this for a baby shower and it was a huge hit! I put chocolate chunks in the brownies, layered toffee bits on both pudding layers and lined the top with Hershey's kisses. Divine!"

TMYERS TASTEOFHOME.COM

CINNAMON-APPLE BROWN BETTY

If I had to define the Betty of Apple Brown Betty, she would be a smart and thrifty Southern gal with a knack for creating simple, soul-comforting desserts. In this sweet dish, spiced apples are slow-cooked between layers of cinnamon-raisin bread cubes for a wonderful twist on the traditional oven-baked classic.
—**HEATHER DEMERITTE** SCOTTSDALE, AZ

PREP: 15 MIN. • **COOK:** 2 HOURS
MAKES: 6 SERVINGS

- 5 medium tart apples, cubed
- 2 tablespoons lemon juice
- 1 cup packed brown sugar
- 1 teaspoon ground cinnamon
- ¼ teaspoon ground nutmeg
- 6 tablespoons butter, melted
- 6 cups cubed day-old cinnamon-raisin bread (about 10 slices)
   Sweetened whipped cream, optional

1. In a large bowl, toss apples with lemon juice. In a small bowl, mix the brown sugar, cinnamon and nutmeg; add to apple mixture and toss to coat. In a large bowl, drizzle butter over bread cubes; toss to coat.
2. Place 2 cups of bread cubes in a greased 3- or 4-qt. slow cooker. Layer with half of apple mixture and 2 cups bread cubes. Repeat layers. Cook, covered, on low 2-3 hours or until apples are tender. Stir before serving. If desired, top with whipped cream.

BUTTERMILK PEACH ICE CREAM

My mother's family owned peach orchards in Missouri, and I live in Tennessee, a top consumer of buttermilk. This summery ice cream combines my past and present.
—**KIM HIGGINBOTHAM** KNOXVILLE, TN

PREP: 15 MIN. + CHILLING
PROCESS: 30 MIN./BATCH + FREEZING
MAKES: 2 QUARTS

- 2 pounds ripe peaches (about 7 medium), peeled and quartered
- ½ cup sugar
- ½ cup packed brown sugar
- 1 tablespoon lemon juice
- 1 teaspoon vanilla extract
   Pinch salt
- 2 cups buttermilk
- 1 cup heavy whipping cream

1. Place peaches in a food processor; process until smooth. Add sugars, lemon juice, vanilla and salt; process until blended.
2. In a bowl, mix buttermilk and cream. Stir in the peach mixture. Refrigerate, covered, 1 hour or until cold.
3. Fill the cylinder of the ice cream maker no more than two-thirds full. Freeze according to manufacturer's directions, refrigerating any remaining mixture to process later. Transfer the ice cream to freezer containers, allowing headspace for expansion. Freeze 2-4 hours or until firm. Let the ice cream stand at room temperature 10 minutes before serving.

6. For filling, in a small bowl, beat cream until it begins to thicken. Add mascarpone cheese and confectioners' sugar; beat until soft peaks form. Fold in ¼ cup of the lemon curd.

7. Line the bottom of tunnel with strawberries. Spoon mascarpone mixture over the berries; top with remaining lemon curd. Replace the cake top; refrigerate, covered, at least 4 hours or overnight.

8. For glaze, in a small bowl, mix confectioners' sugar, lemon peel and enough juice to reach the desired consistency. Unwrap cake; spread the glaze over top, allowing some to drip down sides. Refrigerate until serving.

NOTE *To remove the seeds from a vanilla bean, cut bean lengthwise in half with a sharp knife; scrape out the dark, pulpy seeds.*

⑤ INGREDIENTS

FROZEN LIME CAKE

I've got just the treat for block parties, cookouts or any time you need a cool dessert. The crust is a snap, and the ice cream and sherbet layers are so delicious.

—**KATHY GILLOGLY** SUN CITY, CA

PREP: 15 MIN. + FREEZING
MAKES: 9 SERVINGS

- 1½ cups ground almonds
- ¾ cup crushed gingersnap cookies (about 15 cookies)
- ⅓ cup butter, melted
- 2 pints pineapple-coconut or vanilla ice cream, softened
- 2 pints lime sherbet, softened
  Whipped topping, optional

1. Using a small bowl, combine the almonds, cookies and butter. Press onto the bottom of a 9-in. square pan. Freeze 15 minutes.

2. Spread ice cream over crust. Cover and freeze at least 30 minutes. Top with sherbet. Cover and freeze 4 hours or overnight.

3. Remove from freezer 10 minutes before serving. Garnish servings with whipped topping if desired.

LEMON CURD-FILLED ANGEL FOOD CAKE

For a sunny angel food cake, we make a filling of mascarpone, cream cheese and lemon curd, and then drizzle the cake with a lemony sweet glaze.

—**LEAH REKAU** MILWAUKEE, WI

PREP: 55 MIN. + CHILLING
BAKE: 45 MIN. + COOLING
MAKES: 16 SERVINGS

- 12 large egg whites (about 1⅔ cups)
- 1 cup cake flour
- 1½ cups sugar, divided
- 1 vanilla bean (see Note) or 1 teaspoon vanilla extract
- ½ teaspoon cream of tartar
- ¼ teaspoon salt

FILLING

- ½ cup heavy whipping cream
- ½ cup mascarpone cheese
- 2 tablespoons confectioners' sugar
- 1 jar (10 ounces) lemon curd, divided
- 1 cup sliced fresh strawberries, patted dry

GLAZE

- 2 cups confectioners' sugar
- 1 teaspoon grated lemon peel
- 3 to 4 tablespoons lemon juice

1. Place egg whites in a large bowl; let egg whites stand at room temperature 30 minutes.

2. Preheat oven to 325°. In a small bowl, mix flour and ¾ cup sugar until they are blended.

3. Add seeds from vanilla bean (or extract if using), cream of tartar and salt to egg whites. Beat on medium speed until soft peaks form. Gradually add the remaining ¾ cup of sugar, 1 tablespoon at a time, beating on high after each addition until the sugar is dissolved. Continue beating until soft glossy peaks form. Gradually fold in flour mixture, about ½ cup at a time.

4. Gently transfer the batter to an ungreased 10-in. tube pan. Cut through the batter with a knife to remove air pockets. Bake on the lowest oven rack 45-55 minutes or until the top springs back when it is lightly touched. Immediately invert the pan; cool completely in pan, about 1½ hours.

5. Run a knife around the sides and center tube of pan. Remove cake to a serving plate. Using a serrated knife, cut a 1-in. slice off top of cake. Hollow out remaining cake, leaving a 1-in.-thick shell (save removed cake for another use).

⑤ INGREDIENTS

IRISH CREAM CUSTARDS

Creme brulee is our favorite dessert and we love Irish cream liqueur, so I decided to put them together for a dinner finale we truly love.

—**JOYCE MOYNIHAN** LAKEVILLE, MN

PREP: 20 MIN. + CHILLING • **BAKE:** 20 MIN.
MAKES: 6 SERVINGS

- 2 cups heavy whipping cream
- ¼ cup Irish cream liqueur
- 3 large eggs
- 2 large egg yolks
- ¾ cup plus 2 tablespoons sugar, divided
- 1 teaspoon vanilla extract

1. Preheat oven to 325°. In a saucepan, heat cream and liqueur until bubbles form around sides of pan; remove from heat. In a large bowl, whisk eggs, egg yolks and ¾ cup sugar until blended but not foamy. Slowly stir in hot cream mixture. Stir in vanilla.

2. Place six 6-oz. broiler-safe ramekins in a baking pan large enough to hold them without touching. Pour cream mixture into ramekins. Place pan on oven rack; add very hot water to pan to within ½ in. of tops of ramekins.

3. Bake 20-25 minutes or until a knife inserted near center comes out clean; centers will still be soft. Immediately remove ramekins from water bath to a wire rack; cool 10 minutes. Refrigerate until cold.

4. To caramelize the topping with a kitchen torch, sprinkle custards evenly with remaining sugar. Hold torch flame about 2 in. above custard surface and rotate it slowly until sugar is evenly caramelized. Serve immediately or refrigerate up to 1 hour.

5. To caramelize topping in a broiler, place ramekins on a baking sheet; let stand at room temperature 15 minutes. Preheat broiler. Sprinkle the custards evenly with the remaining sugar. Broil 3-4 in. from the heat 5-7 minutes or until the sugar is caramelized. Serve immediately or refrigerate up to 1 hour.

GRITS PIE

Simple, Southern and scrumptious, this pie will be a definite hit, even with people who normally don't eat grits. It has the perfect custardy texture.

—**VICTORIA HUDSON** PICKENS, SC

PREP: 15 MIN. • **BAKE:** 30 MIN.
MAKES: 10 SERVINGS

- ¾ cup water
- ⅛ teaspoon salt
- ¼ cup quick-cooking grits
- ½ cup butter, cubed
- ¾ cup sugar
- 2 tablespoons all-purpose flour
- 3 large eggs
- ¼ cup buttermilk
- 1 teaspoon vanilla extract
  Pastry for single-crust pie
  (9 inches)
  Whipped cream, orange slices or
  sliced fresh strawberries,
  optional

1. In a small saucepan, bring water and salt to a boil. Slowly stir in grits. Reduce heat; cook and stir for 4-5 minutes or until thickened. Add butter; stir until melted. Remove from the heat; cool to room temperature.
2. In a small bowl, whisk the sugar, flour, eggs, buttermilk and vanilla. Slowly stir into grits. Roll out pastry to fit a 9-in. pie plate. Transfer pastry to pie plate. Trim pastry to ½ in. beyond edge of plate; flute edges. Add filling.
3. Bake at 325° for 30-35 minutes or just until set. Serve warm or cool to room temperature. Garnish with whipped cream and orange slices or strawberries if desired.

SIMPLE TURTLE CHEESECAKE

For an almost instant dessert, I spread homemade ganache and caramel sauce over pre-made cheesecake. It makes the holidays feel slightly less hectic.

—**LAURA MCDOWELL** LAKE VILLA, IL

START TO FINISH: 25 MIN.
MAKES: 8 SERVINGS

- 1 frozen New York-style cheesecake
  (30 ounces), thawed
- ½ cup semisweet chocolate chips
- ½ cup heavy whipping cream, divided
- 3 tablespoons chopped pecans,
  toasted
- ¼ cup butter, cubed
- ½ cup plus 2 tablespoons packed
  brown sugar
- 1 tablespoon light corn syrup

1. Place cheesecake on a serving plate. Place chocolate chips in a small bowl. In a small saucepan, bring ¼ cup of the cream just to a boil. Pour it over the chocolate, stirring with a whisk until smooth. Cool mixture slightly, stirring occasionally. Pour over cheesecake; sprinkle with the pecans. Refrigerate until set.
2. In a small saucepan, melt butter; stir in brown sugar and corn syrup. Bring to a boil. Reduce the heat; cook and stir until sugar is dissolved. Stir in the remaining cream and return to a boil. Remove from the heat. Serve warm with cheesecake or, if desired, cool completely and drizzle the mixture over the cheesecake.
NOTE *To toast nuts, bake in a shallow pan in a 350° oven for 5-10 minutes or cook in a skillet over low heat until lightly browned, stirring occasionally.*

CARAMEL-MOCHA ICE CREAM DESSERT

You can use any kind of ice cream in this frosty dessert—the possibilities are endless! I personally suggest changing it up by substituting chocolate and vanilla for coffee and dulce de leche.

—SCARLETT ELROD NEWNAN, GA

PREP: 45 MIN. + FREEZING
MAKES: 20 SERVINGS

- 10 whole graham crackers
- 1 cup butter, cubed
- 1 cup packed brown sugar
- 1 cup chopped pecans

FILLING

- 1 quart dulce de leche ice cream, softened
- 1 jar (16 ounces) hot fudge ice cream topping, warmed
- 1 quart coffee ice cream, softened
- 1½ cups heavy whipping cream
- ⅓ cup coffee liqueur
  Chocolate curls

1. Preheat oven to 350°. Arrange the crackers in a single layer in a greased 15x10x1-in. baking pan. In a large saucepan, melt butter over medium heat. Stir in brown sugar. Bring to a gentle boil; cook and stir for 2 minutes. Remove from the heat and stir in pecans. Pour over crackers; spread to cover crackers.

2. Bake 8-10 minutes or until bubbly. Cool completely on a wire rack.

3. Crush the cracker mixture into coarse crumbs; sprinkle half into an ungreased 13x9-in. dish. Spread with dulce de leche ice cream. Cover and freeze for 1 hour or until firm.

4. Drizzle with ice cream topping and sprinkle with the remaining crumb mixture. Cover and freeze 30 minutes or until ice cream topping is set.

5. Spread with coffee ice cream; freeze. In a small bowl, beat cream until stiff peaks form. Fold in coffee liqueur. Spread over top of dessert. Cover and freeze 4 hours or until firm.

6. Remove from the freezer 15 minutes before serving time. Garnish it with chocolate curls.

RASPBERRY RUMBLE

My guy is a big raspberry fan, so that's what I use in this cake that features a classic fluffy frosting. Freeze the berries so they don't stain the batter.

—LORRAINE CALAND SHUNIAH, ON

PREP: 40 MIN. • **BAKE:** 25 MIN. + COOLING
MAKES: 12 SERVINGS

- 2 cups fresh raspberries
- ¼ cup butter, softened
- ¾ cup sugar
- 2 large eggs
- 2¼ cups all-purpose flour
- 2 teaspoons baking powder
- 1 teaspoon salt
- ¾ cup 2% milk

TOPPING

- 3 large egg whites
- 1 cup sugar
- ⅛ teaspoon cream of tartar
- ¼ to ½ cup boiling water, optional
- ¼ teaspoon almond extract
  Sliced almonds

1. Place raspberries on a baking sheet; freeze until firm. Preheat oven to 350°.

2. In a large bowl, cream butter and sugar until light and fluffy; beat in eggs. In another bowl, whisk together flour, baking powder and salt; add this to creamed mixture alternately with milk, beating well. Fold in frozen raspberries. Spread into a greased 13x9-in. baking pan.

3. Bake for 25-30 minutes or until a toothpick inserted in the center comes out clean. Cool completely in the pan on a wire rack.

4. For the topping, whisk together the egg whites, sugar and cream of tartar in a large heatproof bowl. Place over simmering water in a large saucepan over medium heat; whisking mixture constantly, heat the mixture until a thermometer reads 160°. Remove from the heat.

5. Beat on high speed until stiff glossy peaks form, about 5 minutes. If desired, thin topping with water by slowly beating in enough boiling water until desired consistency is reached. Fold in extract. Spread over cake. Sprinkle with almonds. Refrigerate leftovers.

BIRTHDAY CAKE FREEZER POPS

On my quest to find birthday cake ice cream—my favorite flavor—I came up with these easy ice pops. Now, instead of going to the store whenever a craving hits, I just head to my freezer.
—**DAWN LOPEZ** WESTERLY, RI

PREP: 20 MIN. + FREEZING
MAKES: 1½ DOZEN

- ⅔ **cup sprinkles, divided**
- 18 **paper or plastic cups (3 ounces each) and wooden pop sticks**
- 2 **cups cold 2% milk**
- 1 **package (3.4 ounces) instant vanilla pudding mix**
- 1 **carton (8 ounces) frozen whipped topping, thawed**
- 2 **cups crushed vanilla wafers (about 60 wafers)**

1. Spoon 1 teaspoon sprinkles into each cup. In a large bowl, whisk the milk and pudding mix 2 minutes. Let stand 2 minutes or until soft-set. Stir in whipped topping, crushed wafers and remaining sprinkles.

2. Cut a 1-in. hole in the tip of a pastry bag or in a corner of a food-safe plastic bag. Transfer mixture to bag. Pipe into prepared cups. Top with foil and insert sticks through foil. Freeze until firm, about 4 hours. Let stand at room temperature 5 minutes before gently removing pops.

NUTELLA HAND PIES

Pint-size Nutella hand pies made with puff pastry are a great way to surprise your family!
—*TASTE OF HOME* TEST KITCHEN

PREP: 10 MIN. • **BAKE:** 20 MIN.
MAKES: 9 SERVINGS

- 1 **large egg**
- 1 **tablespoon water**
- 1 **sheet frozen puff pastry, thawed**
- 3 **tablespoons Nutella**
- 1 **to 2 teaspoons grated orange peel**

ICING
- ⅓ **cup confectioners' sugar**
- ½ **teaspoon orange juice**
- ⅛ **teaspoon grated orange peel**
  Additional Nutella, optional

1. Preheat oven to 400°. In a small bowl, whisk egg with water.

2. Unfold puff pastry; cut into nine squares. Place 1 teaspoon Nutella in center of each; sprinkle with orange peel. Brush edges of pastry with egg mixture. Fold one corner over filling to form a triangle; press edges to seal. Transfer to an ungreased baking sheet.

3. Bake 17-20 minutes or until golden brown. Cool slightly.

4. In a small bowl, mix confectioners' sugar, orange juice and orange peel; drizzle over pies. If desired, warm additional Nutella in a microwave and drizzle over tops.

PEANUT BUTTER SHEET CAKE

I received the recipe for Peanut Butter Sheet Cake from a pastor's wife. My family absolutely loves it.

—**BRENDA JACKSON** GARDEN CITY, KS

PREP: 15 MIN. • **BAKE:** 20 MIN. + COOLING
MAKES: 24 SERVINGS

- 2 **cups all-purpose flour**
- 2 **cups sugar**
- 1 **teaspoon baking soda**
- ½ **teaspoon salt**
- 1 **cup water**
- ¾ **cup butter, cubed**
- ½ **cup chunky peanut butter**
- ¼ **cup canola oil**
- 2 **large eggs**
- ½ **cup buttermilk**
- 1 **teaspoon vanilla extract**

GLAZE
- ⅔ **cup sugar**
- ⅓ **cup evaporated milk**
- 1 **tablespoon butter**
- ⅓ **cup chunky peanut butter**
- ⅓ **cup miniature marshmallows**
- ½ **teaspoon vanilla extract**

1. Preheat the oven to 350°. Grease a 15x10x1-in. baking pan.
2. In a large bowl, whisk the flour, sugar, baking soda and salt. In a small saucepan, combine water and butter; bring just to a boil. Stir in peanut butter and oil until blended. Stir into the flour mixture. In a small bowl, whisk the eggs, buttermilk and vanilla until they are blended; add to flour mixture, whisking constantly.
3. Transfer to prepared pan. Bake 20-25 minutes or until a toothpick inserted in center comes out clean.
4. Meanwhile, for glaze, combine sugar, milk and butter in a saucepan. Bring to a boil, stirring constantly; cook and stir 2 minutes. Remove from heat; stir in peanut butter, marshmallows and vanilla until blended. Spoon over warm cake, spreading evenly. Cool on a wire rack.

BLUEBERRY-BLACKBERRY RUSTIC TART

My dad would always stop the car on the side of the road in Maine and say, "I smell blueberries!" He had a pail ready to go. Then Mom would bake the wild berries in a cornmeal crust.

—**PRISCILLA GILBERT**
INDIAN HARBOUR BEACH, FL

PREP: 20 MIN. + CHILLING • **BAKE:** 55 MIN.
MAKES: 8 SERVINGS

- 2 **cups all-purpose flour**
- ⅓ **cup sugar**
- ¼ **cup yellow cornmeal**
- ⅔ **cup cold butter, cubed**
- ½ **cup buttermilk**

FILLING
- 4 **cups fresh blueberries**
- 2 **cups fresh blackberries**
- ⅔ **cup sugar**
- ⅓ **cup all-purpose flour**
- 2 **tablespoons lemon juice**
- 1 **large egg, beaten**
- 2 **tablespoons turbinado (washed raw) sugar or coarse sugar**
  Whipped cream, optional

1. In a large bowl, mix flour, sugar and cornmeal; cut in butter until crumbly. Gradually add buttermilk, tossing with a fork until the dough holds together when pressed. Shape into a disk; wrap in plastic wrap. Refrigerate 30 minutes or overnight.
2. Preheat oven to 375°. On a lightly floured surface, roll the dough into a 14-in. circle. Transfer to a parchment paper-lined baking sheet.
3. In a large bowl, combine berries, sugar, flour and lemon juice; spoon over pastry to within 2 in. of edges. Fold the pastry edge over the filling, leaving center uncovered. Brush the folded pastry with beaten egg; sprinkle with turbinado sugar.
4. Bake 55-60 minutes or until crust is golden brown and filling is bubbly. Using parchment paper, slide tart onto a wire rack to cool. If desired, serve with whipped cream.

CHERRY GELATIN SUPREME

When I was growing up, this yummy, easy-to-make dessert was always on the menu at holiday get-togethers. Years ago, my aunt gave me the recipe, and now when I make it for my family, I think of her.

—JANICE RATHGEB BRIGHTON, IL

PREP: 20 MIN. + CHILLING
MAKES: 12 SERVINGS

- 2 cups water, divided
- 1 package (3 ounces) cherry gelatin
- 1 can (21 ounces) cherry pie filling
- 1 package (3 ounces) lemon gelatin
- 1 package (3 ounces) cream cheese, softened
- ⅓ cup mayonnaise
- 1 can (8 ounces) crushed pineapple, undrained
- 1 cup miniature marshmallows
- ½ cup heavy whipping cream, whipped
- 2 tablespoons chopped pecans

1. In a large saucepan, bring 1 cup water to a boil. Stir in cherry gelatin until dissolved. Stir in pie filling. Pour into an 11x7-in. dish. Cover and refrigerate for 2 hours or until set.
2. In a small saucepan, bring the remaining water to a boil. Stir in lemon gelatin until dissolved. In a small bowl, beat the cream cheese and mayonnaise until smooth. Beat in lemon gelatin and pineapple. Cover and refrigerate for 45 minutes.
3. Fold in the marshmallows and whipped cream. Spoon over cherry layer; sprinkle with pecans. Cover and refrigerate for 2 hours or until set.

⑤ INGREDIENTS

BLUEBERRY CREAM POPS

Blueberries and cream are such a fun after-school snack. Make it in the morning so the pops are ready to go when the kids come in the door.

—CINDY REAMS PHILIPSBURG, PA

PREP: 15 MIN. + FREEZING
MAKES: 8 POPS

- ⅔ cup sugar
- ⅔ cup water
- 2 cups fresh or frozen blueberries, thawed
- ¼ cup heavy whipping cream
- 8 freezer pop molds or 8 paper cups (3 ounces each) and wooden pop sticks

1. For sugar syrup, in a small saucepan, combine the sugar and water; bring the mixture to a boil, stirring to dissolve sugar. Cool completely.
2. Meanwhile, in a bowl, coarsely mash blueberries; stir in cream and sugar syrup. Spoon into molds or paper cups. Top molds with holders. If using cups, top with foil and insert sticks through foil. Freeze until firm. To serve, let pops stand at room temperature 10 minutes before gently unmolding.

PINEAPPLE UPSIDE-DOWN CHEESECAKE

My mom often made pineapple upside-down cake, but I prefer something creamier. This recipe looks just like her cake, but gets even tastier as pineapple upside-down cheesecake.

—MARILYN MCGINNIS CITRUS HEIGHTS, CA

PREP: 25 MIN. • **BAKE:** 35 MIN. + CHILLING
MAKES: 4 SERVINGS

- ¾ cup packed brown sugar
- 4 slices canned pineapple
- 4 maraschino cherries

FILLING
- 1 package (8 ounces) cream cheese, softened
- ½ cup confectioners' sugar
- 2 teaspoons all-purpose flour
- 1 teaspoon vanilla extract
- 1 large egg, lightly beaten
- ¼ cup crushed pineapple, well drained

CRUST
- 1 tablespoon butter
- ⅓ cup graham cracker crumbs
- ¼ teaspoon ground cinnamon

1. Preheat oven to 325°. Sprinkle brown sugar into an 8-in. ovenproof skillet. Arrange pineapple in a single layer over brown sugar; place a cherry in the center of each pineapple slice.

2. For filling, in a large bowl, beat cream cheese and confectioners' sugar until smooth. Beat in flour and vanilla. Add egg; beat on low speed just until blended. Fold in crushed pineapple. Spoon over fruit.

3. Bake 35-40 minutes or until the center is almost set. Cool on a wire rack 10 minutes. Loosen the sides from the pan with a knife. Cool 1 hour longer. Refrigerate overnight, covering when completely cooled.

4. For crust, in a small skillet, melt butter over medium-low heat. Add cracker crumbs and cinnamon; cook and stir 4-6 minutes or until toasted. Cool. Just before serving, top the cheesecake with toasted crumbs, pressing to adhere. Invert cheesecake onto a serving plate.

CHOCOLATE S'MORES TART

I created this tart for my kids, who love having s'mores on the fire pit. It's truly indulgent. We simply can't get enough of the billowy marshmallow topping.

—DINA CROWELL FREDERICKSBURG, VA

PREP: 55 MIN. + CHILLING
MAKES: 16 SERVINGS

- 1½ cups graham cracker crumbs
- ¼ cup sugar
- ⅓ cup butter, melted

FILLING
- 10 ounces bittersweet chocolate, chopped
- ¼ cup butter, cubed
- 1½ cups heavy whipping cream

TOPPING
- 5 large egg whites
- 1 cup sugar
- ¼ teaspoon cream of tartar

1. In a small bowl, mix the cracker crumbs and sugar; stir in the butter. Press the mixture onto the bottom and ½ in. up the sides of an ungreased 9-in. fluted tart pan with a removable bottom. Refrigerate for 30 minutes.

2. Place chocolate and butter in a large bowl. In a small saucepan, bring cream just to a boil. Pour over the chocolate and butter; let stand 5 minutes. Stir with a whisk until smooth. Pour into prepared tart shell. Refrigerate 1 hour or until set. Place egg whites in a large bowl; let stand at room temperature 30 minutes.

3. In top of a double boiler or a metal bowl over simmering water, combine egg whites, sugar and cream of tartar. Beat on low speed 1 minute. Continue beating on low until a thermometer reads 160°, about 5 minutes. Transfer to a large bowl; beat on high until stiff glossy peaks form and mixture is slightly cooled, about 5 minutes.

4. Spread meringue over the tart. If desired, heat meringue with a kitchen torch or broil 2 in. from heat 30-45 seconds or until meringue is lightly browned. Refrigerate leftovers.

NOTE *For a firmer crust, bake at 350° until crust is lightly browned, 10-12 minutes. Cool on a wire rack.*

BANANA CREAM PIE

Made from our farm-fresh dairy products, this pie was a sensational creamy treat anytime that Mom served it. Her recipe is a real treasure, and I've never found one that tastes better!

—BERNICE MORRIS MARSHFIELD, MO

PREP: 20 MIN. + COOLING
MAKES: 6-8 SERVINGS

- ¾ cup sugar
- ⅓ cup all-purpose flour
- ¼ teaspoon salt
- 2 cups milk
- 3 large egg yolks, lightly beaten
- 2 tablespoons butter
- 1 teaspoon vanilla extract
- 3 medium firm bananas
- 1 pastry shell (9 inches), baked
   Whipped cream and additional sliced bananas

1. In a saucepan, combine sugar, flour and salt; stir in milk and mix well. Cook over medium-high heat until mixture is thickened and bubbly. Cook and stir for 2 minutes longer. Remove from the heat. Stir a small amount into the egg yolks; return all to saucepan. Bring to a gentle boil. Cook for and stir 2 minutes; remove from the heat. Add butter and vanilla; cool slightly.

2. Slice the bananas into pastry shell; pour filling over top. Cool on wire rack for 1 hour. Store in the refrigerator. Before serving, garnish with whipped cream and additional bananas.

PECAN BUTTER TARTS

I searched for the perfect butter tart for ages. After many attempts, I discovered this delightful version that begs for a scoop of ice cream on top.

—SUSAN KIEBOAM STREETSBORO, OH

PREP: 30 MIN. • **BAKE:** 10 MIN + COOLING
MAKES: 1 DOZEN

- 1 package (14.1 ounces) refrigerated pie pastry

FILLING

- ½ cup raisins
- 1 cup water
- 1 large egg, lightly beaten
- ½ cup packed dark brown sugar
- ½ cup packed light brown sugar
- ⅓ cup butter, melted
- 1½ teaspoons vanilla extract
- ¼ teaspoon salt
- ⅓ cup coarsely chopped pecans
   Vanilla ice cream, optional

1. Preheat the oven to 425°. Line 12 muffin cups with foil liners. (Do not use paper-lined foil liners.)

2. On a work surface, unroll pastry sheets. Cut 12 circles with a floured 4-in. round cookie cutter (save the remaining pastry for another use). Gently press pastry circles onto bottom and up sides of foil liners. Refrigerate while preparing filling.

3. In a microwave-safe bowl, combine the raisins and water; microwave on high 2 minutes. Drain; cool slightly.

4. In a small bowl, mix the egg, brown sugars, melted butter, vanilla and salt until they are blended; stir in the pecans and raisins. Spoon into pastry cups, dividing evenly.

5. Bake on a lower oven rack 7-9 minutes or until the filling just begins to bubble up and crusts are light golden brown (do not overbake). Cool completely in pan on a wire rack. If desired, serve with ice cream.

WHOLE WHEAT STRAWBERRY SHORTCAKES

Nothing says spring like fresh strawberry shortcake. It's heavenly. My mother and I usually make this with strawberries we picked ourselves.

—**SARAH HATTER** BRODHEAD, WI

PREP: 45 MIN. + CHILLING
BAKE: 15 MIN. + COOLING
MAKES: 6 SERVINGS

- 2½ cups fresh strawberries, hulled, divided
- 1 to 2 tablespoons maple syrup

SHORTCAKES
- 2 cups whole wheat flour
- 2½ teaspoons baking powder
- ½ teaspoon salt
- ¼ teaspoon baking soda
- ½ cup cold butter, cubed
- 1 large egg
- ½ cup 2% milk
- ¼ cup honey
  Whipped cream

1. In a bowl, thoroughly mash ¾ cup strawberries; stir in syrup. Cut the remaining strawberries into ¼-in. slices; add to the crushed strawberries and toss to coat. Refrigerate, covered, for 1 hour.

2. Meanwhile, preheat oven to 400°. In a large bowl, whisk flour, baking powder, salt and baking soda. Cut in butter until mixture resembles coarse crumbs. In a small bowl, whisk egg, milk and honey until blended; stir into flour mixture just until moistened.

3. Turn onto a lightly floured surface; knead gently 8-10 times. Pat or roll dough to ¾-in. thickness; cut with a floured 2½-in. biscuit cutter. Place 2 in. apart on parchment paper-lined baking sheets. Bake 12-15 minutes or until light brown. Remove to wire racks to cool slightly.

4. To serve, split the shortcakes in half. Fill with the strawberry mixture and whipped cream. Top with additional whipped cream.

CHOCOLATE CHIFFON CAKE

If you want to offer family and friends a dessert that really stands out from the rest, this is the cake you need. Beautiful, high layers of rich sponge cake are drizzled with a succulent chocolate glaze.

—**ERMA FOX** MEMPHIS, MO

PREP: 25 MIN. + COOLING
BAKE: 1 HOUR + COOLING
MAKES: 16-20 SERVINGS

- 7 large eggs, separated
- ½ cup baking cocoa
- ¾ cup boiling water
- 1¾ cups cake flour
- 1¾ cups sugar
- 1½ teaspoons baking soda
- 1 teaspoon salt
- ½ cup canola oil
- 2 teaspoons vanilla extract
- ¼ teaspoon cream of tartar

ICING
- ⅓ cup butter
- 2 cups confectioners' sugar
- 2 ounces unsweetened chocolate, melted and cooled
- 1½ teaspoons vanilla extract
- 3 to 4 tablespoons hot water
  Chopped nuts, optional

1. Let eggs stand at room temperature for 30 minutes. In a bowl, combine cocoa and water until smooth; cool for 20 minutes. In a large bowl, combine flour, sugar, baking soda and salt. In a bowl, whisk egg yolks, oil and vanilla; add to the dry ingredients along with the cocoa mixture. Beat until well blended. In another large bowl and with clean beaters, beat egg whites and cream of tartar on high speed until stiff peaks form. Gradually fold into egg yolk mixture.

2. Gently spoon the batter into an ungreased 10-in. tube pan. Cut through the batter with a knife to remove air pockets. Bake on lowest rack at 325° for 60-65 minutes or until the top springs back when lightly touched. Immediately invert the pan; cool completely. Run a knife around sides and center tube of the pan. Invert cake onto a serving plate.

3. For the icing, melt butter in a saucepan. Remove from heat; stir in the confectioners' sugar, chocolate, vanilla and water. Drizzle over cake. Sprinkle with nuts if desired.

⑤INGREDIENTS

EASY GRASSHOPPER ICE CREAM PIE

This quick pie is such an ego booster! My family compliments me the entire time they're eating it. It's a big hit at work potlucks, too.

—**KIM MURPHY** ALBIA, IA

PREP: 15 MIN. + FREEZING
MAKES: 8 SERVINGS

- 4 cups mint chocolate chip ice cream, softened
- 1 chocolate crumb crust (8 inches)
- 5 Oreo cookies, chopped
- ⅓ cup chocolate-covered peppermint candies
  Chocolate hard-shell ice cream topping

Spread ice cream into crust. Sprinkle with cookies and candies; drizzle with ice cream topping. Freeze until firm. Remove from the freezer 15 minutes before serving.

NOTE *This recipe was tested with Junior Mints chocolate-covered peppermint candies.*

APPLE PIE A LA MODE

I was planning a dinner party and wanted a dessert that would wow. My caramel apple ice cream pie certainly did the trick. Now it's a family favorite.

—**TRISHA KRUSE** EAGLE, ID

PREP: 15 MIN. + FREEZING
MAKES: 8 SERVINGS

- 1 **can (21 ounces) apple pie filling**
- 1 **graham cracker crust (9 inches)**
- 2 **cups butter pecan ice cream, softened if necessary**
- 1 **jar (12 ounces) hot caramel ice cream topping**
- ¼ **cup chopped pecans, toasted**

1. Spread half of the pie filling over crust. Top with half of the ice cream; freeze 30 minutes. Drizzle with half of caramel topping; layer with remaining pie filling. Freeze 30 minutes. Scoop remaining ice cream over top. Freeze, covered, until firm.

2. Remove from freezer 30 minutes before serving. In a microwave, warm remaining caramel topping. Serve pie with warm caramel topping; sprinkle with pecans.

NOTE *To toast nuts, bake in a shallow pan in a 350° oven for 5-10 minutes or cook in a skillet over low heat until lightly browned, stirring occasionally.*

WINNIE'S MINI RHUBARB & STRAWBERRY PIES

Every spring, we had strawberries and rhubarb on our farm outside Seattle. These fruity hand pies remind me of those times and of Grandma Winnie's baking.

—**SHAWN CARLETON** SAN DIEGO, CA

PREP: 25 MIN. + CHILLING
BAKE: 15 MIN. + COOLING
MAKES: 2 DOZEN

- 3 **tablespoons quick-cooking tapioca**
- 4 **cups sliced fresh strawberries**
- 2 **cups sliced fresh rhubarb**
- ¾ **cup sugar**
- 1 **teaspoon grated orange peel**
- 1 **teaspoon vanilla extract**
- ¼ **teaspoon salt**
- ¼ **teaspoon ground cinnamon**
- 3 **drops red food coloring, optional**
  Pastry for double-crust pie (9 inches)

1. Preheat oven to 425°. Place tapioca in a small food processor or spice grinder; process until finely ground.

2. In a large saucepan, combine strawberries, rhubarb, sugar, orange peel, vanilla, salt, cinnamon, tapioca and, if desired, food coloring; bring to a boil. Reduce the heat; simmer, covered, for 15-20 minutes or until strawberries are tender, stirring the mixture occasionally. Transfer to a large bowl; cover and refrigerate overnight.

3. On a lightly floured surface, roll one half of the dough to an 18-in. circle. Cut 12 circles with a 4-in. biscuit cutter, rerolling scraps as necessary; press dough onto bottom and up sides of ungreased muffin cups. Repeat with remaining dough. Spoon strawberry mixture into muffin cups.

4. Bake 12-15 minutes or until filling is bubbly and the crust is golden brown. Cool in pan 5 minutes; remove to wire racks to cool.

PASTRY FOR DOUBLE-CRUST PIE (9 INCHES) *Combine 2½ cups of all-purpose flour and ½ teaspoon salt; cut in 1 cup cold butter until crumbly. Gradually add ⅓ to ⅔ cup ice water, tossing with a fork until dough holds together when pressed. Divide the dough in half. Shape each into a disk; wrap in plastic wrap. Refrigerate 1 hour or overnight.*

BLUEBERRY ZUCCHINI SQUARES

I saw a bar recipe on a muffin mix box that called for apple and lemon peel. I tried it from scratch with shredded zucchini and fresh blueberries instead, and it worked!

—SHELLY BEVINGTON HERMISTON, OR

PREP: 30 MIN. • **BAKE:** 30 MIN. + COOLING
MAKES: 2 DOZEN

- 2 cups shredded zucchini (do not pack)
- ½ cup buttermilk
- 1 tablespoon grated lemon peel
- 3 tablespoons lemon juice
- 1 cup butter, softened
- 2½ cups sugar
- 2 large eggs
- 3¼ cups plus 2 tablespoons all-purpose flour, divided
- 1 teaspoon baking soda
- ½ teaspoon salt
- 2 cups fresh or frozen blueberries

GLAZE
- 2 cups confectioners' sugar
- ¼ cup buttermilk
- 1 tablespoon grated lemon peel
- 2 teaspoons lemon juice
- ⅛ teaspoon salt

1. Preheat oven to 350°. Grease a 15x10x1-in. baking pan.
2. In a small bowl, combine zucchini, buttermilk, lemon peel and lemon juice; toss to combine. In a large bowl, cream butter and sugar until light and fluffy. Beat in eggs, one at a time. In another bowl, whisk 3¼ cups flour, baking soda and salt; gradually add to creamed mixture alternately with zucchini mixture, mixing well after each addition. Toss blueberries with remaining flour; fold into batter.
3. Transfer batter to prepared pan, spreading evenly (pan will be full). Bake 30-35 minutes or until light golden brown and a toothpick inserted in center comes out clean. Cool completely in pan on a wire rack.
4. In a small bowl, mix the glaze ingredients until smooth; spread over top. Let stand until set.

NOTE *If using frozen blueberries, use without thawing to avoid discoloring the batter.*

GIANT PEANUT BUTTER ICE CREAM SANDWICH

I created this treat for my husband. Because it can be made ahead of time and frozen, it cuts stress for busy hostesses—and really, who doesn't love peanut butter?

—JOANN BELACK BRADENTON, FL

PREP: 30 MIN. • **BAKE:** 20 MIN. + FREEZING
MAKES: 12 SERVINGS

- 2 packages (16 ounces each) ready-to-bake refrigerated chocolate peanut butter cookie dough
- 6 whole chocolate graham crackers, crushed
- 1 cup cold milk
- 1 cup heavy whipping cream
- 1 package (3.4 ounces) instant vanilla pudding mix
- 1 package (8 ounces) cream cheese, softened
- 1⅓ cups creamy peanut butter
- 3 cups vanilla ice cream, softened
- ¼ cup Nutella

1. Preheat oven to 350°. Let the dough stand at room temperature 5-10 minutes to soften. Press into two ungreased 9-in. springform pans; sprinkle with graham cracker crumbs. Bake for 20-25 minutes or until set. Cool completely.
2. In a large bowl, whisk the milk, cream and pudding mix 2 minutes. Let stand 2 minutes or until soft-set. In another large bowl, beat the cream cheese and peanut butter until smooth. Add the pudding and ice cream; beat until smooth.
3. Spread over one cookie crust. Remove sides of second pan; place crust, crumb side down, over filling. Wrap in plastic wrap; freeze on a baking sheet 4 hours or until firm.
4. Remove from freezer 15 minutes before serving. Place Nutella in a small microwave-safe bowl; cover and microwave at 50% power 1-2 minutes or until smooth, stirring twice. Remove sides of pan; cut dessert into slices. Drizzle with Nutella.

CHOCOLATE ESPRESSO LAVA CAKE

When a chocolate craving hits, I whip up this cake my aunt inspired. It's gooey and saucy but not too sweet.

—LISA RENSHAW KANSAS CITY, MO

PREP: 15 MIN. • **COOK:** 3 HOURS + STANDING
MAKES: 16 SERVINGS

- 1 package chocolate fudge cake mix (regular size)
- 1 tablespoon instant espresso powder
- 3 cups 2% milk
- 1 package (3.9 ounces) instant chocolate pudding mix
- 1 cup (6 ounces) semisweet chocolate chips
- 1 cup white baking chips

1. Prepare cake mix batter according to package directions, adding espresso powder before mixing. Transfer to a greased 4-qt. slow cooker.
2. In a small bowl, whisk milk and pudding mix 2 minutes. Let stand 2 minutes or until soft-set. Pour over the batter. Cook, covered, on low 3 to 3½ hours or until a toothpick inserted in the cake portion comes out with moist crumbs.
3. Sprinkle top with chocolate chips and baking chips. Turn off slow cooker; remove insert. Let stand, uncovered, 15-30 minutes or until chips are softened. Serve warm.

=== READER REVIEW

"I used a box of sugar-free chocolate pudding for this recipe because that was all I had on hand. It worked out just fine."

GRAMMY DEBBIE TASTEOFHOME.COM

SHORTCUT TRES LECHES CAKE

My mom's favorite cake is tres leches, a butter cake soaked with three kinds of milk. There's so much to love about my no-fuss version. You'll see when you give it a try!

—MARINA CASTLE KELLEY
CANYON COUNTRY, CA

PREP: 20 MIN. + CHILLING
BAKE: 30 MIN. + COOLING
MAKES: 20 SERVINGS

- 1 package butter recipe golden cake or yellow cake mix (regular size)
- 3 large eggs
- ⅔ cup 2% milk
- ½ cup butter, softened
- 1 teaspoon vanilla extract

TOPPING

- 1 can (14 ounces) sweetened condensed milk
- 1 can (12 ounces) evaporated milk
- 1 cup heavy whipping cream

WHIPPED CREAM

- 1 cup heavy whipping cream
- 3 tablespoons confectioners' sugar
- 1 teaspoon vanilla extract

1. Preheat oven to 350°. Grease a 13x9-in. baking pan.
2. In a large bowl, combine cake mix, eggs, milk, softened butter and vanilla; beat on low speed 30 seconds. Beat on medium 2 minutes. Transfer to the prepared pan. Bake 30-35 minutes or until a toothpick inserted in center comes out clean.
3. Cool in the pan on a wire rack 20 minutes. In a 4-cup measuring cup, whisk the topping ingredients until blended. Using a skewer, generously poke holes in top of warm cake. Pour the milk mixture slowly over cake, filling holes. Cool 30 minutes longer. Refrigerate, covered, at least 4 hours or overnight.
4. In a bowl, beat cream until it begins to thicken. Add confectioners' sugar and vanilla; beat until soft peaks form. Spread over cake.

BUTTERY COCONUT BARS

My coconut bars are an American version of a Filipino coconut cake called *bibingka*. These are a crispier, sweeter take on the Christmas tradition I grew up liking.

—**DENISE NYLAND** PANAMA CITY, FL

PREP: 20 MIN. + COOLING
BAKE: 40 MIN. + COOLING
MAKES: 3 DOZEN

    2 cups all-purpose flour
    1 cup packed brown sugar
    ½ teaspoon salt
    1 cup butter, melted
FILLING
    3 large eggs
    1 can (14 ounces) sweetened
       condensed milk
    ½ cup all-purpose flour
    ¼ cup packed brown sugar
    ¼ cup butter, melted
    3 teaspoons vanilla extract
    ½ teaspoon salt
    4 cups flaked coconut, divided

1. Preheat the oven to 350°. Line a 13x9-in. baking pan with parchment paper, letting ends extend up sides.
2. In a large bowl, mix flour, brown sugar and salt; stir in 1 cup melted butter. Press onto bottom of prepared pan. Bake 12-15 minutes or until light brown. Cool 10 minutes on a wire rack. Reduce oven setting to 325°.
3. In a large bowl, whisk the first seven filling ingredients until blended; stir in 3 cups coconut. Pour over the crust; sprinkle with remaining coconut. Bake 25-30 minutes or until light golden brown. Cool in pan on a wire rack. Lifting with parchment paper, remove from pan. Cut into bars.

FUDGE-TOPPED BROWNIES

Why choose between brownies or fudge when you can have them both! These exquisite brownies are the ultimate chocolate dessert.

—**JUDY OLSON** WHITECOURT, AB

PREP: 25 MIN. • **BAKE:** 25 MIN. + FREEZING
MAKES: ABOUT 10 DOZEN

    1 cup butter
    4 ounces unsweetened chocolate,
       chopped
    2 cups sugar
    2 teaspoons vanilla extract
    4 large eggs
   1½ cups all-purpose flour
    1 teaspoon baking powder
    ½ teaspoon salt
    1 cup chopped walnuts
TOPPING
   4½ cups sugar
    1 can (12 ounces) evaporated milk
    ½ cup butter, cubed
    1 package (12 ounces) semisweet
       chocolate chips
    1 package (11½ ounces) milk
       chocolate chips
    1 jar (7 ounces) marshmallow creme
    2 teaspoons vanilla extract
    2 cups chopped walnuts

1. In a heavy saucepan or microwave, melt butter and chocolate; stir until smooth. Remove from heat; blend in sugar and vanilla. Add eggs; mix well. Combine flour, baking powder and salt; add to the chocolate mixture. Stir in walnuts. Pour into a greased 13x9-in. baking pan. Bake at 350° for 25-30 minutes or until top springs back when lightly touched. Cool on a wire rack while preparing topping.
2. Combine sugar, milk and butter in a large heavy saucepan; bring to a boil over medium heat. Reduce the heat; simmer, uncovered, for 5 minutes, stirring constantly. Remove from the heat. Stir in the chocolate chips, marshmallow creme and vanilla until smooth. Add walnuts. Spread over warm brownies. Freeze for 3 hours or until firm. Cut into 1-in. squares. Store in the refrigerator.

TOFFEE-PEAR CRISP BREAD PUDDING

My son loves pear crisp, but one night I was making bread pudding and he asked if I could make both. I compromised by combining two desserts into this one dish. It's fantastic!

—KURT WAIT REDWOOD CITY, CA

PREP: 20 MIN. + STANDING
BAKE: 40 MIN. + COOLING
MAKES: 12 SERVINGS

1¾ cups 2% milk
1 cup butterscotch-caramel ice cream topping
¼ cup butter, cubed
1 teaspoon ground cinnamon
½ teaspoon ground ginger
2 large eggs
4 cups cubed day-old French bread
2 cups sliced peeled fresh pears (about 2 medium)

TOPPING
½ cup all-purpose flour
½ cup packed brown sugar
⅓ cup cold butter
⅓ cup English toffee bits

1. Preheat oven to 350°. In a small saucepan, combine milk, caramel topping, butter, cinnamon and ginger. Cook and stir over medium-low heat until the butter is melted. Remove from heat.

2. Whisk eggs in a large bowl; gradually whisk in a third of the milk mixture. Stir in the remaining milk mixture. Add the cubed bread; stir to coat. Let stand 10 minutes. Gently stir in pears; transfer to a greased 11x7-in. baking dish. Bake, uncovered, 20 minutes.

3. Meanwhile, for the topping, in a small bowl, combine the flour and brown sugar; cut in butter until crumbly. Stir in toffee bits; sprinkle over the bread pudding. Bake, uncovered, 20-25 minutes longer or until puffed, golden and a knife inserted near center comes out clean. Let stand 10 minutes before serving. Serve warm. Refrigerate leftovers.

COCONUT ITALIAN CREAM CAKE

I'd never tasted an Italian cream cake before moving to Colorado. Now I bake for people in the area, and this beauty is one of the most requested.

—**ANN BUSH** COLORADO CITY, CO

PREP: 50 MIN. • **BAKE:** 20 MIN. + COOLING
MAKES: 16 SERVINGS

- 5 large eggs, separated
- 1 cup butter, softened
- 1⅔ cups sugar
- 1½ teaspoons vanilla extract
- 2 cups all-purpose flour
- ¾ teaspoon baking soda
- ½ teaspoon salt
- 1 cup buttermilk
- 1⅓ cups flaked coconut
- 1 cup chopped pecans, toasted

FROSTING
- 12 ounces cream cheese, softened
- 6 tablespoons butter, softened
- 2¼ teaspoons vanilla extract
- 5⅔ cups confectioners' sugar
- 3 to 4 tablespoons heavy whipping cream
- ½ cup chopped pecans, toasted
- ¼ cup toasted flaked coconut, optional

1. Place the egg whites in a small bowl; let stand at room temperature 30 minutes.
2. Preheat oven to 350°. Line the bottoms of three greased 9-in. round baking pans with parchment paper; grease the paper.
3. In a large bowl, cream butter and sugar until light and fluffy. Add egg yolks, one at a time, beating well after each addition. Beat in vanilla. In another bowl, whisk flour, baking soda and salt; add to creamed mixture alternately with buttermilk, beating well after each addition. Fold in the coconut and pecans.
4. With clean beaters, beat egg whites on medium speed until stiff peaks form. Gradually fold into batter. Transfer to the prepared pans. Bake 20-25 minutes or until a toothpick inserted in center comes out clean. Cool in pans 10 minutes before removing to wire racks; remove paper. Cool completely.
5. For frosting, in a large bowl, beat cream cheese and butter until smooth. Beat in vanilla. Gradually beat in the confectioners' sugar and enough cream to reach spreading consistency. Spread frosting between the layers and over the top and sides of cake. Sprinkle with the pecans and, if desired, coconut. Refrigerate the leftovers.
NOTE *To toast pecans and coconut, spread each, one at a time, in a 15x10x1-in. baking pan. Bake at 350° for 5-10 minutes or until lightly browned, stirring occasionally.*

PEACH MELBA TRIFLE

This dream of a dessert tastes extra good on a busy day because you can make it ahead of time. If you don't have fresh peaches handy, use canned ones.

—**CHRISTINA MOORE** CASAR, NC

PREP: 20 MIN. + CHILLING
MAKES: 12 SERVINGS

- 2 packages (12 ounces each) frozen unsweetened raspberries, thawed
- 1 tablespoon cornstarch
- 1½ cups (12 ounces) fat-free peach yogurt
- ⅛ teaspoon almond extract
- 1 carton (8 ounces) frozen reduced-fat whipped topping, thawed
- 2 prepared angel food cakes (8 to 10 ounces each), cut into 1-inch cubes (about 8 cups)
- 4 small peaches, peeled and sliced (about 2 cups)

1. In a large saucepan, mix raspberries and cornstarch until blended. Bring to a boil; cook and stir 1-2 minutes or until thickened. Strain the seeds; cover and refrigerate.
2. In a large bowl, mix yogurt and extract; fold in whipped topping. In a 4-qt. bowl, layer half of the cake cubes, yogurt mixture and peaches. Repeat the layers. Refrigerate, covered, at least 3 hours before serving. Serve with raspberry sauce.

COOKIES & CANDIES

Just about everybody has a sweet tooth. Here you'll find a treasure trove of recipes to satisfy that craving. Whether it's a classic cookie or a mouthwatering candy, these recipes are sure to get people talking. Traditional favorites take on delightful new flavors and spins—like a new go-to cookie inspired by a favorite cake!

EASY OATMEAL CREAM PIES

These are easy to make, use only five ingredients and taste very similar to a store-bought cookie. Of course, everything's better from your own kitchen!

—**CRYSTAL SCHLUETER** NORTHGLENN, CO

PREP: 20 MIN. + CHILLING
BAKE: 10 MIN./BATCH + COOLING
MAKES: 1½ DOZEN

- ¾ cup butter, softened
- 2 large eggs
- 1 package spice cake mix (regular size)
- 1 cup quick-cooking oats
- 1 can (16 ounces) vanilla frosting

1. Beat butter and eggs until blended. Beat in cake mix and oats. Refrigerate, covered, 2 hours or until firm enough to roll, though the dough will remain fairly soft.

2. Preheat oven to 350°. On a well-floured surface, roll half of dough to ¼-in. thickness. Cut with a floured 2½-in. round cookie cutter. Place 1 in. apart on parchment paper-lined baking sheets. Bake 8-10 minutes or until set. Remove from pans to wire racks to cool completely. Repeat with the remaining dough.

3. Spread frosting on bottoms of half of the cookies; cover with remaining cookies.

FREEZE OPTION *Freeze baked and assembled cookies in freezer containers, separating layers with waxed paper. Thaw before serving.*

=== READER REVIEW

"These are especially good with the whipped vanilla frosting! I didn't roll them out, just dropped them with a cookie scoop. They were thicker that way, but still good."

SUGARCRYSTAL TASTEOFHOME.COM

LEMON MELTAWAYS

Both the cookie and the frosting are spiked with lemon juice. The result is a divinely tangy confection!

—MARY HOUCHIN LEBANON, IL

PREP: 15 MIN. + CHILLING
BAKE: 10 MIN./BATCH + COOLING
MAKES: ABOUT 5 DOZEN

¾ cup butter, softened
⅓ cup confectioners' sugar
1 teaspoon lemon juice
1¼ cups all-purpose flour
½ cup cornstarch
FROSTING
¼ cup butter, softened
¾ cup confectioners' sugar
1 teaspoon grated lemon peel
1 teaspoon lemon juice
1 to 3 drops yellow food coloring, optional

1. In a bowl, beat the butter and confectioners' sugar until blended. Beat in lemon juice. In a small bowl, whisk flour and cornstarch; gradually beat into the butter mixture. Divide dough in half; shape each half into an 8-in.-long roll. Wrap rolls in plastic; refrigerate 2 hours or until firm.
2. Preheat oven to 350°. Unwrap dough and cut crosswise into ¼-in. slices. Place slices 2 in. apart on ungreased baking sheets.
3. Bake 8-12 minutes or until firm. Remove from pans to wire racks to cool completely.
4. For frosting, in a small bowl, beat butter and confectioners' sugar until smooth. Beat in lemon peel, lemon juice and, if desired, food coloring. Spread over cookies.

TOP TIP

Lemon Zest in a Flash

The quickest way I know to get grated lemon peel? I slice off big pieces of peel and grind them for just a few seconds in a food processor.

—LARUE H. SAFFORD, AZ

CHOCOLATE MEXICAN WEDDING CAKES

Cinnamon adds warmth to this twist on a traditional Mexican treat. Sometimes I add mini chocolate chips to the dough and, after baking, dip the cooled cookies in melted almond bark.

—JOANNE VALKEMA FREEPORT, IL

PREP: 20 MIN. • **BAKE:** 15 MIN./BATCH
MAKES: ABOUT 3½ DOZEN

- 1 cup butter, softened
- 1¾ cups confectioners' sugar, divided
- 1 teaspoon vanilla extract
- 1½ cups all-purpose flour
- ¼ cup cornstarch
- ¼ cup baking cocoa
- ½ teaspoon salt
- 1¼ cups finely chopped pecans or almonds
- ½ teaspoon ground cinnamon

1. Preheat oven to 325°. In a large bowl, cream the butter and 1 cup of confectioners' sugar until light and fluffy. Beat in vanilla. Combine flour, cornstarch, cocoa and salt; gradually add to creamed mixture and mix well. Stir in nuts.

2. Shape tablespoonfuls of the dough into 1-in. balls. Place 2 in. apart on ungreased baking sheets. Bake for 12-14 minutes or until set.

3. In a small bowl, combine cinnamon and remaining confectioners' sugar. Roll the warm cookies in the sugar mixture; cool on wire racks. Store in an airtight container.

BUTTERY GANACHE COOKIE CUPS

Our family wanted to share our love of ganache-filled cupcakes, so we made them into cookies—and because we bake the cookies in muffin cups, we get the best of both worlds.

—ADELA SRINIVASAN PARKER, CO

PREP: 30 MIN. + CHILLING
BAKE: 10 MIN./BATCH + COOLING
MAKES: ABOUT 4 DOZEN

- 1 cup butter, softened
- 1 cup sugar
- 2 large eggs
- 2 tablespoons orange juice
- 1 teaspoon orange extract
- 3 cups all-purpose flour
- 1 teaspoon baking powder
- ¼ teaspoon salt
- 1 tablespoon confectioners' sugar
- 6 ounces bittersweet chocolate, chopped
- 1 cup heavy whipping cream

1. In a large bowl, cream butter and sugar until light and fluffy. Add eggs, one at a time, beating well after each addition. Beat in orange juice and extract. In another bowl, whisk flour, baking powder and salt; gradually beat into creamed mixture. Refrigerate, covered, for 1 hour or until firm.

2. Preheat oven to 350°. Shape level tablespoons of dough into balls; press evenly onto the bottom and up the sides of greased or foil-lined mini-muffin cups. Bake for 7-9 minutes or until edges are light brown. Cool in pans for 2 minutes. Remove to wire racks to cool completely. Dust with confectioners' sugar.

3. Meanwhile, place chocolate in a small bowl. In a small saucepan, bring cream just to a boil. Pour over the chocolate; whisk until smooth. Cool slightly. Refrigerate, covered, 1 hour or until ganache thickens to a spreading consistency, stirring occasionally. Pipe into cookie cups. Refrigerate in airtight containers.

FREEZE OPTION *Freeze shaped balls of dough on waxed paper-lined baking sheets until firm. Transfer to resealable plastic freezer bags; return to freezer. To use, thaw dough in refrigerator overnight. Bake and fill cookies as directed.*

SUGAR COOKIES

This is truly an oldie, dating back to a Swedish woman born in 1877. Her daughter, Esther Davis, came up with all the exact measurements (the original cookies were mixed by feel and taste) and shared the recipe with me. These are my favorite cookies, and I hope they'll become yours as well.

—HELEN WALLIS VANCOUVER, WA

PREP: 30 MIN. • **BAKE:** 10 MIN./BATCH
MAKES: 5 DOZEN

- ½ cup butter, softened
- ½ cup shortening
- 1 cup sugar
- 1 large egg
- 1 teaspoon vanilla extract
- 2¼ cups all-purpose flour
- ½ teaspoon baking powder
- ½ teaspoon baking soda
  Additional sugar

1. Preheat oven to 350°. Cream the butter, shortening and sugar until light and fluffy. Beat in the egg and vanilla. In another bowl, whisk flour, baking powder and baking soda; gradually beat into creamed mixture.

2. Shape into 1-in. balls. Roll in the additional sugar. Place on greased baking sheets; flatten with a glass. Bake until set, 10-12 minutes. Remove to wire racks to cool.

(5) INGREDIENTS
MINI S'MORES

I created my s'mores at a time when I couldn't afford store-bought gifts. They're awesome for parties and bake sales—and kids love to help put them together.

—STEPHANIE TEWELL ELIZABETH, IL

PREP: 50 MIN. + STANDING • **COOK:** 5 MIN.
MAKES: ABOUT 4 DOZEN

- 2 cups milk chocolate chips
- ½ cup heavy whipping cream
- 1 package (14.4 ounces) graham crackers, quartered
- 1 cup marshmallow creme
- 2 cartons (7 ounces each) milk chocolate for dipping
- 4 ounces white candy coating, melted, optional

1. Place chocolate chips in a bowl. In a small saucepan, bring cream just to a boil. Pour over chocolate; whisk until smooth. Cool to room temperature or until mixture reaches a spreading consistency, about 10 minutes.

2. Spread the chocolate mixture over one side of half of the graham crackers. Spread marshmallow creme over one side of the remaining graham crackers; place over chocolate-covered crackers, pressing to adhere.

3. Melt dipping chocolate according to package directions. Dip each s'more halfway into dipping chocolate; allow excess to drip off. Place on waxed paper-lined baking sheets; let stand until dipping chocolate is set.

4. If desired, drizzle tops with melted white candy coating; let stand until set. Store in an airtight container in the refrigerator.

CHEWY OATMEAL COOKIES

I pack chocolate chips, raisins, nuts and cinnamon into my oatmeal cookies. Our kids love them!

—**JANIS PLAGEMAN** LYNDEN, WA

PREP: 15 MIN.
BAKE: 10 MIN./BATCH + COOLING
MAKES: ABOUT 5 DOZEN

- 1 cup butter, softened
- 1 cup sugar
- 1 cup packed brown sugar
- 2 large eggs
- 1 tablespoon molasses
- 2 teaspoons vanilla extract
- 2 cups all-purpose flour
- 2 cups quick-cooking oats
- 1½ teaspoons baking soda
- 1 teaspoon ground cinnamon
- ½ teaspoon salt
- 1 cup raisins
- 1 cup chopped pecans
- 1 cup semisweet chocolate chips

1. In a large bowl, cream butter and sugars until light and fluffy. Add the eggs, molasses and vanilla; beat well.
2. Combine flour, oats, baking soda, cinnamon and salt; gradually add to creamed mixture and mix well. Stir in the raisins, pecans and chocolate chips. Drop by tablespoonfuls 2 in. apart onto greased baking sheets.
3. Bake at 350° for 9-10 minutes or until lightly browned. Cool on pans for 2 minutes before removing to wire racks to cool completely.

(5)INGREDIENTS

CRUNCHY CANDY CLUSTERS

Before I retired, I'd take these peanut butter bites to work for special occasions. I still make them for holidays; my family looks forward to the coated cereal and marshmallow clusters.

—**FAYE O'BRYAN** OWENSBORO, KY

PREP: 15 MIN. • **COOK:** 1 HOUR
MAKES: 6½ DOZEN

- 2 pounds white candy coating, coarsely chopped
- 1½ cups peanut butter
- ½ teaspoon almond extract, optional
- 4 cups Cap'n Crunch cereal
- 4 cups crisp rice cereal
- 4 cups miniature marshmallows

1. Place candy coating in a 5-qt. slow cooker. Cover and cook on high for 1 hour. Add peanut butter. Stir in extract, if desired.
2. In a large bowl, combine the cereals and marshmallows. Stir in the peanut butter mixture until well coated. Drop by tablespoonfuls onto waxed paper. Let stand until set. Store at room temperature.

CREAMY PEPPERMINT PATTIES

These smooth chocolate candies fill the bill for folks who like a little sweetness after a meal but don't want a full serving of a rich dessert.

—**DONNA GONDA** NORTH CANTON, OH

PREP: 40 MIN. + CHILLING
MAKES: ABOUT 8 DOZEN

- 1 package (8 ounces) cream cheese, softened
- 1 teaspoon peppermint extract
- 9 cups confectioners' sugar
- 1½ cups milk chocolate chips
- 1½ cups semisweet chocolate chips
- 3 tablespoons shortening

1. Beat cream cheese and extract until smooth. Gradually add confectioners' sugar, beating well.
2. Shape dough into 1-in. balls. Place on waxed paper-lined baking sheets. Flatten into patties about 1½-1¾ in. in diameter. Cover and refrigerate until chilled, about 1 hour.
3. In a microwave, melt chips and shortening; stir until smooth. Cool slightly. Dip patties in the melted chocolate, allowing excess to drip off; place on waxed paper until set. Store in the refrigerator.

PEANUT BUTTER CHIPPERS

My cookie-loving family always comes running to the kitchen when they smell peanut butter and chocolate baking. This recipe is so quick and easy, I often stir up a batch while making dinner.

—PAT DOERFLINGER CENTERVIEW, MO

PREP: 10 MIN. • **BAKE:** 15 MIN./BATCH
MAKES: 3½ DOZEN

- 6 tablespoons butter, softened
- ¼ cup peanut butter
- ½ cup sugar
- ½ cup packed brown sugar
- 1 large egg
- 1 teaspoon vanilla extract
- 1¼ cups all-purpose flour
- ½ teaspoon baking soda
- ¼ teaspoon salt
- 1 cup milk chocolate chips

1. In a small bowl, cream the butter, peanut butter and sugars until light and fluffy. Beat in egg and vanilla. Combine the flour, baking soda and salt; gradually add to creamed mixture and mix well. Stir in chocolate chips.
2. Drop by tablespoonfuls 2 in. apart onto ungreased baking sheets. Bake at 350° for 11-14 minutes or until golden brown. Remove to wire racks.
NOTE *Reduced-fat peanut butter is not recommended for this recipe.*

ALMOND CRUNCH

Once you start eating this treat, you may not be able to stop! Matzo crackers are topped with caramel, chocolate and almonds, then baked to perfection.

—SHARALYN ZANDER JACKSONVILLE, AL

PREP: 20 MIN. • **BAKE:** 15 MIN. + CHILLING
MAKES: 1 POUND

- 4 to 6 unsalted matzo crackers
- 1 cup butter, cubed
- 1 cup packed brown sugar
- ¾ cup semisweet chocolate chips
- 1 teaspoon shortening
- 1 cup slivered almonds, toasted

1. Line a 15x10x1-in. baking pan with foil; line the foil with parchment paper. Arrange crackers in pan; set aside.
2. In a large heavy saucepan over medium heat, melt the butter. Stir in brown sugar. Bring to a boil; cook and stir for 3-4 minutes or until the sugar is dissolved. Spread mixture evenly over crackers.
3. Bake at 350° for 15-17 minutes (cover loosely with foil if the top browns too quickly). Cool on a wire rack for 5 minutes. Meanwhile, melt chocolate chips and shortening; stir until smooth. Stir in almonds; spread chocolate mixture over the top of the cracker base. Cool for 1 hour.
4. Break into pieces. Cover and refrigerate for at least 2 hours or until chocolate is set. Store in an airtight container.

COFFEEHOUSE CARAMEL-DARK CHOCOLATE-LATTE COOKIES

These taste like my favorite coffeehouse beverage. In cookie form, they're crispy on the outside but nice and soft in the middle.

—**ANGELA SPENGLER** TAMPA, FL

PREP: 20 MIN. • **BAKE:** 10 MIN./BATCH
MAKES: ABOUT 3 DOZEN

- 6 tablespoons butter, softened
- ⅓ cup shortening
- ½ cup packed brown sugar
- ⅓ cup sugar
- 1 large egg
- 2 tablespoons hot caramel ice cream topping
- 1 teaspoon vanilla extract
- 1½ cups all-purpose flour
- 4 teaspoons dark roast instant coffee granules
- ½ teaspoon baking soda
- ½ teaspoon salt
- 1½ cups dark chocolate chips

1. Preheat oven to 350°. In a large bowl, cream butter, shortening and sugars until light and fluffy. Beat in egg, ice cream topping and vanilla. In another bowl, whisk flour, coffee granules, baking soda and salt; gradually beat into creamed mixture. Fold in chocolate chips.
2. Drop dough by rounded tablespoonfuls 2 in. apart onto ungreased baking sheets. Bake for 8-10 minutes or until set. Cool on pans for 2 minutes, then remove to wire racks to cool completely.
FREEZE OPTION *Drop dough by rounded tablespoonfuls onto waxed paper-lined baking sheets; freeze until firm. Transfer to resealable plastic freezer bags; return to freezer. Bake frozen cookies as directed, increasing time by 1-2 minutes.*

WHITE CHOCOLATE MACADAMIA COOKIES

White baking chips and macadamia nuts make a fantastic duo in these buttery cookies. They are a nice change from the classic chocolate chip cookies.

—**CATHY LENNON** NEWPORT, TN

PREP: 15 MIN. • **BAKE:** 10 MIN./BATCH
MAKES: 4½ DOZEN

- ½ cup butter, softened
- ⅔ cup sugar
- 1 large egg
- 1 teaspoon vanilla extract
- 1 cup plus 2 tablespoons all-purpose flour
- ½ teaspoon baking soda
- 1 cup macadamia nuts, chopped
- 1 cup white baking chips

1. Preheat oven to 350°. In a large bowl, cream butter and sugar until light and fluffy. Beat in egg and vanilla. In another bowl, whisk flour and baking soda; gradually beat into the creamed mixture. Stir in nuts and baking chips.
2. Drop by heaping teaspoonfuls 2 in. apart onto ungreased baking sheets. Bake for 10-12 minutes or until golden brown. Cool on pans for 1 minute, then remove to wire racks to cool completely.
FREEZE OPTION *Freeze baked cookies, layered between waxed paper, in freezer containers. To use, thaw before serving or, if desired, reheat on a baking sheet in a preheated 350° oven for 3-4 minutes.*

MINI PEANUT BUTTER SANDWICH COOKIES

Peanut butter lovers go nuts for these rich little sandwich cookies. To cool down on a hot day, sandwich ice cream instead of frosting between the cookies.

—**KERI WOLFE** NAPPANEE, IN

PREP: 25 MIN.
BAKE: 15 MIN./BATCH + COOLING
MAKES: ABOUT 3½ DOZEN

- 1 **cup shortening**
- 1 **cup creamy peanut butter**
- 1 **cup sugar**
- 1 **cup packed brown sugar**
- 3 **large eggs**
- 1 **teaspoon vanilla extract**
- 3½ **cups all-purpose flour**
- 2 **teaspoons baking soda**
- ½ **teaspoon salt**
FILLING
- ¾ **cup creamy peanut butter**
- ½ **cup 2% milk**
- 1½ **teaspoons vanilla extract**
- 4 **cups confectioners' sugar**

1. Preheat oven to 350°. In a large bowl, cream shortening, peanut butter and sugars until blended. Beat in eggs and vanilla. In another bowl, whisk flour, baking soda and salt; gradually beat into creamed mixture.

2. Shape dough into 1-in. balls; place 2 in. apart on ungreased baking sheets. Bake for 11-13 minutes or until set. Remove from pans to wire racks to cool completely.

3. In a small bowl, beat peanut butter, milk and vanilla until blended. Beat in confectioners' sugar until smooth. Spread filling on bottoms of half of the cookies; cover with remaining cookies.

FREEZE OPTION *Freeze baked, unfilled cookies in freezer containers. To use, thaw cookies and fill as directed.*

NOTE *Reduced-fat peanut butter is not recommended for this recipe.*

CHOCOLATE PECAN CARAMELS

I haven't missed a year making this candy for the holidays since a friend first gave me the recipe in 1964!

—**JUNE HUMPHREY** STRONGSVILLE, OH

PREP: 20 MIN. • **COOK:** 15 MIN. + COOLING
MAKES: ABOUT 2½ POUNDS (ABOUT 6¾ DOZEN)

- 1 **tablespoon plus 1 cup butter, softened, divided**
- 1½ **cups coarsely chopped pecans, toasted**
- 1 **cup semisweet chocolate chips**
- 2 **cups packed brown sugar**
- 1 **cup light corn syrup**
- ¼ **cup water**
- 1 **can (14 ounces) sweetened condensed milk**
- 2 **teaspoons vanilla extract**

1. Line a 13x9-in. pan with foil; grease foil with 1 tablespoon butter. Sprinkle with pecans and chocolate chips; set aside.

2. In a heavy saucepan, melt the remaining butter over medium heat. Add the brown sugar, corn syrup and water. Cook and stir until mixture comes to a boil. Stir in milk. Cook, stirring constantly, until a candy thermometer reads 248° (firm-ball stage).

3. Remove from heat and add vanilla. Pour into prepared pan (do not scrape saucepan). Cool completely before cutting.

NOTE *Test your candy thermometer before each use by bringing water to a boil; the thermometer should read 212°. Adjust your recipe temperature up or down based on your test.*

⑤ INGREDIENTS

DARK CHOCOLATE RASPBERRY FUDGE

Something about the combination of dark chocolate and raspberry is so appealing. This fudge makes a heartfelt homemade gift, or a treat that's worth sharing in the candy dish.

—**BARBARA LENTO** HOUSTON, PA

PREP: 15 MIN. + FREEZING
COOK: 5 MIN. + CHILLING
MAKES: 3 POUNDS (81 PIECES)

- 1 package (10 to 12 ounces) white baking chips
- 1 teaspoon butter, softened
- 3 cups dark chocolate chips
- 1 can (14 ounces) sweetened condensed milk
- ¼ cup raspberry liqueur
- ⅛ teaspoon salt

1. Place baking chips in a single layer on a small baking sheet. Freeze for 30 minutes. Line a 9-in. square pan with foil; grease foil with butter.
2. In a large microwave-safe bowl, combine dark chocolate chips and milk. Microwave, uncovered, on high for 2 minutes; stir. Microwave in additional 30-second intervals, stirring until smooth. Stir in liqueur and salt. Add white baking chips; stir just until partially melted. Spread into prepared pan. Refrigerate 1 hour or until firm.
3. Using foil, lift fudge out of the pan. Remove foil; cut the fudge into 1-in. squares. Store in an airtight container in the refrigerator.
NOTE *This recipe was tested in a 1,100-watt microwave.*

APRICOT-FILLED TRIANGLES

It's a good thing this recipe makes a big batch, because no one can stop after eating just one. These crisp, buttery cookies truly do melt in your mouth.

—**MILDRED LORENCE** CARLISLE, PA

PREP: 1¼ HOURS + CHILLING
BAKE: 10 MIN./BATCH + COOLING
MAKES: 6 DOZEN

- 1 pound dried apricots (2½ cups)
- 1½ cups water
- ½ cup sugar
DOUGH
- ⅔ cup shortening
- 3 tablespoons 2% milk
- 1⅓ cups sugar
- 2 large eggs
- 1 teaspoon lemon extract
- 4 cups cake flour
- 2 teaspoons baking powder
- 1 teaspoon salt

1. In a small saucepan, cook apricots and water over low heat for 45 minutes or until the water is absorbed and apricots are soft. Cool slightly; transfer to a blender. Cover and process until smooth. Add sugar; cover and process until blended. Set aside.
2. In a large saucepan over low heat, melt shortening and milk. Remove from the heat; stir in sugar. Add eggs, one at a time, whisking well after each addition. Stir in extract. Combine the flour, baking powder and salt; gradually add to the saucepan and mix well. Cover and refrigerate for 4 hours or until easy to handle.
3. On a lightly floured surface, roll out dough to ⅛-in. thickness. Cut with a floured 3-in. round cookie cutter. Place 1 teaspoon apricot filling in the center of each. Bring three edges together over the filling, overlapping slightly (a portion of the filling will show in the center); pinch edges gently. Place 1 in. apart on ungreased baking sheets.
4. Bake at 400° for 8-10 minutes or until golden brown. Remove to wire racks to cool.

194 TASTEOFHOME.COM

SALTED TOFFEE CASHEW COOKIES

I just might be addicted to the sweet and salty flavor combo of these nutty cookies. Lucky for me, they're also quick to make.
—**CRYSTAL SCHLUETER** NORTHGLENN, CO

PREP: 25 MIN. • **BAKE:** 10 MIN./BATCH
MAKES: ABOUT 5 DOZEN

- 1 **cup butter, softened**
- 1½ **cups packed brown sugar**
- 2 **large eggs**
- 1 **teaspoon vanilla extract**
- 2⅔ **cups all-purpose flour**
- 1 **teaspoon salt**
- 1 **teaspoon baking soda**
- 1½ **cups chopped salted cashews**
- 1 **cup brickle toffee bits**
- 1 **cup butterscotch chips**
  Salted whole cashews

1. Preheat oven to 375°. In a large bowl, cream butter and brown sugar until light and fluffy. Beat in eggs and vanilla. In another bowl, whisk flour, salt and baking soda; gradually beat into the creamed mixture. Stir in chopped cashews, toffee bits and butterscotch chips.

2. Drop by rounded tablespoonfuls 2 in. apart onto ungreased baking sheets. Press a whole cashew into the top of each cookie. Bake for 7-9 minutes or until golden brown. Cool on pans 2 minutes, then remove to wire racks to cool completely.

FREEZE OPTION *Freeze cookies in freezer containers. Thaw before serving.*

HOW-TO

Make Softer Cookies

When making cookies, be sure to measure the flour carefully; adding too much can make cookies firm, dry and tough. Also, avoid overmixing the dough, and check for doneness at the minimum baking time.

CHOCOLATE LINZER COOKIES

Living where I do, it's no surprise I enjoy holiday baking. My mom and I used to make these cookies together. Now that I'm married and living in Alaska, I love to bake them for my own family.

—**HEATHER PETERS** NORTH POLE, AK

PREP: 30 MIN. + CHILLING
BAKE: 10 MIN./BATCH + COOLING
MAKES: 2 DOZEN

- ¾ **cup butter, softened**
- 1 **cup sugar**
- 2 **large eggs**
- ½ **teaspoon almond extract**
- 2⅓ **cups all-purpose flour**
- 1 **teaspoon baking powder**
- ½ **teaspoon salt**
- ½ **teaspoon ground cinnamon**
- 1 **cup semisweet chocolate chips, melted**
  Confectioners' sugar
- 6 **tablespoons seedless raspberry jam**

1. In a small bowl, cream butter and sugar until light and fluffy. Add eggs, one at a time, beating well after each addition. Beat in extract. Combine the flour, baking powder, salt and cinnamon; gradually add to creamed mixture and mix well. Refrigerate for 1 hour or until easy to handle.

2. Divide dough in half. On a lightly floured surface, roll out one portion to ⅛-in. thickness; cut with a floured 2½-in. round cookie cutter. Roll out remaining dough; cut with a 2½-in. floured doughnut cutter so the center is cut out of each cookie.

3. Place 1 in. apart on ungreased baking sheets. Bake at 350° for 8-10 minutes or until edges are lightly browned. Remove to wire racks to cool.

4. Spread melted chocolate over the bottoms of the solid cookies. Place cookies with cutout centers over the chocolate. Sprinkle with confectioners' sugar. Spoon ½ teaspoon raspberry jam in the center of each cookie.

MARSHMALLOW PUFFS

With peanut butter, chocolate and marshmallows, these treats were very popular with our three children when they were growing up. Now I make them for our grandchildren. The puffs are quick to make, too, so they're perfect for the holidays when time is so precious.

—**DODY CAGENELLO** SIMSBURY, CT

PREP: 10 MIN. + CHILLING
MAKES: 3 DOZEN

- 36 **large marshmallows**
- 1½ **cups semisweet chocolate chips**
- ½ **cup chunky peanut butter**
- 2 **tablespoons butter**

Line a 9-in. square pan with foil; grease the foil with butter. Arrange marshmallows in pan. In a microwave, melt the chocolate chips, peanut butter and butter; stir until smooth. Pour and spread over the marshmallows. Chill completely. Cut into 1½-in. squares.
NOTE *This recipe was tested in a 1,100-watt microwave.*

SALTED PECAN SHORTBREAD SQUARES

My shortbread squares are the ultimate sweets for cookie trays and gift-giving. The buttery caramel and toasted nuts make it tough to eat just one.

—**DIANA ASHCRAFT** MONMOUTH, OR

PREP: 25 MIN. • **BAKE:** 25 MIN. + COOLING
MAKES: 4 DOZEN

- 1½ cups all-purpose flour
- 1 cup confectioners' sugar
- ½ cup cornstarch
- 1 teaspoon sea salt
- 1 cup cold unsalted butter, cubed

FILLING
- ¾ cup unsalted butter, cubed
- 1½ cups packed brown sugar
- ½ cup dark corn syrup
- ½ teaspoon sea salt
- ½ cup milk chocolate chips
- ¼ cup heavy whipping cream
- 1 teaspoon vanilla extract
- 4 cups coarsely chopped pecans, toasted

1. Preheat oven to 350°. Line two 13x9-in. baking pans with foil, letting ends extend up sides of pan.

2. Place flour, confectioners' sugar, cornstarch and salt in a food processor; pulse until blended. Add butter; pulse until butter is the size of peas. Divide mixture between the prepared pans; press onto bottom of pans. Bake for 10-12 minutes or until light brown. Cool on a wire rack.

3. For filling, melt butter in a large saucepan. Stir in brown sugar, corn syrup and salt; bring to a boil. Reduce heat to medium; cook and stir until sugar is completely dissolved, about 3 minutes. Remove from heat; stir in chocolate chips, cream and vanilla until smooth. Stir in pecans. Spread filling over crusts.

4. Bake 12-15 minutes or until the filling is bubbly. Cool completely in pans on wire racks. Using foil, lift the shortbread out of pans. Gently peel off foil; cut shortbread into bars. Store in an airtight container.

NOTE *To toast nuts, bake in a shallow pan in a 350° oven for 5-10 minutes or cook in a skillet over low heat until lightly browned, stirring occasionally.*

TRUFFLE CHERRIES

My family and I are a bunch of chocolate lovers, especially during the holidays. Double-chocolate gems like these don't stand a chance at our house.

—**ANNE DROUIN** DUNNVILLE, ON

PREP: 20 MIN. + CHILLING
MAKES: ABOUT 2 DOZEN

- ⅓ cup heavy whipping cream
- 2 tablespoons butter
- 2 tablespoons sugar
- 4 ounces semisweet chocolate, chopped
- 1 jar (8 ounces) maraschino cherries with stems, well drained

COATING
- 6 ounces semisweet chocolate, chopped
- 2 tablespoons shortening

1. In a small saucepan, bring the cream, butter and sugar to a boil, stirring constantly. Remove from the heat; stir in chocolate until melted. Cover and refrigerate for at least 4 hours or until easy to handle.

2. Pat cherries with paper towels until very dry. Shape a teaspoonful of the chocolate mixture around each cherry, forming a ball. Cover and refrigerate for 2-3 hours or until firm.

3. In a microwave, melt chocolate and shortening; stir until smooth. Dip cherries until coated; allow excess to drip off. Place on waxed paper to set.

CONFETTI CAKE BATTER COOKIES

Mom and I took up cake decorating. Funfetti was our favorite cake, so we used the mix to make cutout cookies. Plain or decorated, they're a favorite at parties.

—**DANIELLE DEMARCO** BASKING RIDGE, NJ

PREP: 15 MIN. + CHILLING
BAKE: 10 MIN./BATCH + COOLING
MAKES: ABOUT 2 DOZEN

- ½ **cup butter, softened**
- 2 **large eggs**
- 1 **teaspoon vanilla extract**
- 1 **package Funfetti cake mix**

1. In a large bowl, beat butter, eggs and vanilla until combined. Beat in cake mix. Refrigerate dough, covered, 2 hours or until firm enough to roll.
2. Preheat oven to 350°. On a well-floured surface, roll dough to ¼-in. thickness. Cut with a floured 2½-in. cookie cutter. Place 1 in. apart on ungreased baking sheets. Bake for 8-10 minutes or until set. Remove from pans to wire racks to cool completely. Decorate as desired.
FREEZE OPTION *Transfer dough to a resealable plastic freezer bag; freeze. To use, thaw dough in refrigerator until soft enough to roll. Prepare and bake cookies as directed; decorate as desired.*

AUNT ROSE'S FANTASTIC BUTTER TOFFEE

I don't live in the country, but I love everything about it—especially good old-fashioned home cooking! Every year, you'll find me at our County Fair, entering a different recipe contest. This toffee is a family favorite.

—**KATHY DORMAN** SNOVER, MI

PREP: 25 MIN. • **COOK:** 15 MIN.
MAKES: ABOUT 2 POUNDS

- 2 **cups unblanched whole almonds**
- 11 **ounces milk chocolate, chopped**
- 1 **cup butter, cubed**
- 1 **cup sugar**
- 3 **tablespoons cold water**

1. Preheat oven to 350°. In a shallow baking pan, toast the almonds until golden brown, 5-10 minutes, stirring occasionally. Cool. Pulse chocolate in a food processor until finely ground (do not overprocess); transfer to a bowl. Pulse almonds in food processor until coarsely chopped. Sprinkle 1 cup almonds over the bottom of a greased 15x10-in. pan. Sprinkle with 1 cup of the chocolate.
2. In a heavy saucepan, combine butter, sugar and water. Cook over medium heat until a candy thermometer reads 290° (soft-crack stage), stirring occasionally.
3. Immediately pour the mixture over almonds and chocolate in pan. Sprinkle with the remaining chocolate and almonds. Refrigerate until set; break into pieces.
NOTE *We recommend that you test your candy thermometer before each use by bringing water to a boil; the thermometer should read 212°. Adjust your recipe temperature up or down based on your test.*

SACHER TORTE SQUARES

Sacher torte is a Viennese cake that requires several steps. My squares are an easy alternative, but they still feature the classic apricot and chocolate flavors.

—ARLENE ERLBACH MORTON GROVE, IL

PREP: 30 MIN. • **BAKE:** 30 MIN. + CHILLING
MAKES: 20 SERVINGS

- 1 package devil's food cake mix (regular size)
- 2 cans (12 ounces each) apricot cake and pastry filling
- 3 large eggs
- 2 teaspoons vanilla extract
- 1 cup dark chocolate chips

TOPPINGS
- ½ cup apricot preserves
- 2 teaspoons vanilla extract
- ⅓ cup butter, cubed
- 1 cup sugar
- 1 cup heavy whipping cream
- 1 cup dark chocolate chips
- ¼ cup sliced almonds

1. Preheat oven to 350°. Grease a 13x9-in. baking pan.
2. In a large bowl, combine cake mix, apricot filling, eggs and vanilla; beat on low speed for 30 seconds. Beat on medium speed for 2 minutes. Fold in chocolate chips. Transfer to the prepared pan. Bake 30-35 minutes or until a toothpick inserted in center comes out clean.
3. Remove pan from oven and place on a wire rack. In a small bowl, mix preserves and vanilla; spread over warm cake.
4. In a small saucepan, combine butter, sugar and cream; bring to a boil, stirring to dissolve the sugar. Remove from heat; stir in chocolate chips until melted. Spread over the cake; sprinkle with almonds. Refrigerate until set, about 1 hour.

MAPLE WHOOPIE PIES

In New York, we have a huge maple syrup industry. I took a basic whoopie pie and gave it a local twist using our beloved maple flavor.

—HOLLY HARZ MALONE, NY

PREP: 40 MIN.
BAKE: 10 MIN./BATCH + COOLING
MAKES: ABOUT 2 DOZEN

- ⅓ cup butter, softened
- ¾ cup sugar
- 1 large egg
- 1 teaspoon vanilla extract
- 1 teaspoon maple flavoring
- 2¼ cups all-purpose flour
- 1¼ teaspoons baking powder
- 1 teaspoon salt
- ½ cup heavy whipping cream
- ½ cup maple syrup
- ½ cup chopped pecans

FILLING
- ½ cup butter, softened
- ½ cup shortening
- 1 teaspoon maple flavoring
- 4 cups confectioners' sugar
- ¼ cup heavy whipping cream
- 2 tablespoons maple syrup

1. Preheat oven to 375°. In a large bowl, cream butter and sugar until light and fluffy. Beat in egg, vanilla and flavoring. In another bowl, whisk the flour, baking powder and salt; add to creamed mixture alternately with cream and syrup, beating well after each addition. Stir in pecans.
2. Drop the dough by rounded tablespoonfuls 2 in. apart onto greased baking sheets. Bake for 8-10 minutes or until the edges are light brown and the tops spring back when lightly touched. Remove from pans to wire racks to cool completely.
3. For filling, in a large bowl, beat butter, shortening and flavoring until creamy. Beat in confectioners' sugar alternately with cream and syrup until smooth. Spread filling on the bottoms of half of the cookies; cover with the remaining cookies. Store in airtight containers.

WALNUT SANDWICH COOKIES

I've made this recipe many times over the years, and the cookies are always a hit with my family and friends.

—**SHIRLEY BARKER** NORMAL, IL

PREP: 15 MIN.
BAKE: 15 MIN./BATCH + COOLING
MAKES: 2 DOZEN

- ¾ **cup butter, softened**
- 1 **cup sugar**
- 1 **tablespoon water**
- 1½ **cups all-purpose flour**
- ½ **teaspoon salt**
- ¾ **cup ground walnuts**

FILLING

- 3 **ounces cream cheese, softened**
- 1 **tablespoon butter, softened**
- 1½ **cups confectioners' sugar**
- ½ **teaspoon grated orange peel**

1. In a large bowl, cream butter and sugar until light and fluffy. Beat in water. Combine the flour and salt; gradually add to creamed mixture and mix well. Stir in walnuts. Roll dough into 1-in. balls.

2. Place balls 1 in. apart on ungreased baking sheets. Coat the bottom of a glass with cooking spray, then dip in sugar. Flatten cookies with prepared glass, redipping in sugar as needed.

3. Bake at 350° for 12-15 minutes or until edges are lightly browned. Cool for 2 minutes, then remove to wire racks to cool completely.

4. For filling, in a small bowl, beat cream cheese and butter until fluffy. Gradually add confectioners' sugar and orange peel; beat until smooth. Spread filling over the bottoms of half of the cookies; top with remaining cookies. Store in the refrigerator.

---

⑤ INGREDIENTS

CHERRY DIVINITY

It's not a Valentine's Day party without these light and airy confections on my dessert platter. You can replace the cherry gelatin with any flavor to suit your tastes.

—**CRYSTAL RALPH-HAUGHN** BARTLESVILLE, OK

PREP: 35 MIN.
COOK: 25 MIN. + STANDING
MAKES: 5 DOZEN

- 2 **large egg whites**
- 3 **cups sugar**
- ¾ **cup water**
- ¾ **cup light corn syrup**
- 1 **package (3 ounces) cherry gelatin**
- 1 **cup chopped walnuts**

1. Place egg whites in the bowl of a large stand mixer; let stand at room temperature for 30 minutes. Meanwhile, line three 15x10x1-in. baking pans with waxed paper.

2. In a heavy saucepan, combine the sugar, water and corn syrup; cook and stir until sugar is dissolved and the mixture comes to a boil. Cook over medium heat, without stirring, until a candy thermometer reads 250° (hard-ball stage).

3. Just before the temperature is reached, beat egg whites until foamy. Gradually beat in gelatin. Beat until stiff peaks form. With mixer running on high speed, carefully pour hot syrup in a slow, steady stream into the bowl. Beat just until the candy loses its gloss and holds its shape, about 5 minutes. Immediately stir in walnuts.

4. Quickly drop by tablespoonfuls onto prepared pans. Let stand at room temperature overnight or until dry to the touch. Store in an airtight container at room temperature.

NOTE *We recommend that you test your candy thermometer before each use by bringing water to a boil; the thermometer should read 212°. Adjust your recipe temperature up or down based on your test.*

LAYERED MINT CANDIES

These melt-in-your-mouth candies have the perfect amount of mint nestled between layers of mild chocolate. Even when I make a double batch at Christmas, the supply doesn't last long.

—RHONDA VAUBLE SAC CITY, IA

PREP: 15 MIN. + CHILLING
MAKES: ABOUT 2 POUNDS (ABOUT 9½ DOZEN)

- 1 tablespoon butter
- 1½ pounds white candy coating, coarsely chopped, divided
- 1 cup semisweet chocolate chips
- 1 teaspoon peppermint extract
- 4 drops green food coloring, optional
- 3 tablespoons heavy whipping cream

1. Line a 13x9-in. pan with foil. Grease foil with butter.

2. Microwave 1 pound of the candy coating and the chocolate chips until smooth, stirring every 30 seconds. Spread half into the prepared pan, reserving half. Microwave remaining candy coating until melted; stir in extract and, if desired, food coloring. Stir in cream until smooth (mixture will be stiff). Spread over the first layer; refrigerate until firm, about 10 minutes. Warm reserved chocolate mixture if necessary; spread over mint layer. Refrigerate until firm, about 1 hour.

3. Using foil, lift candy out of pan, then remove foil. Cut candy into 1-in. squares. Refrigerate in an airtight container.

READER REVIEW

"I have been making this candy for many years; it's always a favorite. I vary the flavor by using cherry, almond or orange—and then color the middle layer accordingly."

MERRYSTITCH2003 TASTEOFHOME.COM

AUNT MYRTLE'S COCONUT OAT COOKIES

These cookies are the stuff of happy memories. Coconut and oatmeal give them rich flavor and texture. Store them in your best cookie jar.

—**CATHERINE CASSIDY** MILWAUKEE, WI

PREP: 30 MIN. • **BAKE:** 10 MIN./BATCH
MAKES: ABOUT 5 DOZEN

- 1 cup butter, softened
- 1 cup packed brown sugar
- 2 large eggs
- 2 teaspoons vanilla extract
- 2⅓ cups all-purpose flour
- 1 teaspoon salt
- 1 teaspoon baking soda
- ¾ teaspoon baking powder
- 2 cups flaked coconut
- 1 cup old-fashioned or quick-cooking oats
- ¾ cup chopped walnuts, toasted

1. Preheat oven to 375°. In a large bowl, cream butter and brown sugar until light and fluffy. Beat in eggs and vanilla. In another bowl, whisk flour, salt, baking soda and baking powder; gradually beat into creamed mixture. Stir in coconut, oats and walnuts.

2. Drop dough by tablespoonfuls 2 in. apart onto ungreased baking sheets. Bake 8-10 minutes or until light brown. Remove from pans to wire racks to cool.

NOTE *To toast nuts, bake in a shallow pan in a 350° oven for 5-10 minutes or cook in a skillet over low heat until lightly browned, stirring occasionally.*

ANISE ICEBOX COOKIES

Enjoy these old-fashioned crisp cookies that have just the right accent of anise.

—**SHARON NICHOLS** BROOKINGS, SD

PREP: 25 MIN. + CHILLING
BAKE: 10 MIN./BATCH
MAKES: ABOUT 5½ DOZEN

- 1 cup butter, softened
- 1 cup sugar
- 1 cup packed brown sugar
- 1 large egg
- 2½ cups all-purpose flour
- 1 teaspoon baking soda
- ½ teaspoon salt
- ½ teaspoon ground cinnamon
- ½ teaspoon ground cloves
- ½ cup finely chopped pecans
- 1 tablespoon aniseed

1. In a large bowl, cream butter and sugars until light and fluffy. Beat in egg. Combine the flour, baking soda, salt, cinnamon and cloves; gradually add to the creamed mixture and mix well. Stir in pecans and aniseed.

2. Shape dough into two 10-in. rolls; wrap each in plastic. Refrigerate for 4 hours.

3. Unwrap; cut ¼ in. off the ends of each roll. Cut dough into ¼-in. slices. Place slices 2 in. apart on ungreased baking sheets. Bake at 375° for 8-10 minutes or until golden brown. Remove to wire racks to cool.

FAST FIX ▶
GERMAN SPICE COOKIES

These chewy spice cookies are great with coffee and taste even better the next day. The recipe has been in my family for more than 40 years.

—**JOAN TYSON** BOWLING GREEN, OH

START TO FINISH: 20 MIN.
MAKES: 3½ DOZEN

- 3 large eggs
- 2 cups packed brown sugar
- 1 teaspoon ground cloves
- 1 teaspoon ground cinnamon
- ½ teaspoon pepper
- 2 cups all-purpose flour
- ½ teaspoon baking soda
- ½ teaspoon salt
- 1 cup raisins
- 1 cup chopped walnuts

1. In a large bowl, beat the eggs. Add the brown sugar, cloves, cinnamon and pepper. Combine the flour, baking soda and salt; gradually add to the egg mixture. Stir in raisins and walnuts.

2. Drop by tablespoonfuls 2 in. apart onto lightly greased baking sheets. Bake at 400° for 8-10 minutes or until the surface cracks. Remove to wire racks to cool.

SEASONAL SPECIALTIES

Winter, spring, summer or fall—the recipes here will cover them all! This year, spread the love with homemade goodies on Valentine's Day, and confidently take on the responsibility of hosting Easter. Celebrate the return of warm weather with a festive Cinco de Mayo fiesta or a simple picnic. Once autumn rolls in, welcome it back with cozy fall-themed recipes, then prepare for Halloween with spooky-good eats! Finally, when it's time for Thanksgiving and Christmas, introduce your family to dishes that'll become new holiday traditions.

CHOCOLATE CHIP RED VELVET WHOOPIE PIES

Baking a fun treat is a must when my four grandchildren come to stay at "Grandma Camp."

—LINDA SCHEND KENOSHA, WI

PREP: 45 MIN.
BAKE: 10 MIN./BATCH + COOLING
MAKES: ABOUT 2 DOZEN

- 1 **package red velvet cake mix (regular size)**
- 3 **large eggs**
- ½ **cup canola oil**
- 2 **teaspoons vanilla extract**

FILLING

- 8 **ounces cream cheese, softened**
- ½ **cup butter, softened**
- 2 **cups confectioners' sugar**
- 1 **cup (6 ounces) miniature semisweet chocolate chips**

1. Preheat oven to 350°. In a large bowl, combine cake mix, eggs, oil and vanilla; beat on low speed 30 seconds. Beat on medium speed 2 minutes.
2. Cut a ½-in. hole in the tip of a pastry bag or in a corner of a food-safe plastic bag. Transfer dough to bag. Pipe the dough into 1½x1-in. heart shapes onto parchment paper-lined baking sheets, spacing hearts 1 in. apart.
3. Bake 6-8 minutes or until edges are set. Cool on pans 2 minutes. Remove to wire racks to cool completely.
4. For filling, in a large bowl, beat the cream cheese and butter until blended. Gradually beat in confectioners' sugar until smooth. Stir in chocolate chips. Spread filling on bottoms of half of the cookies. Top with remaining cookies. Refrigerate leftovers.

TOP TIP

Use Different Flavored Chips

Want to change this cookie recipe ever so slightly? Feel free to try butterscotch or white chocolate chips instead of the called-for chocolate chips. You may discover a new winning combo!

MOLTEN MOCHA CAKE

When I first made this slow cooker chocolate cake, my husband and daughter loved it—it's one of my daughter's favorite desserts. I also shared the cake with my next door neighbor's son, who liked it so much that he ate the whole thing without telling anyone!

—AIMEE FORTNEY FAIRVIEW, TN

PREP: 10 MIN. • **COOK:** 2½ HOURS
MAKES: 4 SERVINGS

    4   large eggs
 1½   cups sugar
   ½   cup butter, melted
    3   teaspoons vanilla extract
    1   cup all-purpose flour
   ½   cup baking cocoa
    1   tablespoon instant coffee granules
   ¼   teaspoon salt
        Fresh raspberries or sliced
          fresh strawberries and vanilla
          ice cream, optional

1. In a large bowl, beat eggs, sugar, butter and vanilla until blended. In another bowl, whisk flour, cocoa, coffee granules and salt; gradually beat into egg mixture.

2. Transfer to a greased 1½-qt. slow cooker. Cook, covered, on low 2½-3 hours or until a toothpick comes out with moist crumbs. If desired, serve warm cake with berries and ice cream.

PEANUT BUTTER CUTOUT COOKIES

I used peanut butter in place of the butter for this take on a traditional cutout cookie, and it turned out super nutty and soft. My children love to decorate the cookies with frosting, sprinkles and some youthful creativity.

—CINDI BAUER MARSHFIELD, WI

PREP: 30 MIN. + CHILLING
BAKE: 10 MIN./BATCH + COOLING
MAKES: ABOUT 4½ DOZEN

    1   cup creamy peanut butter
   ¾   cup sugar
   ¾   cup packed brown sugar
    2   large eggs
   ⅓   cup 2% milk
    1   teaspoon vanilla extract
 2½   cups all-purpose flour
   ½   teaspoon baking powder
   ½   teaspoon baking soda
        Vanilla frosting
        Red food coloring
        Assorted colored sprinkles

1. In a large bowl, cream peanut butter and sugars until light and fluffy, about 4 minutes. Beat in the eggs, milk and vanilla. Combine the flour, baking powder and baking soda; add to the creamed mixture and mix well. Cover and refrigerate for 2 hours or until the dough is easy to handle.

2. On a lightly floured surface, roll out dough to ¼-in. thickness. Cut with 2- to 4-in. cookie cutters. Place cookies 2 in. apart on ungreased baking sheets.

3. Bake at 375° for 7-9 minutes or until edges are browned. Cool for 1 minute before removing from pans to wire racks to cool completely. Once cool, frost and decorate cookies as desired.

In these ultra-fudgy brownies, coffee granules bump up the chocolate flavor. Add chocolate chips to the batter to make them even more irresistible!
—**SARAH THOMPSON** GREENFIELD, WI

PREP: 20 MIN. • **BAKE:** 40 MIN. + COOLING
MAKES: 16 SERVINGS

- 1 **cup sugar**
- ½ **cup packed brown sugar**
- ⅔ **cup butter, cubed**
- ¼ **cup water**
- 2 **teaspoons instant coffee granules, optional**
- 2¾ **cups bittersweet chocolate chips, divided**
- 4 **large eggs**
- 2 **teaspoons vanilla extract**
- 1½ **cups all-purpose flour**
- ½ **teaspoon baking soda**
- ½ **teaspoon salt**

1. Preheat oven to 325°. Line a 9-in. square baking pan with parchment paper, letting the ends of the paper extend up the sides of the pan. In a large heavy saucepan, combine sugars, butter, water and, if desired, instant coffee granules; bring to a boil, stirring constantly. Remove from heat; add 1¾ cups chocolate chips and stir until melted. Cool slightly.
2. In a large bowl, whisk eggs until foamy, about 3 minutes. Add vanilla; gradually whisk in chocolate mixture. In another bowl, whisk flour, baking soda and salt; stir into the chocolate mixture. Fold in the remaining chocolate chips.
3. Pour into the prepared pan. Bake on a lower oven rack 40-50 minutes or until a toothpick inserted in the center comes out with moist crumbs (do not overbake). Cool completely in pan on a wire rack.
4. Lifting with parchment paper, remove the brownies from the pan. Cut into squares.

⑤ INGREDIENTS
NUTELLA-STUFFED STRAWBERRIES

Gourmet strawberries are pricey to purchase but easy to make. We serve fresh strawberries with hazelnut spread as a crowd-pleasing appetizer or dessert.
—**DARLENE BRENDEN** SALEM, OR

PREP: 15 MIN. + CHILLING
MAKES: 1 DOZEN

- 12 **large fresh strawberries**
- ¼ **cup Nutella**
- 1 **cup milk chocolate chips, melted**
- ¼ **cup chopped hazelnuts**
  Confectioners' sugar

1. Remove stems from strawberries. Using a paring knife, cut out centers; pipe Nutella into strawberries.
2. Insert a toothpick into the side of each strawberry. One at a time, hold the toothpick and dip the stem end of the strawberry into melted chocolate; allow excess to drip off. Sprinkle with hazelnuts. Place strawberries on a waxed paper-lined baking sheet, point side up. Remove toothpicks; refrigerate the strawberries until set. Just before serving, dust with confectioners' sugar.

LEMON-BLUEBERRY POUND CAKE

Pair a slice of this moist cake with a scoop of vanilla ice cream. It's a staple at our family barbecues.

—REBECCA LITTLE PARK RIDGE, IL

PREP: 25 MIN. • **BAKE:** 55 MIN. + COOLING
MAKES: 12 SERVINGS

- ⅓ **cup butter, softened**
- 4 **ounces cream cheese, softened**
- 2 **cups sugar**
- 3 **large eggs**
- 1 **large egg white**
- 1 **tablespoon grated lemon peel**
- 2 **teaspoons vanilla extract**
- 2 **cups fresh or frozen unsweetened blueberries**
- 3 **cups all-purpose flour, divided**
- 1 **teaspoon baking powder**
- ½ **teaspoon baking soda**
- ½ **teaspoon salt**
- 1 **cup (8 ounces) lemon yogurt**

GLAZE
- 1¼ **cups confectioners' sugar**
- 2 **tablespoons lemon juice**

1. Preheat oven to 350°. Grease and flour a 10-in. fluted tube pan. In a large bowl, cream the butter, cream cheese and sugar until blended. Add the eggs and egg white, one at a time; beat well after each addition. Beat in lemon peel and vanilla.

2. Toss blueberries with 2 tablespoons of flour. In another bowl, mix the remaining flour with baking powder, baking soda and salt; add to creamed mixture alternately with yogurt, beating after each addition just until combined. Fold in blueberry mixture.

3. Transfer the batter to the prepared pan. Bake 55-60 minutes or until a toothpick inserted in the center comes out clean. Cool in pan 10 minutes, then remove to wire rack to cool completely.

4. In a small bowl, mix confectioners' sugar and lemon juice until smooth. Drizzle over cake.

NOTE *For easier removal of cake, use solid shortening when greasing a fluted or plain tube pan.*

BOURBON-GLAZED HAM

Smoky and sweet flavors come through in every bite of this Kentucky-style ham. Since I found this recipe, it's the only ham I make.

—SUSAN SCHILLER TOMAHAWK, WI

PREP: 15 MIN.
BAKE: 2½ HOURS + STANDING
MAKES: 16 SERVINGS

- 1 **fully cooked bone-in ham (8 to 10 pounds)**
- ¾ **cup bourbon, divided**
- 2 **cups packed brown sugar**
- 1 **tablespoon ground mustard**
- 1 **tablespoon orange marmalade**
- ⅛ **teaspoon ground coriander**

1. Place ham on a rack in a shallow roasting pan. Score the surface of the ham, making diamond-shaped cuts ½ in. deep. Brush with 2 tablespoons bourbon. Bake, uncovered, at 325° for 2 hours.

2. In a small bowl, combine the brown sugar, mustard, marmalade, coriander and remaining bourbon; spoon over ham. Bake 30 minutes longer or until a thermometer reads 140°. Let stand for 15 minutes before slicing.

SIMPLE GLAZED HAM *Score ham. Bake as directed, brushing with a mixture of 1¼ cups brown sugar, 2 tablespoons cider vinegar and 2½ teaspoons prepared mustard during last hour of baking.*

HORSERADISH HAM *Score ham; stud with cloves. Bake as directed, brushing with a mixture of 1¼ cups brown sugar, ⅓ cup plus 1 tablespoon prepared horseradish and ⅓ cup lemon juice during last hour of baking.*

ORANGE-GLAZED HAM *Score ham. Combine 3½ teaspoons ground mustard and 1¼ teaspoons ground allspice; rub over ham. Bake as directed, brushing with 1 cup orange marmalade during last hour of baking.*

TRIPLE CITRUS SCONES

I love the bright and buttery flavor of these tender scones. Serve them with a yummy jam, or try them as a base for strawberry shortcake.

—ANGELA LEMOINE HOWELL, NJ

PREP: 20 MIN. • **BAKE:** 15 MIN.
MAKES: 8 SCONES

- 2¼ cups all-purpose flour
- ¼ cup plus 1 tablespoon sugar, divided
- 4 teaspoons grated orange peel
- 2 teaspoons grated lemon peel
- 1½ teaspoons grated lime peel
- 3 teaspoons baking powder
- ½ teaspoon salt
- 6 tablespoons cold butter, cubed
- 1 large egg
- ¼ cup orange juice
- ¼ cup buttermilk
- 1 tablespoon butter, melted

GLAZE

- ¼ cup confectioners' sugar
- 1½ teaspoons grated lime peel
- 1 tablespoon lime juice
- 1 tablespoon orange juice

1. Preheat oven to 400°. Place flour, ¼ cup sugar, citrus peels, baking powder and salt in a food processor; pulse until blended. Add cold butter; pulse until butter is the size of peas. Transfer to a large bowl. In a small bowl, whisk egg, orange juice and buttermilk until blended; stir into crumb mixture just until moistened.
2. Turn onto a lightly floured surface; knead gently 6-8 times. Pat dough into a 6-in. circle. Cut into eight wedges. Place wedges on a parchment paper-lined baking sheet. Brush with melted butter; sprinkle with remaining sugar.
3. Bake for 14-18 minutes or until golden brown. Meanwhile, in a small bowl, mix the glaze ingredients until smooth. Remove the scones from oven; immediately brush with the glaze. Serve warm.

FAST FIX
SNAP PEA SALAD

When snap peas are in season, we can't resist making this crunchy salad. I usually serve it cold, but it's also good warm, with the peas straight from the pot.

—JEAN ECOS HARTLAND, WI

START TO FINISH: 20 MIN.
MAKES: 12 SERVINGS (¾ CUP EACH)

- ¼ cup white wine vinegar
- ¼ cup Dijon mustard
- 2 tablespoons minced fresh parsley
- 2 tablespoons olive oil
- 2 tablespoons honey
- 1 tablespoon lemon juice
- 1 teaspoon salt
- ½ teaspoon pepper
- 3 pounds fresh sugar snap peas
  Grated lemon peel, optional

1. For vinaigrette, in a small bowl, whisk the first eight ingredients until blended. In a 6-qt. stockpot, bring 16 cups of water to a boil. Add the snap peas; cook, uncovered, for 2-3 minutes or just until the peas turn bright green. Remove the peas and immediately drop them into ice water. Drain and pat dry; place in a large bowl.
2. Drizzle peas with vinaigrette and toss to coat. Serve immediately or refrigerate, covered, up to 4 hours before serving. If desired, sprinkle with lemon peel.

FISH TACOS WITH GUACAMOLE

Fish tacos with guacamole is my new favorite recipe; they're lighter than beef tacos smothered in cheese. Try hot sauce, onions, tomatoes or jalapenos on top, depending on your preference for spice!

—**DEB PERRY** TRAVERSE CITY, MI

PREP: 25 MIN. • **COOK:** 10 MIN.
MAKES: 4 SERVINGS

- 2 cups angel hair coleslaw mix
- 1½ teaspoons canola oil
- 1½ teaspoons lime juice

GUACAMOLE

- 1 medium ripe avocado, peeled and quartered
- 2 tablespoons fat-free sour cream
- 1 tablespoon finely chopped onion
- 1 tablespoon minced fresh cilantro
- ⅛ teaspoon salt
  Dash pepper

TACOS

- 1 pound tilapia fillets, cut into 1-inch pieces
- ¼ teaspoon salt
- ⅛ teaspoon pepper
- 2 teaspoons canola oil
- 8 corn tortillas (6 inches), warmed
  Optional toppings: hot pepper sauce and chopped tomatoes, green onions and jalapeno pepper

1. In a small bowl, toss the coleslaw mix with oil and lime juice; refrigerate until serving. In another bowl, mash the avocado with a fork; stir in sour cream, onion, cilantro, salt and pepper.
2. Sprinkle the tilapia fillets with salt and pepper. In a large nonstick skillet, heat oil over medium-high heat. Add tilapia; cook 3-4 minutes on each side or until fish just begins to flake easily with a fork. Serve in tortillas with coleslaw, guacamole and toppings as desired.

FRUIT SALAD SALSA WITH CINNAMON TORTILLA CHIPS

Salsa with strawberries, blueberries and nectarines makes a refreshing side dish. We scoop it up with cinnamon sugar tortilla chips.

—**ADAN FRANCO** MILWAUKEE, WI

PREP: 15 MIN. • **COOK:** 5 MIN./BATCH
MAKES: 6 CUPS SALSA (80 CHIPS)

- 2 **medium apples, finely chopped**
- 2 **medium nectarines or peaches, finely chopped**
- 2 **cups chopped fresh strawberries**
- 1 **cup fresh blueberries**
- 2 **tablespoons lemon juice**
  Dash salt

CHIPS
- ½ **cup sugar**
- 2 **tablespoons ground cinnamon**
- 10 **flour tortillas (8 inches)**
  Oil for frying

1. In a large bowl, combine the first six ingredients. Refrigerate until serving.
2. In a small bowl, mix the sugar and cinnamon. Cut each tortilla into eight wedges. In an electric skillet, heat 1 in. of oil to 375°. Fry chips, several at a time, 2-3 minutes on each side or until golden brown. Drain on paper towels.
3. Transfer chips to a large bowl; sprinkle with sugar mixture and gently toss to coat. Serve with salsa.

TRES LECHES CAKE

A staple dessert in Mexican kitchens for generations, this cake gets its name from the three types of milk—evaporated, sweetened condensed and heavy whipping cream—that are used to create its moist and tender texture.

—*TASTE OF HOME* TEST KITCHEN

PREP: 45 MIN. • **BAKE:** 20 MIN. + CHILLING
MAKES: 10 SERVINGS

- 4 **large eggs, separated**
- ⅔ **cup sugar, divided**
- ⅔ **cup cake flour**
  Dash salt
- ¾ **cup heavy whipping cream**
- ¾ **cup evaporated milk**
- ¾ **cup sweetened condensed milk**
- 2 **teaspoons vanilla extract**
- ¼ **teaspoon rum extract**

TOPPING
- 1¼ **cups heavy whipping cream**
- 3 **tablespoons sugar**
  Sliced fresh strawberries and dulce de leche, optional

1. Place egg whites in a large bowl; let stand at room temperature for 30 minutes. Line the bottom of a 9-in. springform pan with parchment paper; grease the paper.
2. Meanwhile, preheat oven to 350°. In another large bowl, beat egg yolks until slightly thickened. Gradually add ⅓ cup sugar, beating on high speed until thick and lemon-colored. Fold in the flour, a third at a time.
3. Add salt to egg whites; with clean beaters, beat on medium until soft peaks form. Add the remaining sugar, 1 tablespoon at a time, beating on high after each addition until the sugar is dissolved. Continue beating until soft glossy peaks form. Fold a third of the whites into the batter, then fold in the remaining whites. Gently spread batter into the prepared pan.
4. Bake until the top springs back when lightly touched, 20-25 minutes. Cool 10 minutes before removing from pan to a wire rack to cool completely.
5. Place cake on a serving plate. Poke holes in top with a skewer. In a small bowl, mix the cream, evaporated milk, sweetened condensed milk and both extracts; spoon slowly over cake. Refrigerate, covered, for 2 hours.
6. Beat cream until it begins to thicken. Add sugar; beat until peaks form. Spread over cake. If desired, top with strawberries and dulce de leche just before serving.

FAST FIX ▶

HOT DOG SLIDERS WITH MANGO-PINEAPPLE SALSA

For parties, we shrink down lots of foods to slider size, including these quick hot dogs. Pile on the easy but irresistible fruit salsa for a burst of fresh flavor.

—**CAROLE RESNICK** CLEVELAND, OH

START TO FINISH: 30 MIN.
MAKES: 2 DOZEN (2 CUPS SALSA)

- 3 tablespoons lime juice
- 2 tablespoons honey
- ¼ teaspoon salt
- 1 cup cubed fresh pineapple (½ inch)
- 1 cup cubed peeled mango (½ inch)
- ¼ cup finely chopped red onion
- 2 tablespoons finely chopped sweet red pepper
- 12 hot dogs
- 12 hot dog buns, split

1. In a small bowl, whisk lime juice, honey and salt until blended. Add the pineapple, mango, onion and red pepper; toss to coat.

2. Grill the hot dogs, covered, over medium heat or broil 4 in. from heat 7-9 minutes or until heated through, turning occasionally.

3. Place hot dogs in buns; cut each crosswise in half. Serve with fruit salsa.

FAST FIX ▶

FAJITA IN A BOWL

Get out the skewers and take a stab at grilling peppers, onions and corn for an awesome steak salad that's pure summer.

—**PEGGY WOODWARD** SHULLSBURG, WI

START TO FINISH: 30 MIN.
MAKES: 4 SERVINGS

- 1 tablespoon brown sugar
- 1 tablespoon chili powder
- ½ teaspoon salt
- 1 beef flank steak (1 pound)
- 12 miniature sweet peppers, halved and seeded
- 1 medium red onion, cut into thin wedges
- 2 cups cherry tomatoes
- 2 medium ears sweet corn, husks removed

SALAD

- 12 cups torn mixed salad greens
- 1 cup fresh cilantro leaves
- ½ cup reduced-fat lime vinaigrette
   Optional ingredients: cotija cheese, lime wedges and tortillas

1. In a small bowl, mix brown sugar, chili powder and salt. Rub onto both sides of the steak.

2. Place the peppers and onion on a grilling grid; place on grill rack over medium heat. Grill, covered, for 9-11 minutes or until crisp-tender, stirring occasionally; add the tomatoes during the last 2 minutes. Remove from grill.

3. Place the steak and corn directly on the grill rack; close lid. Grill the steak for 8-10 minutes on each side or until a thermometer reads 145° for medium rare; grill the corn for 10-12 minutes or until lightly charred, turning occasionally.

4. Divide the greens and cilantro among four bowls. Cut the corn from cobs and thinly slice the steak across the grain; place in bowls. Top with vegetables; drizzle with vinaigrette. If desired, serve with cotija cheese, lime wedges and tortillas.

NOTE *If you do not have a grilling grid, use a disposable foil pan with holes poked into the bottom with a meat fork.*

WATERMELON SALAD WITH FETA

Our family celebrates the Fourth of July each year with a watermelon salad arranged to resemble the flag. Here's an all-American centerpiece that truly is red, white and blue.
—**JAN WHITWORTH** ROEBUCK, SC

START TO FINISH: 25 MIN.
MAKES: 12 SERVINGS (¾ CUP EACH)

- ¼ **cup red wine vinegar**
- 1 **tablespoon Dijon mustard**
- 1 **tablespoon grated lemon peel**
- 1 **teaspoon sugar**
- ¼ **teaspoon salt**
- ¼ **teaspoon pepper**
- ⅓ **cup olive oil**
- ¼ **cup finely chopped red onion**

SALAD
- 6 **cups fresh arugula (about 5 ounces)**
- 1½ **cups fresh blueberries**
- 5 **cups cubed seedless watermelon**
- 1 **package (8 ounces) feta cheese, cut into ½-in. cubes**

1. For the vinaigrette, in a small bowl, whisk together the first six ingredients; gradually whisk in oil until blended. Stir in onion.

2. In a large bowl, lightly toss arugula with ¼ cup vinaigrette. Arrange evenly in a large rectangular serving dish.

3. For stars, place blueberries over the top left corner of the arugula. Arrange watermelon and cheese in alternating stripes. Drizzle with the remaining vinaigrette. Serve immediately.

FIESTA COLESLAW

Coleslaw with a touch of heat makes a zesty side for barbecue chicken or pork. I also pile it on fish tacos and po'boys.
—**FAY MORELAND** WICHITA FALLS, TX

START TO FINISH: 20 MIN.
MAKES: 10 SERVINGS

- 1 **package (14 ounces) coleslaw mix**
- 1 **cup chopped peeled jicama**
- 6 **radishes, halved and sliced**
- 4 **jalapeno peppers, seeded and finely chopped**
- 1 **medium onion, chopped**
- ⅓ **cup minced fresh cilantro**
- ½ **cup mayonnaise**
- ¼ **cup cider vinegar**
- 2 **tablespoons sugar**
- ½ **teaspoon salt**
- ½ **teaspoon celery salt**
- ¼ **teaspoon coarsely ground pepper**
  Lime wedges, optional

1. In a large bowl, combine the first six ingredients. In a small bowl, whisk the mayonnaise, vinegar, sugar and seasonings. Pour over the coleslaw mixture; toss to coat.

2. Refrigerate, covered, until serving. If desired, serve with lime wedges.

NOTE *Wear disposable gloves when cutting hot peppers; the oils can burn skin. Avoid touching your face.*

SWEET POTATO, ORANGE & PINEAPPLE CRUNCH

I combined my two favorite sweet potato casseroles in the world to create my own special version for the holiday table.

—LISA VARNER EL PASO, TX

PREP: 35 MIN. • **BAKE:** 40 MIN.
MAKES: 12 SERVINGS (½ CUP EACH)

- 2 pounds sweet potatoes, peeled and cubed (about 6 cups)
- ¾ cup sugar
- 1 can (8 ounces) crushed pineapple, drained
- 2 large eggs, lightly beaten
- ½ cup sour cream or plain yogurt
- ½ teaspoon grated orange peel
- ¼ cup orange juice
- ¼ cup butter, melted
- 1 teaspoon vanilla extract

TOPPING
- 1 cup flaked coconut
- 1 cup chopped pecans
- 1 cup packed brown sugar
- ½ cup all-purpose flour
- ¼ cup butter, melted

1. Preheat oven to 350°. Place the sweet potatoes in a large saucepan; add water to cover. Bring to a boil over high heat. Reduce heat to medium; cook, uncovered, for 10-15 minutes or until tender. Drain.

2. Place sweet potatoes in a large bowl and mash them. Stir in sugar, pineapple, eggs, sour cream, orange peel, juice, butter and vanilla; transfer to a greased 13x9-in. baking dish. In a large bowl, mix coconut, pecans, brown sugar and flour. Add butter; mix until crumbly. Sprinkle over top.

3. Bake, uncovered, 40-45 minutes or until heated through and topping is golden brown.

CREAMY BUTTERNUT SQUASH & SAGE SOUP

I recently started experimenting with new recipes, and I created this rich squash soup that omits heavy cream altogether, making it a healthier way to satisfy my craving for creaminess.

—NITHYA KUMAR DAVIS, CA

PREP: 20 MIN. • **COOK:** 50 MIN.
MAKES: 4 SERVINGS

- 4 cups cubed peeled butternut squash
- 1 tablespoon olive oil
- 2 tablespoons minced fresh sage
- ¼ teaspoon salt
- ¼ teaspoon pepper

SOUP
- 1 tablespoon olive oil
- 2 tablespoons butter, divided
- 1 medium onion, chopped
- 1 garlic clove, minced
- ¾ teaspoon salt
- ¼ to ½ teaspoon crushed red pepper flakes
- ⅛ teaspoon pepper
- 4 cups water
- 1 medium sweet potato, chopped
- 1 medium carrot, chopped

1. Preheat oven to 400°. Place squash in a foil-lined 15x10x1-in. baking pan. Drizzle with oil; sprinkle with sage, salt and pepper. Toss to coat. Roast for 30-35 minutes or until tender, stirring occasionally.

2. Meanwhile, in a large saucepan, heat oil and 1 tablespoon butter over medium heat. Add onion and garlic; cook and stir for 3-4 minutes or until softened. Reduce heat to medium-low; cook for 30-40 minutes or until deep golden brown, stirring occasionally. Stir in salt, pepper flakes and pepper.

3. Add water, sweet potato and carrot to saucepan. Bring to a boil. Reduce heat; cook, uncovered, 10-15 minutes or until the vegetables are tender. Add the squash mixture and remaining butter to soup. Puree the soup using an immersion blender. Or, cool the soup slightly and puree in batches in a tabletop blender; return to the pan and heat through.

TURKEY SAUSAGE-STUFFED ACORN SQUASH

Finding healthy recipes the family will eat is a challenge. This elegant squash is one dish we all love. It works with pork, turkey or chicken sausage.
—**MELISSA PELKEY HASS** WALESKA, GA

PREP: 30 MIN. • **BAKE:** 50 MIN.
MAKES: 8 SERVINGS

- 4 **medium acorn squash (about 1½ pounds each)**
- 1 **cup cherry tomatoes, halved**
- 1 **pound Italian turkey sausage links, casings removed**
- ½ **pound sliced fresh mushrooms**
- 1 **medium apple, peeled and finely chopped**
- 1 **small onion, finely chopped**
- 2 **teaspoons fennel seed**
- 2 **teaspoons caraway seeds**
- ½ **teaspoon dried sage leaves**
- 3 **cups fresh baby spinach**
- 1 **tablespoon minced fresh thyme**
- ¼ **teaspoon salt**
- ⅛ **teaspoon pepper**
- 8 **ounces fresh mozzarella cheese, chopped**
- 1 **tablespoon red wine vinegar**

1. Preheat oven to 400°. Cut squash lengthwise in half; remove and discard seeds. Using a sharp knife, cut a thin slice from the bottom of each half to allow it to lie flat. Place squash in a shallow roasting pan, hollow side down; add ¼ in. of hot water and halved tomatoes. Bake, uncovered, for 45 minutes.
2. Meanwhile, in a large skillet, cook the sausage, mushrooms, apple, onion and dried seasonings over medium heat 8-10 minutes or until sausage is no longer pink, breaking up sausage into crumbles; drain. Add spinach, thyme, salt and pepper; cook and stir for 2 minutes. Remove from heat.
3. Carefully remove the squash from the roasting pan. Drain cooking liquid, reserving tomatoes. Return squash to pan, hollow side up.
4. Stir the cheese, vinegar and reserved tomatoes into the sausage mixture. Spoon into squash cavities. Bake 5-10 minutes longer or until heated through and squash is easily pierced with a fork.

(5) INGREDIENTS
ROASTED FRESH PUMPKIN SEEDS

I learned to roast pumpkin seeds from my mother, who learned it from her mother. It's a healthy snack and fun to make after you finish carving jack-o'-lanterns!
—**MARGARET DRYE** PLAINFIELD, NH

PREP: 20 MIN. + SOAKING
BAKE: 1½ HOURS + COOLING
MAKES: 1½ CUPS

- 2 **cups fresh pumpkin seeds**
- 1 **teaspoon salt**
- 1 **tablespoon olive oil**
- ¾ **teaspoon kosher or fine sea salt**

1. Place the seeds in a 1-qt. bowl; cover with water. Stir in salt; let stand, covered, overnight.
2. Preheat oven to 200°. Drain and rinse the seeds; drain again and pat them dry. Transfer to a 15x10x1-in. baking pan. Toss with oil and kosher salt; spread in a single layer.
3. Roast 1½-1¾ hours or until crisp and lightly browned, stirring occasionally. Cool completely. Store in an airtight container.

APPLE MAPLE PECAN SALAD

A well-made salad has good flavor and a pleasing crunch. This one with cabbage, apples and pecans gets high marks in both departments, with extra points for color.
—**EMILY TYRA** MILWAUKEE, WI

PREP: 15 MIN. + STANDING
MAKES: 12 SERVINGS

- ¼ **cup lemon juice**
- ¼ **cup canola oil**
- ¼ **cup maple syrup**
- 1½ **teaspoons Dijon mustard**
- ½ **teaspoon coarsely ground pepper**
- 4 **cups shredded cabbage**
- 3 **large Granny Smith apples, julienned**
- ½ **cup crumbled Gorgonzola cheese**
- 1 **cup chopped pecans, toasted**

Whisk the first five ingredients until blended. Combine the cabbage, apples and Gorgonzola; toss with dressing to coat. Let the salad stand for 30 minutes before serving. Sprinkle with pecans.
NOTE *To toast nuts, bake them in a shallow pan in a 350° oven for 5-10 minutes or cook them in a skillet over low heat until lightly browned, stirring occasionally.*

⑤ INGREDIENTS

JACK-O'-LANTERN CAKE

I pieced two Bundt cakes together to make this gap-toothed grinner—the best Halloween centerpiece ever!

—JULIANNE JOHNSON GROVE CITY, MN

PREP: 35 MIN. • **BAKE:** 30 MIN. + COOLING
MAKES: 12-16 SERVINGS

- 2 packages spice cake mix (regular size)
- 4 cans (16 ounces each) vanilla frosting
  Red and yellow food coloring
- 1 ice cream cake cone (about 3 inches tall)
- 2 Oreo cookies
- 1 package (24 ounces) ready-to-use rolled black fondant

1. Prepare and bake cakes according to package directions using two 10-in. fluted tube pans. Cool. Meanwhile, tint frosting orange using red and yellow food coloring.

2. Cut thin slice off the bottom of each cake. Spread the bottom of one cake with frosting; press flat sides together to make a pumpkin shape. Place a foil ball in the center to support the stem; top with an ice cream cake cone. Frost cake with remaining frosting.

TO DECORATE FACE *Roll out fondant to ⅛-in. thickness; cut into desired shapes for mouth and nose. Remove the tops from two Oreo cookies; cut half-circles in filling for eyes. Press cookies and fondant into frosting to make the face.*

CARAMEL APPLE DOUGHNUT MUFFINS

Welcome autumn and Halloween into your kitchen with these muffins. The recipe will remind you of cinnamon-sugar cake doughnuts.

—JULIE RUBLE CHARLOTTE, NC

PREP: 50 MIN. • **BAKE:** 15 MIN.
MAKES: 4 DOZEN (SCANT 1 CUP SAUCE)

- 1½ cups all-purpose flour
- ¾ cup sugar
- 2 teaspoons baking powder
- ¼ teaspoon salt
- ¼ teaspoon ground nutmeg
- 1 large egg
- ¾ cup 2% milk
- ¼ cup canola oil
- 1 teaspoon vanilla extract
- 1 medium apple, peeled and finely chopped (about 1 cup)

CARAMEL SAUCE
- ¾ cup sugar
- 2 tablespoons water
- ½ cup heavy whipping cream, warmed
- 2 tablespoons creme fraiche or sour cream
- ¼ teaspoon vanilla extract
- ⅛ teaspoon salt

COATING
- ⅓ cup sugar
- 1 tablespoon ground cinnamon
- 3 tablespoons butter, melted

1. Preheat oven to 350°. In a large bowl, whisk flour, sugar, baking powder, salt and nutmeg. In another bowl, whisk egg, milk, oil and vanilla until blended. Add to flour mixture; stir just until moistened. Fold in apple.

2. Fill greased mini-muffin cups three-fourths full. Bake for 15-17 minutes or until a toothpick inserted in center comes out clean. Cool 5 minutes before removing from pans to wire racks.

3. Meanwhile, for caramel sauce, in a small heavy saucepan, combine sugar and water; stir gently to moisten the sugar. Cook over medium heat, gently swirling pan occasionally, until the syrup turns a medium amber color, 8-10 minutes.

4. Remove from heat; gradually stir in warm cream. Transfer to a small bowl. Place the bowl in an ice water bath, stirring frequently until cooled, about 5 minutes. Remove bowl from ice water. Whisk in creme fraiche, vanilla and salt.

5. For the coating, combine sugar and cinnamon. Dip tops of warm muffins in butter, then coat in cinnamon-sugar. Serve muffins with caramel sauce.

CANDY CORN QUESADILLAS

Celebrate the season with a savory touch. These candy corn triangles will be a smash hit. Let kids join in the fun by using a rolling pin to crush a bag filled with tortilla chips while you do the rest.

—MARIE PARKER MILWAUKEE, WI

PREP: 25 MIN. • **COOK:** 10 MIN.
MAKES: 2 DOZEN

- 1 rotisserie chicken, cut up
- 1 jar (16 ounces) salsa
- 1 cup frozen corn, thawed
- ¼ cup barbecue sauce
- ½ teaspoon ground cumin
- ½ cup butter, melted
- 8 flour tortillas (10 inches)
- 1 jar (15½ ounces) salsa con queso dip, warmed
- 4 cups shredded Mexican cheese blend
- 2⅔ cups crushed nacho-flavored tortilla chips
- ½ cup sour cream

1. In a Dutch oven, combine the first five ingredients; heat through, stirring occasionally. Brush butter over one side of each tortilla.

2. Place one tortilla in a large skillet, buttered side down. Spread with 1 cup chicken mixture; top with another tortilla, buttered side up. Cook over medium heat for 1-2 minutes or until bottom is lightly browned. Turn quesadilla.

3. Spread ½ cup queso dip over the quesadilla; carefully sprinkle cheese along the outer edge. Cook, covered, for 1-2 minutes or until the cheese begins to melt.

4. Remove to a cutting board. Sprinkle crushed chips over queso dip. Cut quesadilla into six wedges. Place a small dollop of sour cream at the point of each wedge. Repeat with remaining ingredients.

BUTTERNUT SQUASH ROLLS

With their cheery yellow color and delicious aroma, these rolls will brighten your buffet table. This recipe is a great way to use the squash from my garden.
—**BERNICE MORRIS** MARSHFIELD, MO

PREP: 30 MIN. + RISING • **BAKE:** 20 MIN.
MAKES: 2 DOZEN

- 1 **package (¼ ounce) active dry yeast**
- 1 **cup warm whole milk (110° to 115°)**
- ¼ **cup warm water (110° to 115°)**
- 3 **tablespoons butter, softened**
- 2 **teaspoons salt**
- ½ **cup sugar**
- 1 **cup mashed cooked butternut squash**
- 5 **to 5½ cups all-purpose flour, divided**

1. In a large bowl, dissolve yeast in milk and water. Add the butter, salt, sugar, squash and 3 cups flour; beat until smooth. Add enough remaining flour to form a soft dough.
2. Turn dough onto a floured surface; knead until it is smooth and elastic, 6-8 minutes. Place in a greased bowl, turning once to grease top. Cover and let rise in a warm place until doubled, about 1 hour.
3. Punch dough down. Form into rolls; place in two greased 10-in. cast-iron skillets or 9-in. round baking pans. Cover and let rise until doubled, about 30 minutes.
4. Bake at 375° for 20-25 minutes or until golden brown.

CITRUS & HERB ROASTED TURKEY BREAST

This recipe will make you love turkey in a whole new way. Brining with lemon, rosemary and orange juice makes it so flavorful. It's the star attraction at our Thanksgiving table.
—**FAY MORELAND** WICHITA FALLS, TX

PREP: 1 HOUR + CHILLING
BAKE: 2 HOURS + STANDING
MAKES: 10 SERVINGS

- 4 **cups water**
- ¾ **cup kosher salt**
- ¾ **cup sugar**
- 2 **medium lemons, quartered**
- 6 **fresh rosemary sprigs**
- 6 **fresh thyme sprigs**
- 8 **garlic cloves, halved**
- 1 **tablespoon coarsely ground pepper**
- 2 **cups cold apple juice**
- 2 **cups cold orange juice**
- 2 **large oven roasting bags**
- 1 **bone-in turkey breast (5 to 6 pounds)**

HERB BUTTER
- ⅓ **cup butter, softened**
- 4 **teaspoons grated lemon peel**
- 1 **tablespoon minced fresh rosemary**
- 1 **tablespoon minced fresh thyme**
- 1½ **teaspoons coarsely ground pepper**

SEASONED SALT BUTTER
- ¼ **cup butter, melted**
- 1½ **teaspoons seasoned salt**

1. In a 6-qt. stockpot, combine the first eight ingredients and bring them to a boil. Remove from heat. Add cold juices to the brine; cool to room temperature.
2. Place one oven roasting bag inside the other. Place turkey breast inside both bags; pour cooled brine over turkey. Seal bags, pressing out as much air as possible, and turn to coat. Place in a roasting pan. Refrigerate 8 hours or overnight, turning occasionally.
3. In a small bowl, beat herb butter ingredients until blended. Remove turkey from brine; rinse and pat dry. Discard brine. Place turkey on a rack in a 15x10x1-in. baking pan. With your fingers, carefully loosen skin from turkey breast; rub the herb butter under the skin. Use toothpicks to secure the skin to the underside of the breast. Refrigerate, covered, for 18-24 hours.
4. Preheat oven to 425°. In a small bowl, mix butter and seasoned salt; brush over outside of turkey. Roast 15 minutes.
5. Reduce oven setting to 325°. Roast turkey 1¾-2¼ hours longer or until a thermometer reads 170°. (Cover turkey loosely with foil if it browns too quickly.) Remove turkey from oven; tent with foil. Let stand for 15 minutes before carving.

APPLE BUTTER & PUMPKIN PIE

I'm proud of this pie because I made it up in my head, and it turned out so well! It's a little different from traditional pumpkin or pecan pie, which makes it a nice surprise for the holidays.

—SHERRY LITTLE SHERWOOD, AR

PREP: 45 MIN. + CHILLING
BAKE: 45 MIN. + COOLING
MAKES: 8 SERVINGS

- 1¾ cups all-purpose flour
- ½ teaspoon salt
- ½ cup cold butter, cubed
- ¼ cup shortening
- 3 to 5 tablespoons ice water

FILLING

- 3 large eggs, lightly beaten
- 1 cup apple butter
- 1 cup canned pumpkin
- ⅔ cup packed light brown sugar
- ½ teaspoon salt
- ¾ teaspoon ground cinnamon
- ½ teaspoon ground ginger
- ¼ teaspoon ground nutmeg
- ¾ cup half-and-half cream

Optional toppings: sugared cranberries (see note below), toasted chopped pecans and sweetened whipped cream

1. In a bowl, mix flour and salt; cut in butter and shortening until crumbly. Gradually add ice water, tossing with a fork until the dough holds together when pressed. Reserve one-fourth of the dough for cutouts; shape into a disk. Shape remaining dough into a separate disk. Wrap each disk in plastic; refrigerate 1 hour or overnight.

2. On a lightly floured surface, roll the large disk of dough to a ⅛-in.-thick circle; transfer to a 9-in. pie plate. Trim pastry to ½ in. beyond rim of plate; flute the edge. Roll the small disk of dough to a ¼-in. thickness; cut into desired shapes with floured 1-in. cookie cutters. Place cutouts on an ungreased baking sheet. Refrigerate crust and cutouts while preparing the filling.

3. Preheat oven to 425°. Mix eggs, apple butter, pumpkin, brown sugar, salt and spices; stir in cream. Pour into crust. Bake on a lower oven rack for 15 minutes. Reduce oven setting to 350°; bake until the center is almost set, 30-35 minutes. Bake pastry cutouts on an upper oven rack until golden brown, 12-15 minutes.

4. Cool pie and pastry cutouts on a wire rack; serve or refrigerate within 2 hours. Decorate the pie with cutouts and toppings as desired.

NOTE *To make sugared cranberries, place ⅓ cup sugar in a small bowl. In a microwave, warm 1 tablespoon light corn syrup for about 10 seconds; toss with 1 cup fresh cranberries. Add to sugar and toss; let stand on waxed paper until set, about 1 hour.*

FAST FIX ▶
HARVARD BEETS

The bright, citrusy flavors of this pretty side dish make it a great contrast for earthy, savory entrees—and appealing to people who usually shy away from beets.

—JEAN ANN PERKINS NEWBURYPORT, MD

START TO FINISH: 15 MIN.
MAKES: 4-6 SERVINGS

- 1 can (16 ounces) sliced beets
- ¼ cup sugar
- 1½ teaspoons cornstarch
- 2 tablespoons vinegar
- 2 tablespoons orange juice
- 1 tablespoon grated orange peel

Drain beets, reserving 2 tablespoons of the juice; set beets and reserved juice aside. In a saucepan, combine sugar and cornstarch. Add vinegar, orange juice and beet juice; bring to a boil. Reduce heat; simmer for 3-4 minutes or until thickened. Add beets and orange peel; heat through.

TOP TIP

Spice Up Your Pie Crust

For enhanced flavor in your pie crust, add a bit of sugar and a few drops of vanilla to the basic recipe. If you're making an apple or pumpkin pie, add cinnamon to the crust, too. It's delicious!

—BONNIE G. BRUNSWICK, OH

WALNUT PUMPKIN CAKE ROLL

This is one of my family's favorite dessert recipes, especially for holiday gatherings.

—MARY GECHA CENTER RUTLAND, VT

PREP: 20 MIN. + CHILLING
BAKE: 15 MIN. + COOLING
MAKES: 10-12 SERVINGS

- 3 large eggs
- 1 cup sugar
- ⅔ cup canned pumpkin
- 1 teaspoon lemon juice
- ¾ cup all-purpose flour
- 2 teaspoons ground cinnamon
- 1 teaspoon baking powder
- 1 teaspoon ground ginger
- ½ teaspoon salt
- ½ teaspoon ground nutmeg
- 1 cup finely chopped walnuts
  Confectioners' sugar

FILLING

- 6 ounces cream cheese, softened
- 1 cup confectioners' sugar
- ¼ cup butter, softened
- ½ teaspoon vanilla extract

1. Line a greased 15x10x1-in. baking pan with waxed paper. Grease the paper; set aside. In a bowl, beat eggs for 3 minutes. Gradually add sugar; beat for 2 minutes or until mixture becomes thick and lemon-colored. Stir in pumpkin and lemon juice. Combine dry ingredients; fold into the pumpkin mixture. Spread batter evenly in the prepared pan. Sprinkle with walnuts.

2. Bake at 375° for 12-14 minutes or until cake springs back when lightly touched in center. Cool for 5 minutes. Turn cake out of pan onto a kitchen towel dusted with confectioners' sugar. Gently peel off waxed paper. Roll up cake in towel jelly-roll style, starting with a long side. Cool completely on a wire rack.

3. In a bowl, combine the filling ingredients and beat until smooth. Unroll cake; spread evenly with filling to within ½ in. of edges. Roll up again. Cover and refrigerate for 1 hour before slicing. Refrigerate any leftovers.

DRESSING

- 1 tablespoon canola oil
- 1 medium onion, chopped
- 2 celery ribs, chopped
- 3 large eggs
- 2 cans (10¾ ounces each) condensed cream of chicken soup, undiluted
- 3 teaspoons poultry seasoning
- 1 teaspoon pepper
- ½ teaspoon salt
- 2 cups chicken broth

1. Preheat oven to 400°. In a large bowl, whisk flour, cornmeal, baking powder and salt. In another bowl, whisk eggs and buttermilk. Pour oil into an 8-in. ovenproof skillet; place skillet in hot oven for 4 minutes.
2. Meanwhile, add buttermilk mixture to the flour mixture; stir together just until moistened.
3. Carefully tilt and rotate skillet to coat bottom with oil; add batter. Bake 20-25 minutes or until a toothpick inserted in center comes out clean. Cool completely in pan on a wire rack.
4. Reduce oven setting to 350°. For dressing, in a large skillet, heat oil over medium-high heat. Add onion and celery; cook and stir 4-6 minutes or until tender. Remove from heat. Coarsely crumble corn bread into the skillet; toss to combine. In a small bowl, whisk the eggs, condensed soup and seasonings; stir into bread mixture. Stir in broth.
5. Transfer to a greased 13x9-in. baking dish. Bake for 45-55 minutes or until lightly browned.

5 INGREDIENTS

CREAM CHEESE MASHED POTATOES

When I serve this easy mash, the bowl is always scraped clean. Before holiday feasts, I make it early and keep it warm in a slow cooker so I can focus on last-minute details.

—**JILL THOMAS** WASHINGTON, IN

PREP: 20 MIN. • **COOK:** 15 MIN.
MAKES: 20 SERVINGS

- 8 pounds russet potatoes
- 1 package (8 ounces) cream cheese, softened
- ½ cup butter, melted
- 2 teaspoons salt
- ¾ teaspoon pepper
  Additional melted butter, optional
- ¼ cup finely chopped green onions

1. Peel and cube potatoes. Place in a large stockpot; add water to cover. Bring to a boil. Reduce heat; cook, uncovered, until tender, 12-15 minutes. Drain.

2. With a mixer, beat cream cheese, ½ cup melted butter, salt and pepper until smooth. Add potatoes; beat until light and fluffy. If desired, top with additional melted butter. Sprinkle with green onions.

GRANDMA'S CORN BREAD DRESSING

Growing up, we didn't have turkey for Thanksgiving—we had chicken chopped and baked in my grandmother's dressing. Now we leave out the chicken and keep the corn bread dressing.

—**SUZANNE MOHME** BASTROP, TX

PREP: 40 MIN. + COOLING • **BAKE:** 45 MIN.
MAKES: 12 SERVINGS (⅔ CUP EACH)

- 1 cup all-purpose flour
- 1 cup cornmeal
- 2 teaspoons baking powder
- 1 teaspoon salt
- 2 large eggs
- 1 cup buttermilk
- ¼ cup canola oil

HONEY GARLIC GREEN BEANS

Green beans are great, but they can seem somewhat ordinary on their own. Just a couple extra ingredients give them sweet and salty attitude.

—**SHANNON DOBOS** CALGARY, AB

START TO FINISH: 20 MIN.
MAKES: 8 SERVINGS

- 4 **tablespoons honey**
- 2 **tablespoons reduced-sodium soy sauce**
- 4 **garlic cloves, minced**
- ¼ **teaspoon salt**
- ¼ **teaspoon crushed red pepper flakes**
- 2 **pounds fresh green beans, trimmed**

1. Whisk together the first five ingredients; set aside. In a 6-qt. stockpot, bring 10 cups water to a boil. Add beans in batches; cook, uncovered, 2-3 minutes or just until crisp-tender. Remove beans and immediately drop into ice water. Drain and pat dry.
2. Coat stockpot with cooking spray. Add beans; cook, stirring constantly, over high heat until slightly blistered, 2-3 minutes. Add sauce; continue stirring until beans are coated and sauce starts to evaporate slightly, 2-3 minutes. Remove from heat.

CROWN ROAST WITH APRICOT DRESSING

I have been making crown roasts for many years but was only satisfied with the results after combining a few recipes to come up with this version. It's beautifully roasted with an apricot glaze and a nicely browned apricot stuffing.

—**ISABELL COOPER** CAMBRIDGE, NS

PREP: 20 MIN.
BAKE: 2½ HOURS + STANDING
MAKES: 12 SERVINGS

- 1 **pork crown roast (12 ribs, about 8 pounds)**
- ½ **teaspoon seasoned salt**
- ⅓ **cup apricot preserves**

APRICOT DRESSING
- ¼ **cup butter, cubed**
- 1 **cup sliced fresh mushrooms**
- 1 **medium onion, finely chopped**
- 1 **celery rib, finely chopped**
- 1 **cup chopped dried apricots**
- ½ **teaspoon dried savory**
- ½ **teaspoon dried thyme**
- ¼ **teaspoon salt**
- ¼ **teaspoon pepper**
- 3 **cups soft bread crumbs**

1. Preheat oven to 350°. Place roast on a rack in a shallow roasting pan. Sprinkle with seasoned salt. Bake, uncovered, 1 hour.
2. Brush sides of roast with preserves. Bake 1½-2 hours longer or until the meat reaches desired doneness (for medium-rare, a thermometer should read 145°; medium, 160°). Transfer roast to a serving platter. Let stand for 20 minutes before carving.
3. For dressing, in a large skillet, heat butter over medium-high heat. Add mushrooms, onion and celery; cook and stir for 6-8 minutes or until tender. Stir in apricots and seasonings. Add bread crumbs; toss to coat. Transfer to a greased 8-in. square baking dish. Bake 15-20 minutes or until lightly browned. Carve roast between ribs; serve with dressing.

NOTE *For presentation purposes, if desired, spoon dressing into center of roast.*

APPLE-CRANBERRY STUFFED CROWN ROAST *Omit stuffing ingredients. Melt ½ cup butter in a large skillet. Add 1 chopped large onion and 1 chopped celery rib ; saute until tender. Transfer to a large bowl; stir in 2 chopped peeled medium apples, ½ cup dried cranberries, ½ teaspoon dried thyme, ½ teaspoon salt and ½ teaspoon pepper. Add 8 cups soft whole grain bread crumbs and toss to coat. Stir in ½ cup chicken broth. Proceed as recipe directs.*

LITTLE BUTTER COOKIE SANDWICHES

This recipe originally came from my sister-in-law, but I tweaked it a bit to make doubly delicious cookies. You can make all different kinds of shapes.

—**PATRICIA KUTCHINS** LAKE ZURICH, IL

PREP: 30 MIN.
BAKE: 10 MIN./BATCH + COOLING
MAKES: 7 DOZEN

- 2 cups butter, softened
- 1 cup sugar
- 1 large egg
- 1 teaspoon almond extract
  Food coloring, optional
- 4 cups all-purpose flour
  Colored sugar, optional

FILLING
- 2 cups confectioners' sugar
- ¼ cup plus 2 tablespoons apricot preserves
- ½ teaspoon almond extract
- 3 to 4 teaspoons orange juice

1. Preheat oven to 350°. In a large bowl, cream butter and sugar until light and fluffy. Beat in egg, extract and, if desired, food coloring. Gradually beat flour into creamed mixture (dough will be sticky).

2. Using a cookie press fitted with a disk of your choice, press dough 1 in. apart onto ungreased baking sheets. Decorate as desired with colored sugar. Bake for 7-9 minutes or until set. Remove from pans to wire racks to cool completely.

3. Mix confectioners' sugar, preserves, extract and enough orange juice for the mixture to reach a spreading consistency. Spread about ½ teaspoon filling on the bottoms of half of the cookies; top with remaining cookies.

FREEZE OPTION *Transfer unbaked dough to a resealable plastic freezer bag; freeze. To use, thaw dough in refrigerator overnight or until soft enough to press. Prepare and bake cookies as directed.*

CHRISTMAS GINGERBREAD TRIFLE

Trifle desserts make eye-catching centerpieces. To add color, I sometimes garnish mine using candy canes and red and green M&M's. All the possibilities make this a very merry, kid-friendly project.

—**CHERYL TOMPKINS** KINGSVILLE, MO

PREP: 45 MIN. + CHILLING
MAKES: 14 SERVINGS

- 1 package (14½ ounces) gingerbread cake/cookie mix
- 2 cups cold 2% milk
- 2 cups cold eggnog
- 2 packages (3.4 ounces each) instant French vanilla pudding mix
- 1 package (5 ounces) gingerbread man cookies
- 1 carton (16 ounces) frozen whipped topping, thawed

1. Prepare the cake mix according to package directions and bake in a 9-in. square baking pan. Cool completely on a wire rack. Cut into 1-in. cubes.

2. In a large bowl, whisk milk, eggnog and pudding mix 2 minutes. Let stand 2 minutes or until soft-set.

3. Arrange nine cookies around sides of a 4-qt. glass bowl, using a third of the cake cubes to stand cookies upright. Top with a third of the pudding and whipped topping. Repeat layers. Top with the remaining cake, pudding and whipped topping. Refrigerate, covered, 4 hours or overnight.

4. Just before serving, top with the remaining cookies.

NOTE *This recipe was tested with commercially prepared eggnog.*

MY CHRISTMAS FUDGE

I've searched for years for the richest fudge, and this one does it for me. It's virtually foolproof and so creamy you won't believe it. Add just about anything you like to customize it.

—BARB MILLER OAKDALE, MN

PREP: 15 MIN. • **COOK:** 10 MIN. + COOLING
MAKES: 5¾ POUNDS (96 PIECES)

- 4½ cups sugar
- 1 can (12 ounces) evaporated milk
- ½ cup butter, cubed
- 2 packages (11½ ounces each) milk chocolate chips
- 4½ cups miniature marshmallows
- 2 ounces unsweetened chocolate, chopped
- 3 cups chopped walnuts, toasted
- 2 teaspoons vanilla extract
- 4 ounces white baking chocolate, melted

1. Line a 13x9-in. pan with foil; coat with cooking spray.
2. In a heavy Dutch oven, combine the sugar, evaporated milk and butter. Bring to a rapid boil over medium heat, stirring constantly. Cook and stir 5 minutes. Remove from heat.
3. Stir in the chocolate chips, marshmallows and chopped chocolate until melted. Fold in walnuts and vanilla. Immediately spread into the prepared pan. Drizzle with melted white baking chocolate; cool completely.
4. Using foil, lift fudge out of the pan. Remove foil; cut fudge into 96 squares. Store between layers of waxed paper in airtight containers.
NOTE *To toast nuts, bake in a shallow pan in a 350° oven for 5-10 minutes or cook in a skillet over low heat until lightly browned, stirring occasionally.*

FUDGY PEPPERMINT STICK TORTE

I created this cake based on one that a friend made for me. I love that it uses brown sugar rather than granulated. The flavors are great, and it makes a spectacular Christmastime presentation.

—MARY SHIVERS ADA, OK

PREP: 25 MIN. • **BAKE:** 20 MIN. + CHILLING
MAKES: 16 SERVINGS

- 1½ cups butter, softened
- 3¾ cups packed brown sugar
- 4 large eggs
- 2 teaspoons vanilla extract
- 4 cups all-purpose flour
- 1¼ cups baking cocoa
- 2 teaspoons baking powder
- 1 teaspoon salt
- 1 teaspoon baking soda
- 2½ cups cold water

FROSTING
- 4½ cups heavy whipping cream
- 1½ cups confectioners' sugar, divided
- ¾ teaspoon peppermint extract
- 3 packages (8 ounces each) cream cheese, softened
- 1 cup crushed peppermint candies, divided

1. In a large bowl, cream butter and brown sugar until light and fluffy. Add eggs, one at a time, beating well after each addition. Beat in vanilla. Combine the flour, cocoa, baking powder, salt and baking soda; add to the creamed mixture alternately with water, beating well after each addition.
2. Transfer to four greased and floured 9-in. round baking pans. Bake at 350° for 18-22 minutes or until a toothpick inserted in the center comes out clean. Cool for 10 minutes, then remove from pans to wire racks to cool completely.
3. In a small bowl, beat the whipping cream until it begins to thicken. Add ¾ cup confectioners' sugar and the peppermint extract; beat until soft peaks form. In another bowl, beat cream cheese and the remaining confectioners' sugar until smooth. Fold in whipped cream, then ¾ cup crushed candies.
4. Spread frosting between layers and over the top and sides of the cake. Refrigerate for at least 1 hour. Just before serving, sprinkle the remaining candies over the top.

5. Cover dough with plastic wrap; let rise until almost doubled, about 30 minutes. Preheat oven to 375°. Bake until golden brown, 18-22 minutes. (Watch during final 5 minutes for any dripping.) Remove from oven; brush with melted butter, avoiding areas where jam is visible. Cool completely on a wire rack, then dust bread with confectioners' sugar.

NOTE *Vary the flavor by trying blueberry jam and 1 teaspoon grated lemon peel, or blackberry jam and ½ teaspoon cardamom.*

⑤INGREDIENTS FAST FIX▶

FESTIVE HOLIDAY PUNCH

This refreshing holiday punch has a gorgeous raspberry color and tangy flavor. To complete the magic, garnish the glasses with lime wedges.

—**TAHNIA FOX** TRENTON, MI

START TO FINISH: 5 MIN.
MAKES: 14 SERVINGS (¾ CUP EACH)

- 1 **bottle (64 ounces) cranberry-raspberry juice, chilled**
- 1 **can (12 ounces) frozen raspberry lemonade concentrate, thawed**
- 1 **bottle (2 liters) lemon-lime soda, chilled**
  Fresh raspberries
  Ice cubes
  Lime wedges, optional

In a punch bowl, blend juice and lemonade concentrates. Stir in soda; top with raspberries. Serve over ice. If desired, garnish glasses with lime wedges.

CHRISTMAS STAR TWISTED BREAD

This gorgeous sweet bread swirled with jam may look tricky, but it's not. The best part is opening the oven to find this star-shaped beauty in all its glory.

—**DARLENE BRENDEN** SALEM, OR

PREP: 45 MIN. + RISING
BAKE: 20 MIN. + COOLING
MAKES: 16 SERVINGS

- 1 **package (¼ ounce) active dry yeast**
- ¼ **cup warm water (110° to 115°)**
- ¾ **cup warm whole milk (110° to 115°)**
- 1 **large egg**
- ¼ **cup butter, softened**
- ¼ **cup granulated sugar**
- 1 **teaspoon salt**
- 3¼ to 3¾ **cups all-purpose flour**
- ¾ **cup seedless raspberry jam**
- 2 **tablespoons butter, melted**
  Confectioners' sugar

1. Dissolve yeast in warm water until foamy. In another bowl, combine milk, egg, butter, sugar and salt; add yeast mixture and 3 cups flour. Beat on medium speed until smooth, about 1 minute. Stir in enough of the remaining flour to form a soft dough.

2. Turn dough onto a floured surface; knead until it is smooth and elastic, 6-8 minutes. Place in a greased bowl, turning once to grease top. Cover with plastic wrap; let rise in a warm place until doubled, about 1 hour.

3. Punch down dough. Turn onto a lightly floured surface; divide into four portions. Roll one portion into a 12-in. circle. Place on a greased 14-in. pizza pan. Spread with one-third of the jam to within ½ in. from edge. Repeat twice, layering dough and jam, and ending with final portion of dough.

4. Place a 2½-in. round cutter in the center of the circle; do not press down. With a sharp knife, make 16 evenly spaced cuts outward from the cutter to the edge of the dough, forming a starburst. Remove the cutter; grasp two adjacent strips and twist them, rotating twice outward. Pinch ends together. Repeat with remaining strips.

Chunky Taco Soup, 53

Cranberry Limeade, 8

Walnut Pumpkin Cake Roll, 220

Dad's Greek Salad, 81

Fudge-Topped Brownies, 181

Skillet Herb Bread, 155

Fruit Salad Salsa with Cinnamon Tortilla Chips, 211

Nutty Stuffed Mushrooms, 10

Artichoke & Lemon Pasta, 103

Chicken Noodle Casserole, 112

Saturn's Pizza Ring, 89

Barbecue Pork Tacos
with Apple Slaw, 129

Mushroom & Onion Grilled
Cheese Sandwiches, 50

Sausage Hash
Brown Bake, 123

Stuffed Flank Steak, 141

Sweet Potato, Orange &
Pineapple Crunch, 214

Toffee Brownie
Trifle, 163

ALPHABETICAL INDEX

Cheesy Broccoli Soup
in a Bread Bowl, 45

Fajita in a Bowl, 212

Mini S'mores, 188

Quick & Easy Turkey
Sloppy Joes, 54

Zucchini
Egg Skillet, 43

INGREDIENT SUBSTITUTIONS

WHEN YOU NEED:	IN THIS AMOUNT:	SUBSTITUTE:
Baking Powder	1 teaspoon	½ teaspoon cream of tartar plus ¼ teaspoon baking soda
Broth	1 cup	1 cup hot water plus 1 teaspoon bouillon granules *or* 1 bouillon cube
Buttermilk	1 cup	1 tablespoon lemon juice *or* white vinegar plus enough milk to measure 1 cup (let stand 5 minutes), *or* 1 cup plain yogurt
Cajun Seasoning	1 teaspoon	¼ teaspoon cayenne pepper, ½ teaspoon dried thyme, ¼ teaspoon dried basil and 1 minced garlic clove
Chocolate	1 ounce	3 tablespoons baking cocoa plus 1 tablespoon shortening *or* canola oil
Chocolate, Semisweet	1 ounce	1 ounce unsweetened chocolate plus 1 tablespoon sugar, *or* 3 tablespoons semisweet chocolate chips
Corn Syrup, Dark	1 cup	¾ cup light corn syrup plus ¼ cup molasses
Corn Syrup, Light	1 cup	1 cup sugar plus ¼ cup water
Cornstarch	1 tablespoon	2 tablespoons all-purpose flour (for thickening)
Cracker Crumbs	1 cup	1 cup dry bread crumbs
Cream, Half-and-Half	1 cup	1 tablespoon melted butter plus enough whole milk to measure 1 cup
Egg, Large	1 whole	2 large egg whites *or* 2 large egg yolks *or* ¼ cup egg substitute
Flour, Cake	1 cup	1 cup minus 2 tablespoons (⅞ cup) all-purpose flour
Flour, Self-Rising	1 cup	1½ teaspoons baking powder, ½ teaspoon salt and enough all-purpose flour to measure 1 cup
Garlic, Fresh	1 clove	⅛ teaspoon garlic powder
Gingerroot, Fresh	1 teaspoon	¼ teaspoon ground ginger
Honey	1 cup	1¼ cups sugar plus ¼ cup water
Lemon Juice	1 teaspoon	¼ teaspoon cider vinegar
Lemon Peel	1 teaspoon	½ teaspoon lemon extract
Milk, Whole	1 cup	½ cup evaporated milk plus ½ cup water, *or* 1 cup water plus ⅓ cup nonfat dry milk powder
Molasses	1 cup	1 cup honey
Mustard, Prepared	1 tablespoon	½ teaspoon ground mustard plus 2 teaspoons cider *or* white vinegar
Onion	1 small onion (⅓ cup chopped)	1 teaspoon onion powder *or* 1 tablespoon dried minced onion
Poultry Seasoning	1 teaspoon	¾ teaspoon rubbed sage plus ¼ teaspoon dried thyme
Sour Cream	1 cup	1 cup plain yogurt
Sugar	1 cup	1 cup packed brown sugar *or* 2 cups sifted confectioners' sugar
Tomato Juice	1 cup	½ cup tomato sauce plus ½ cup water
Tomato Sauce	2 cups	¾ cup tomato paste plus 1 cup water

GET COOKING WITH A WELL-STOCKED KITCHEN

In a perfect world, you would plan weekly or even monthly menus and have all the ingredients on hand to make each night's dinner. The reality, however, is that you likely haven't thought about dinner until you've walked through the door.

With a reasonably stocked pantry, refrigerator and freezer, you'll still be able to serve a satisfying meal in short order. Consider these tips:

QUICK-COOKING MEATS—such as boneless chicken breasts, chicken thighs, pork tenderloin, pork chops, ground meats, Italian sausage, sirloin and flank steaks, fish fillets and shrimp—should be stocked in the freezer. Wrap them individually (except shrimp), so you can remove only the amount you need. For the quickest defrosting, wrap meats for freezing in small, thin packages.

FROZEN VEGETABLES packaged in plastic bags are a real time-saver. Simply pour out the amount needed—no additional preparation is required.

PASTAS, RICE, RICE MIXES AND COUSCOUS are great staples to have in the pantry—and they generally have a long shelf life. Remember that thinner pastas, such as angel hair, cook faster than thicker pastas, and fresh (refrigerated) pasta cooks faster than dried.

DAIRY PRODUCTS like milk, sour cream, cheeses (shredded, cubed or crumbled), eggs, yogurt, butter and margarine are perishable, so check the use-by date on packages and replace as needed.

CONDIMENTS such as ketchup, mustard, mayonnaise, salad dressings, salsa, taco sauce, soy sauce, stir-fry sauce and lemon juice add flavor to many dishes. Personalize the list to suit your family's tastes.

FRESH FRUIT AND VEGETABLES can make a satisfying pre-dinner snack. Oranges and apples are not as perishable as bananas. Ready-to-use salad greens are perfect for an instant salad.

DRIED HERBS, SPICES, VINEGARS and seasoning mixes add lots of flavor and keep for months.

PASTA SAUCES, OLIVES, BEANS, broths, canned tomatoes, canned vegetables and canned or dried soups are ideal to have on hand for a quick meal—and many of these items are common recipe ingredients.

GET YOUR FAMILY INTO THE HABIT of posting a grocery list. When an item is used up or is almost gone, just add it to the list for your next shopping trip. This way you're less likely to run completely out of an item, and you'll also save time when writing your grocery list.

MAKE THE MOST OF YOUR TIME EVERY NIGHT

With recipes in hand and the kitchen stocked, you're well on the way to a relaxing family meal. Here are some pointers to help get dinner on the table fast:

PREHEAT THE OVEN OR GRILL before starting on the recipe.

PULL OUT THE REQUIRED INGREDIENTS, mixing tools and cooking tools before beginning any prep work.

USE CONVENIENCE ITEMS whenever possible. Think pre-chopped garlic, onion and peppers, shredded or cubed cheese, seasoning mixes and jarred sauces.

MULTITASK! While the meat is simmering for a main dish, toss a salad together, cook a side dish or start on dessert.

ENCOURAGE HELPERS. Have younger children set the table. Older ones can help with ingredient preparation or can even assemble the recipes themselves.

TAKE CARE OF TWO MEALS IN ONE NIGHT by planning main-dish leftovers or making a double batch of favorite sides.

TRICKS TO TAME HUNGER WHEN IT STRIKES

Are the kids begging for a pre-supper snack? Calm their rumbling tummies with nutritious, not-too-filling noshes.

START WITH A SMALL TOSSED SALAD. Try a ready-to-serve salad mix, and add their favorite salad dressing and a little protein, like cubed cheese or julienned slices of deli meat.

CUT UP AN APPLE and smear a little peanut butter on each slice, or offer other fruits such as seedless grapes, cantaloupe, oranges or bananas. For variety, give kids vanilla yogurt or reduced-fat ranch dressing as a dipper, or combine a little reduced-fat sour cream with a sprinkling of brown sugar. Too busy to cut up the fruit? A fruit snack cup will also do the trick.

DURING THE COLD MONTHS, a small mug of soup with a few oyster crackers on top can really hit the spot.

RAW VEGGIES such as carrots, cucumbers, mushrooms, broccoli and cauliflower are tasty treats, especially when served with a little hummus for dipping. Many of these vegetables can be purchased already cut.

OFFER A SMALL SERVING of cheese and crackers. Look for sliced cheese, and cut the slices into smaller squares to fit the crackers. Choose a cracker that's made from whole wheat such as an all-natural seven-grain cracker.